Praise for *Maximizing ASP.NET*

"Whether you want to improve your existing ASP.NET skills or are looking for a book that will give you the grounding and support you need to get started in ASP.NET development, this is the book for you! Jeff's approach is simple—he explains new methods in a logical, no-nonsense way and includes real examples that demonstrate the .NET way to perform a traditional activity."

—John Timney, Microsoft MVP, ASP.NET
Web Services Senior Consultant, British Telecom Consulting & Systems Integration

"I was excited about this book from the moment I first heard about it. I strongly believe ASP.NET developers will benefit greatly from understanding object-oriented fundamentals. Jeff has done a great job of introducing important object-oriented concepts clearly and concisely, enhancing the reader's understanding with some excellent real-life code examples."

—Gordon Barrs, Independent Developer and Technical Training Consultant

"This book covers a great spectrum of ASP.NET topics for those interested in discovering what ASP.NET has to offer. I particularly enjoyed the inclusion of ASP.NET 2.0, IIS 6.0, and Visual Studio 2005 information."

—Tad Anderson, Enterprise Architect, Corporate Systems & Solutions

"A great book for ASP developers wanting to learn an object-oriented methodology.

—Eric Landes, Microsoft MVP, ASP.NET, http://blogs.aspadvice.com/elandes

"This is an excellent resource for developers making the move from ASP to ASP.NET, as well as a good read for developers new to coding web pages on the IIS platform. I particularly appreciated the effort the author took to develop all the sample code in both C# and VB.NET."

—William "mac" McLuskie, Senior Solution Architect, Enterprise Consulting Services, Hewlett-Packard, Inc.

Maximizing ASP.NET

Maximizing ASP.NET
Real World, Object-Oriented Development

Jeffrey Putz

✦Addison-Wesley

Upper Saddle River, NJ • Boston • Indianapolis • San Francisco
New York • Toronto • Montreal • London • Munich • Paris • Madrid
Capetown • Sydney • Tokyo • Singapore • Mexico City

The publisher offers excellent discounts on this book when ordered in quantity for bulk purchases or special sales, which may include electronic versions and/or custom covers and content particular to your business, training goals, marketing focus, and branding interests. For more information, please contact:

U. S. Corporate and Government Sales
(800) 382-3419
corpsales@pearsontechgroup.com

For sales outside the U. S., please contact:

International Sales
international@pearsoned.com

Visit us on the Web: www.awprofessional.com

Library of Congress Catalog Number: 2004116048

Copyright © 2005 Pearson Education, Inc.

ISBN 0-32-129447-5
Text printed in the United States on recycled paper at R.R. Donnelley, Crawfordsville, Indiana.
First printing, March, 2005

For Stephanie

This book, and indeed the wonderful lives we lead, would not be possible without your constant support and love. I can't imagine a universe without you.

Contents

Preface

Microsoft has endowed Web developers with a gift. Since its introduction to the masses in beta form in 2001, the .NET Framework and its ASP.NET subset have changed the way we look at building Web applications. Indeed, before this time, many of us didn't even think in terms of "applications" but rather collections of loosely related scripts that together formed a Web site.

Making this transition required a serious leap of faith and a great deal of new learning for a lot of developers. Scripting languages such as ASP 3.0, ColdFusion, and PHP made it fairly easy for someone with little or no programming experience to quickly learn about the platform and start building dynamic Web sites. Years of experience as a developer or an academic background in computer science were not necessary.

That background still isn't necessary, but with ASP.NET, script developers need to make some fairly radical changes in their thinking to get the most out of this amazing platform. This book aims to help you with that transition, or to get you familiar with the platform's architecture if you're already well versed in object-oriented design.

Why Was This Book Written?

In watching the various message boards and newsgroups around the Internet, it became clear to me that a lot of very smart developers are having some problems making the transition to the object-oriented world of ASP.NET. As much as we praise Microsoft for delivering the platform to us, we can also curse them for making it so inviting and safe because it doesn't force you to follow the "best practices" they envisioned. You can do things in almost the same way you did when you were using a scripting platform.

It would be easy to create a straight book on techniques or a "cookbook" of sorts to help you along, but what I'm really after is a guide that helps you understand the underlying concepts and architecture to the platform so that you can apply the same concepts to your own applications. Indeed, I point out in the second chapter that the code you write isn't any different than the code that Microsoft wrote into the thousands of existing .NET base classes. A cookbook or overview wouldn't help you understand this.

This book is not meant to evangelize object-oriented techniques. The idea is to show you enough rationale behind the concepts to encourage you to use them. I want light bulbs to go off in your head that say, "Oh yeah, I get it!" Using OOP just for the sake of doing so is not good.

Who Is This Book For?

This book assumes that you've already taken the first steps in learning about ASP.NET and have a relatively basic grasp of either the C# or Visual Basic .NET languages. It is also assumed that you have some basic understanding of how to use Microsoft SQL Server and understand what a relational database is. You might be a developer who in a previous life was primarily a script developer and wants to "get" the platform and its strong object-oriented architecture. You might also be a more seasoned developer who just wants to get into some of the platform-specific details of ASP.NET that make things tick under the hood. These developers may choose to skip around a bit.

Regardless of the camp you might be in, this book is all about context. Developers are generally very smart people, and they don't learn by memorization, they learn by understanding. This book takes the basics of object-oriented programming and applies them to ASP.NET and Visual Studio to give the reader a more rounded skillset that includes application design, test-driven development, code reuse, modularization, and an eye on performance. The book puts Microsoft's platform into context by moving beyond the "how" and into the "why," not just explaining the concepts but also selling them as the best way to solve real problems. If you come from a scripting background or want to make your skills more applicable to other areas of .NET programming, this book is for you.

If you are totally new to ASP.NET, this book isn't for you—yet. You should start with one of the many ASP.NET books that have "beginner" or "introduction" in the title. When you've got the basics, come back to this book to round out and strengthen your knowledge. We won't cover basics such as master pages, user controls, connecting to a database, configuring `FormsAuthentication`, and so on.

I want to say up front that the term "best practice" is a bit of a misnomer. Some concepts and methodologies are certainly better than others, but this term implies that universal truths abound in the world of programming. Some might believe that the only real universal truths are death and taxes, so while you read about what I believe are best practices, keep in mind that there's plenty of room for interpretation based on your experience and the business problems you're trying to solve. As with anything else, use what works and adapt it to your needs.

Conventions

Whenever there is a bit of code to show you, it will look like this:

C#
```csharp
public class ThisIsAGreatClass
{
   // lots of code here
}
```

VB.NET
```vbnet
Public Class ThisIsAGreatClass
   ' lots of code here
End Class
```

Special points, sidebars, important notes, and other tangents will be separated from the rest of the text like this:

> This is something you should take into consideration.

Play-by-Play

The following is a brief outline of what you can expect to find in the rest of this book:

Part I: The Leap to Object-Oriented Programming

Chapter 1, "The Object Model." Object-oriented programming has been around for ages, but it's a new concept for developers with a scripting background. You'll learn that everything is an object in .NET, including your own code. We'll analogize the concept of object-oriented programming to the classic example of the structure and use of cars.

Chapter 2, "Classes: The Code Behind the Objects." After you see what an object is and how it contains some kind of functionality, we'll get into the nuts and bolts of writing a class. You'll learn about the instantiation of objects, inheritance, protection levels, static methods, enumerations, and interfaces.

Chapter 3, "Class Design." A class can serve many different purposes in an application. Your classes can execute a block of code, much as the familiar `System.Web.UI.Page` class does, and at times they can do nothing other than group data together. More useful classes can do all these things.

Chapter 4, "Application Architecture." Apart from ASP.NET, the n-tier approach to application development can make even the largest projects easier to build, deploy, and maintain. We'll take a look at this common design pattern and address when and when not to use it.

Chapter 5, "Object-Oriented Programming Applied: A Custom Data Class." This chapter presents you with a practical example of class design that manipulates database data and even caches it for better performance. This model shows you the payoff of object-oriented code, where you write it once and use it many times.

Part II: The ASP.NET Architecture

Chapter 6, "The Nuts and Bolts of IIS and Web Applications." Regardless of how you code your application, the files, folders, and assemblies need to be in the right places to make everything work.

Chapter 7, "The ASP.NET Event Model." Every request by users of your application has a fascinating life cycle. By understanding and following that life cycle, you can intervene or perform certain actions at just the right time to get the most out of your application. The execution of page, application, and control events is covered.

Chapter 8, "HttpHandlers and HttpModules." ASP.NET can do so much more than produce pages, and HttpHandlers and HttpModules are just the tools you'll need for special requests. I'll give you an example of a handler that will protect your images from being bandwidth leeched.

Chapter 9, "Server Controls." You might find that you use the same combination of controls frequently or that an existing control doesn't meet your needs. Building your own isn't that hard, and it's exactly the same process used by Microsoft to create many of the controls you already use.

Chapter 10, "Web Services as Objects." It's easy to create a Web service from your existing code, and it's easy to create a proxy class that consumes the service. What might not be as obvious is that Web services enable you to use that remote code as if it were an object local to your application.

Chapter 11, "Membership and Security." ASP.NET has a rich set of classes to help you control access to your site and verify who your users are. You can use little or no code to identify your users, or extend the system to make your own custom solution. You'll learn how to develop a custom Membership provider to connect the system to your own data.

Chapter 12, "Profiles, Themes, and Skins." Chances are you'll want to keep more than just a user's email and password, and again the ASP.NET team has made it possible to store this data with little effort on your part. You can also take the leap to extend the system with your own provider. Your users' preferences can be tied into an extensive skinning system so they don't have to live with your site's "look."

Chapter 13, "Declarative Programming." With all this talk of object-oriented code, what is declarative programming, and where does it fit? We'll cover some of the common controls and their uses available in ASP.NET.

Part III: Development Issues

Chapter 14, "Developing with Visual Studio." Heralded by many as the greatest development tool ever made, it's not without its nuances and quirks. It quite possibly is the greatest tool, but you'll have to start thinking a little like a desktop application developer. We'll look at the approach the software takes to making your events happen and how to debug with the best of them.

Chapter 15, "Performance, Scalability, and Metrics." There are probably hundreds of things you can do to make your code industrial-strength, but there are a few basics you should know and live by. A number of tools and techniques provide the foundation for measuring the performance of your application.

Chapter 16, "Testing, Deployment, and Code Management." The bigger a project gets, the harder it can be to maintain and deploy. There are a number of ways to keep everything organized while testing and versioning your code. We'll discuss the basics of test-driven development here.

Chapter 17, "More Advanced Topics." The .NET Framework has more classes than you can shake a stick at. Here are a few of the more useful ones in a high-level overview, including streams, networking, and threading.

Code Downloads, Errata, and Feedback

You can download the code from this book, check for errata, and give feedback at this site:

http://www.uberasp.net/books/

Acknowledgments

There are a lot of people who made this book possible, starting with my wife, Stephanie Gall. Her constant support and encouragement gave me the will to leave a cushy high-paying job to write this book.

Special thanks go to Walt Schmidt, my partner on *PointBuzz: The Ultimate Guide to Cedar Point* (http://www.pointbuzz.com). Through the many discussions we had about our "little" hobby site, my programming advice to Walt was met with the advice that I should write a book.

A lot of people I've worked with over the years were crucial to my professional development as an Internet code monkey. Perry Trunick at Penton Media gave me my first job in this role over someone with certifications, all on a gut feeling. Tim Walsh, Bob Eck, Tony D'Avino, Jay Davis, Mike Freeze, Mary Aichlmayr and others had an impact as well. We were involved in really great things during the Internet boom!

Katie and Mark Bruno of Website Design and Development in Wadsworth, Ohio, also helped me realize my potential as a teacher of sorts by giving me the opportunity to teach their staff in the ways of .NET.

I'd like to thank the people who did the editorial reviews for Addison-Wesley, especially Gordon Barrs, for making sure I was covering the right things.

Finally, congratulations to the many people involved with .NET at Microsoft. It's through their hard work and vision that we all have this great platform to work with. Their products have had a profound impact on my professional life and indirectly on the users of my own software and Web sites. I'd specifically like to acknowledge Brian Goldfarb at Microsoft for keeping me in the loop through changes leading up to production for this book. Writing about software that isn't yet done was a lot easier with his help.

About the Author

Jeff Putz is the founder of POP World Media, LLC, a company formed originally to organize several hobby Web sites into a bona fide business. Jeff started programming in grade six on a TRS-80 and moved up through an Atari 600XL and Apple II+ later. After flirting with various jobs in the broadcast world, Jeff returned to computers and welcomed the Internet in 1998, working in various programming and management roles for several companies specializing in vertical market content.

Jeff's POP Forums application (http://www.popforums.com) has been downloaded tens of thousands of times and was featured in *MSDN Magazine* (Feb. 2004). His company is in the process of developing several products using ASP.NET and continues to operate CoasterBuzz (http://www.coasterbuzz.com), the world's most popular roller coaster enthusiast site.

The Leap to Object-Oriented Programming

CHAPTER 1

The Object Model

The single greatest leap of faith a developer needs to make in the world of ASP.NET is to accept the object-oriented nature of this technology. It can be a hard sell because much of what you build from day to day is easily accomplished by writing very procedural code. Why fix what isn't broken?

In this chapter we'll make our sales pitch for object-oriented programming by defining it and comparing it to script-style programming.

Breaking Away from the Linear Script Way of Thinking

The use of scripting languages on the Web can be credited with bringing us out of the dark ages, causing us to move from static HTML pages to rich applications that let us solve problems, all from a relatively lightweight application—the browser. Script is easy to write, which is precisely the reason that ASP, PHP, Cold Fusion, and other scripting languages have been so popular over the years, drawing in people who otherwise might not have been developing for the Web.

Scripting platforms of course have their disadvantages. The worst of them is "spaghetti code," where programming code is mixed in with HTML in little blocks. It's hard to read and maintain. The classic example of this is getting records from a database and then looping through them to create a table. Listing 1.1 shows how we did it in ASP.

Listing 1.1 Old-fashioned ASP

```
<table>
<%Set db = Server.CreateObject("ADODB.Connection")
db.Open strConnectionString
Set ThePosts = Server.CreateObject("ADODB.Recordset")
```

(Continues)

3

Listing 1.1 Old-fashioned ASP   *(Continued)*

```
sql = "SELECT * FROM MyTable"
ThePosts.Open sql, db, adOpenStatic, adLockReadOnly, adCmdText
Do While Not ThePosts.EOF%>
  <tr>
    <td><%=rsThePosts("Field1")%></td>
    <td><%=rsThePosts("Field2")%></td>
    <td><%=rsThePosts("Field3")%></td>
    <td><%=rsThePosts("Field4")%></td>
  </tr>
  <%rsThePosts.MoveNext
Loop
ThePosts.Close
db.Close
Set db = Nothing%>
</table>
```

Listing 1.2 Getting data in ASP.NET

C#

```
SqlConnection objConnection = new SqlConnection(myConnectionString);
objConnection.Open();
SqlCommand objCommand = new SqlCommand("SELECT * FROM MyTable",
objConnection);
MyDataGrid.DataSource = objCommand.ExecuteReader();
MyDataGrid.DataBind();
objConnection.Close();
```

In our ASP.NET example (Listing 1.2), we have no HTML. We reference a `DataGrid` object on the page, and we're done. This is exactly what you need to be thinking about. Instead of going through a sequence of events as you did in ASP to get the desired output, you'll create some objects and give them something to do, probably by making use of some other objects.

Let's push the concept even further and preview a code sample from Chapter 5, "Object-Oriented Programming Applied: A Custom Data Class." In that chapter, we'll give you an example of how to encapsulate data access to a particular table that you can use repeatedly in your application, writing SQL and data plumbing only once. Listing 1.3 shows you how the process of instantiating and using a class works.

People often confuse the terms "class," "instance," (or the act of instantiating) and "object." A class is the code itself, or the blueprint, if you will. An instance of the class (a piece of running code) is an object. You can have many instances of the same class. That object in memory is basically its own miniature running program, and you can create as many as you want. Listing 1.3, for example, has two instances of the `Customer` class. They are two objects that execute the same code. We'll cover classes and objects in more detail later.

The term "encapsulation" gets thrown around a lot, and in a nutshell (if you'll pardon the pun), it's used to describe the wrapping of some bit of functionality into a discrete package. In the object-oriented world, this package is a class.

Listing 1.3 Instantiating and using a class

C#

```
// Instantiate the Customer class using the default constructor
Customer objCustomer = new Customer();
// Assign some of its properties
objCustomer.LastName = "Jones";
objCustomer.FirstName = "Jeff";
// Call its Create() method to save the values in the database,
// and get its new primary key (CustomerID) value
int intCustomerID = objCustomer.Create();

// Instantiate the Customer class using the constructor that takes
// the CustomerID as a parameter
Customer objCustomer2 = new Customer(intCustomerID);
Trace.Write("LastName: " + objCustomer2.LastName);
Trace.Write("FirstName: " + objCustomer2.FirstName);

// Change the value of the first name then save the changes
// to the database
objCustomer2.FirstName = "Stephanie";
objCustomer2.Update();

// On second thought, let's just delete the record entirely
objCustomer2.Delete();
```

(Continues)

Listing 1.3 Instantiating and using a class   *(Continued)*

VB.NET
```
' Instantiate the Customer class using the default constructor
Dim objCustomer As New Customer()
' Assign some of its properties
objCustomer.LastName = "Jones"
objCustomer.FirstName = "Jeff"
' Call its Create() method to save the values in the database,
' and get its new primary key (CustomerID) value
Dim intCustomerID As Integer = objCustomer.Create()

' Instantiate the Customer class using the constructor that takes
' the CustomerID as a parameter
Dim objCustomer2 As New Customer(intCustomerID)
Trace.Write(("LastName: " + objCustomer2.LastName))
Trace.Write(("FirstName: " + objCustomer2.FirstName))

' Change the value of the first name then save the changes
' to the database
objCustomer2.FirstName = "Stephanie"
objCustomer2.Update()

' On second thought, let's just delete the record entirely
objCustomer2.Delete()
```

In this example, we never see anything about connections, readers, or queries, even though we manipulate data several times. We've written a class that does all of these things for us and encapsulates that functionality into a nice little package that we can use repeatedly in our application. We'll get to the specifics of that class later in the book.

These examples illustrate that you can look at object-oriented programming in two different ways. On one hand, there's the "user" view of a class. To a user, the internal implementation of a class is unimportant as long as the user knows that it does what he or she needs it to do. On the other hand, you have the "programmer" view of a class, where the design and code that makes the class work is important. If you look at it from both sides, you may better understand the benefits of object-oriented programming.

Classes and Objects

So what are classes and objects? A class is a piece of code that does something by manipulating its members. Members include methods and properties (other types of members exist, but they will be discussed later). Methods do something, and properties hold data.

An object is an instantiation of a class. An object is a living, breathing entity that does things. In our previous example, we have `Customer` objects that have properties, such as `FirstName` and `LastName`, and methods, such as `Update()` and `Delete()`.

This is a somewhat abstract view of classes and objects. Developers like to know what the nuts and bolts are. Classes are compiled into assemblies. As you're probably aware from your beginning ASP.NET books and training, all of your pages are compiled into assemblies that are cached on the server. This compiled code will execute significantly faster than interpreted code, where the server must go through every line of code and figure out what to do every time the page executes.

Your classes are compiled as well and are stored in an assembly that has a .dll file extension. It's important to understand that any number of classes may "live" in an assembly. It doesn't matter what assembly your class lives in, as long as it's in the `/bin` folder of your application. Any class can be called by any other class in your application as long as it can be found in the `/bin` folder.

> Actually, your classes can live in the machine's global assembly cache (GAC) as well, but for simplicity's sake, let's pretend for now that your compiled classes must live in the `/bin` folder.

Analogy to a Car

People have compared objects to cars as long as object-oriented programming has been around. Hopefully we can push that analogy further by connecting the benefits of using a car with the concept of object-oriented programming.

Think of the blueprints for a car as your class. When your automaker needs to create a car, it instantiates that class (the blueprints) into an object (an actual car). The code might look like this in C#:

```
Car MyCar = new Car();
```

Before the manufacturer is done with the car, they'll set some of its properties. It has properties for `Color`, `Vin` (vehicle identification number), and so on.

```
MyCar.Color = Red;
MyCar.Vin = "1234567890";
```

So now that you have this car, wouldn't it be fun to drive it? Before we get into it, we want to pull up the antenna so we can listen to the radio. The car object already exists, so we're going to call its `RaiseAntenna()` method like this:

```
MyCar.RaiseAntenna();
```

If the distinction isn't already clear, a property holds some kind of data, while a method executes some code.

We need to unlock the car, but that's a little trickier. For that we need a key. The car has an `Unlock()` method, but that method takes a key parameter. Our car object has those fancy key-code pads on it, so all we need to know is that the code is "1234." We'll unlock the car by passing in that code with the `Unlock()` method.

```
MyCar.Unlock("1234");
```

You can see that manipulating our car object (making it do something with methods) is pretty easy. We could go on like this with examples that call other methods to accelerate, brake, and so on, but you've probably seen examples like these before.

What's the benefit of this car object? To start with, the data associated with the car, such as its color, is easily changed. As a user of the object, you don't need to know how to paint a car; you only need to assign a value to its `Color` property. You don't need to know about the inner workings of the

car's locking mechanism; you only need to know that there's an Unlock()
method and that it requires a key.

Going back to our spot of code that manipulates Customer objects, we
don't need to know anything about the underlying code or the data store
where our customer information is kept. All that matters is that we have
this object that we know is supposed to manipulate data in a database.

How would you do this in script? In the best-case scenario, you would
use an include that has some functions you can call to act on this data
(which isn't really best-case at all because the interpreter has to interpret
all that code every time, even if you don't use it). In the worst case, you're
writing the same kind of code every time you need it in every page on the
site. This is not a good use of your time, and making a simple global change
like this becomes a nightmare.

Object Inheritance

Objects are everywhere. Everything in .NET is an object. There are thousands of classes in the .NET Framework, ready to be instantiated into
objects in the world's greatest Web application that you're going to write.
Can you imagine having to write the code from scratch for every one of
those classes? I can't either, and because of inheritance, the clever folks in
Redmond avoided this duplication of effort.

One of the great things about inheritance is that you get something for
free, including all of the benefits that go along with it. When you inherit a
class, your new class gets all of that functionality instantly, plus whatever
new functionality you pile on top of it.

When you browse the .NET SDK documentation, every class shows
that it is derived from another class. These classes inherit members and
structure from another class, for better or worse, much in the way that you
might inherit blue eyes or heart disease from your parents. In .NET, everything ultimately inherits from System.Object, the mother of the entire
class library. It has a couple of methods and a constructor that is inherited
by every single class.

Keeping with our car analogy, let's say that we want our car to be more
secure. We want to replace the unlock code with our own system, and we
want to add keyless entry. It would be silly to design our new car from
scratch because we already have a Car class. We'll create a new class that
inherits the old car as our base class, replace the Unlock() method, and
add an entirely new method called WirelessUnlock().

Listing 1.4 Unlocking your car

C#

```csharp
public class BetterCar : Car
{
   public override void Unlock(string newCode)
   {
      // better unlock code here
   }

   public void WirelessUnlock(string newCode)
   {
      Unlock(newCode);
         }
}
```

VB.NET

```vbnet
Public Class BetterCar
    Inherits Car

    Public Overrides Sub Unlock(newCode As String)
       ' better unlock code here
    End Sub

    Public Sub WirelessUnlock(newCode As String)
        Unlock(newCode)
    End Sub
End Class
```

Let's look at each part of the code. The beginning looks just like any other class declaration, except that we indicate that we'll inherit from the Car class. You've seen this before if you've used a code-behind class for your v1.x ASP.NET pages, where you inherit from System.Web.UI.Page, thus making available all of the events and properties common to the page class.

Next we declare our own Unlock() method by overriding it. Any time code instantiates our BetterCar class, our replacement Unlock() method will be used instead of the original version.

> Overriding is the process of replacing one method with another in a derived class. Whenever the method is called, the original version, for all practical purposes, does not exist unless you explicitly call the original version from the new one (as we'll discuss in a moment).

Finally, we've added a `WirelessUnlock()` method. This method also takes a key code (imagine that it's transmitted from our `WirelessRemote` object), and that key code is passed off to our new `Unlock()` method.

> The old `Unlock()` isn't actually gone. We can still get to it by referring to `base.Unlock()` (or `MyBase.Unlock()` in VB.NET). This is handy when you want the base implementation to do something else in addition to the original action. For example, if we wanted to leave the `Unlock()` implementation the same and flash the lights, we might write our new method like this:
>
> **C#**
> ```
> public override void Unlock(string newCode)
> {
>   base.Unlock(newCode);
>   FlashLights();
> }
> ```
>
> **VB.NET**
> ```
> Public Overrides Sub Unlock(newCode As String)
>   MyBase.Unlock(newCode)
>   FlashLights()
> End Sub
> ```

How would you use inheritance in real life? Let's consider the user control. The user controls that you build (ending in `.ascx`) are, like anything else, classes that are instantiated into objects when the code executes. Imagine for a moment that you have a user control that has a label and code to assign it a value, as in Listing 1.5.

Listing 1.5 Assigning a value to a Label control

```
<%@ Control Language="c#" %>
<script runat="server">
  private void Page_Load(object sender, System.EventArgs e)
  {
    MyLabel.Text = _NewLabelText;
  }

  private string _NewLabelText;
  public string NewLabelText
```

(Continues)

Listing 1.5 Assigning a value to a Label control   *(Continued)*

```
   {
      get {return _NewLabelText;}
      set {_NewLabelText = value;}
   }
</script>
<asp:Label id="MyLabel" runat="server" />
```

For the moment, don't worry about the code syntax; just take note that this user control has a property called `NewLabelText`. Now let's use this user control in a page, shown in Listing 1.6.

Listing 1.6 Using a user control in a page

```
<%@ Page language="c#" %>
<%@ Register TagPrefix="uc1" TagName="WebUserControl1"
Src="WebUserControl1.ascx" %>
<html>
   <body>
      <form id="Form1" method="post" runat="server">
         <uc1:WebUserControl1 id="WebUserControl11" runat="server"
NewLabelText="Look at my text!" />
      </form>
   </body>
</html>
```

Don't look now, but you just practiced inheritance! Your user control inherits from the `UserControl` class. ASP.NET performs this inheritance for you, and while you may not be aware of it, it is going on under the hood. You've added a new property to the user control class called `NewLabelText`. When the page executes, it copies the value "Look at my text!" to the `Label` control in the user control.

Let's look at the same example from another point of view. Let's say that you want several user controls to inherit from a base class that has this special property. We'll create a class that inherits from `UserControl` to accomplish this (Listing 1.7).

Listing 1.7 Creating a class that inherits from UserControl for use by other controls

C#
```
public class BetterUserControl : System.Web.UI.UserControl
{
   private string _NewLabelText;
```

```
   public string NewLabelText
   {
      get {return _NewLabelText;}
      set {_NewLabelText = value;}
   }
}
```

VB.NET

```
Public Class BetterUserControl
Inherits System.Web.UI.UserControl

Private _NewLabelText As String
Public Property NewLabelText() As String
   Get
      Return _NewLabelText
   End Get
   Set
      _NewLabelText = value
   End Set
End Property
End Class
```

Notice that we inherit `UserControl` in our class declaration. You can have your user controls all use this class by changing the `Control` directive:

```
<%@ Control Language="c#" Inherits="BetterUserControl" %>
```

This user control will have a `NewLabelText` property even though we haven't declared it. In fact, just as if it was a normal user control, it will have all of the other properties (such as `ID` and `Page`) and methods (such as `FindControl()`) you've come to know and love. Your user control inherits from `BetterUserControl`, which inherits from `System.Web.UI.UserControl`, which inherits from `System.Web.UI.TemplateControl`, which inherits from `System.Web.UI.Control`, which finally inherits from `System.Object`. Get it? Table 1.1 shows the inheritance tree and the improvements made at each new derived class.

Another example of inheritance that is easier to implement and more relevant to stand-alone class design is to add a method to our `Customer` class. We might want to add a `MailCustomer()` method to the class, or perhaps we might want to override the `Update()` method to execute the base method and then email the customer.

Table 1.1 The Inheritance Sequence for Our User Control

`System.Object`	The base from which all other objects are inherited.
`System.Web.UI.Control`	Inherits `Object`'s members, and adds a wealth of new properties (`ID`, `EnableViewState`, `Visible`, etc.) as well as its own methods (`DataBind()`, `RenderControl()`, etc.) and events (`Init`, `Load`, etc.).
`System.Web.UI.TemplateControl`	Adds a few more members such as the `LoadControl()` method and `Error` event. `Object`'s and `Control`'s members are still available.
`System.Web.UI.UserControl`	Many new members are added including the `Request` property `MapPath()` method, while all of the members of the inherited classes are still available.
`BetterUserControl`	This is where we add our `NewLabelText` property. It joins the ranks of all of the other members from the underlying four inherited classes.

Your Classes Are as Special as Microsoft's

This might sound obvious, but the classes you write are not any different from those written by Microsoft in the .NET Framework. Even though you don't explicitly declare it, your classes ultimately inherit from `System.Object`, just like those found in the vast class library in the framework.

Don't believe me? Open up a class you've written in Visual Studio with Intellisense on and type "this" (or "Me" in VB.NET), followed by a period. (Note: This has to be in a non-static/shared method to work.) Intellisense will pop up a list of methods that are in fact the same methods in the base `Object` class. You've been using inheritance all this time and didn't even realize it!

You can start to see the potential for object-oriented programming when you see how easy it is to put a load of functionality into a discrete little package that can be used repeatedly. You've no doubt used or experimented with the `Calendar` control on your pages. Consider that there are thousands of lines of code that enable you to infinitely alter the look and display of calendars, and you don't need to know a single thing about how it's achieved under the hood.

Summary

Shifting away from the scripting mindset isn't easy, but it yields many benefits when you take an object-oriented approach to development. In this chapter, we showed how encapsulating common functionality into a class enables us to reuse the same code, while the calling code doesn't need to know anything about its implementation. Whether it is a car object or a customer object, these logical units do something for us. Their functionality is exposed through a number of members that describe the object and make it do things.

A class is the physical code we group together to make an object do its thing. The object is the instantiation, or manifestation, of the underlying code in the class. Classes are compiled and stored in assemblies, available to be called by any other code in our application.

Inheritance enables us to extend and alter an existing class without having to know anything about its underlying logic. This makes adding a feature to a class a piece of cake, removing the need to reinvent the wheel.

In the next chapter, we'll get into the real nuts and bolts of a class.

CHAPTER 2

Classes: The Code Behind the Objects

In the last chapter, we briefly described the code structure for classes. Now we'll look at the underlying structures of a class that enable you to get things done. This is not an exhaustive list of members or other structures (we will not, for example, cover structs, generics, or delegates), but these are the nuts and bolts you should be most familiar with.

For more specific and thorough explanations, check out *Professional C#, 3rd Edition* (Wrox Press, 2004) or *Professional Visual Basic .NET, 3rd Edition* (Wrox Press, 2004).

It's easy to get overwhelmed by all of the information in this chapter. Take the topics one at a time, and don't worry if you don't see how it all fits into the big picture. Until you've had a lot of opportunities to apply these concepts, they may not sink in. Most developers I know learn by doing, not just by reading about the subject! As we get more into class design in the next chapter, you may refer back to some topics here.

You'll hear different parts of a class referred to as "members." Members include all of the little parts of a class, including properties, methods, and internally used variables that have class scope (more on that later). Think of it this way: anything indented one tab in from your class declaration in Visual Studio is a class member. The drop-down list in the Visual Studio code editor (at the top, on the right) enables you to quickly jump around to your various class members.

Access Modifiers

There are four modifiers for class members: public, private, protected, and internal (plus the combination of protected internal). These control whether a member is accessible to other code inside and outside the class. You already know public members, which can be called from any instance of the class. Private members can only be accessed from within the class. Protected members may be accessed from within the class or from within a derived class. Internal members may only be accessed from within other classes in the same assembly.

You'll see these modifiers in use right away in the chapter, starting with public constructors and private variables.

The Class Declaration

Just to cover our bases, you already know that declaring a class and putting it in a particular namespace looks like Listing 2.1.

Listing 2.1 The basic class declaration

C#
```
namespace MyNamespace
{
  public class Car
  {
    // class members
  }
}
```

VB.NET
```
Namespace MyNamespace
   Public Class Car
      ' class members
   End Class
End Namespace
```

We use namespaces because the .NET Framework is strongly typed. That means we give every class a fully qualified name to make sure that it's not duplicated and that there's no confusion about the class we're referencing. For example, both ASP.NET and Windows Forms have a TextBox class. The framework knows the difference because one lives in the `System.Web.UI.WebControls` namespace and the other in the `System.Windows.Forms.Control` namespace. We don't need to use its fully qualified name because we make `using` (`Imports` in VB.NET) declarations at the top of our code files so the compiler knows what we're talking about.

Constructors

Constructors are the "setup" methods of your classes. They are fired whenever your class is instantiated. You are not required to write code for a constructor, but if you do not, the base class constructor will fire anyway. At the very least, the base class is `System.Object`, so the constructor for this class will fire.

> Notice the syntax of a constructor. In C#, it's simply the name of the class. In VB.NET, it's a special `Sub` called `New`. This is true for every class, and it's what differentiates it from other methods in the class.

One of the most typical uses for a constructor is to set initial values for different properties in the class. If you have a `Name` property, for example, its value will be `null` when the class is instantiated, unless you specify some value for it (maybe an empty string) in the constructor.

You don't call a constructor directly. It's fired when you instantiate the object. Recall the creation of our car:

Listing 2.2 Instantiating an object

C#
```
Car myCar = new Car();
```

VB.NET
```
Dim myCar As New Car()
```

The car's constructor method, if there is one, is fired as soon as we create this new car object called `myCar`. In our class, the code is simply a method with the same name as the class in C#, or the `New` keyword in VB:

Listing 2.3 A basic constructor

C#
```
public Car()
{
  // code
}
```

VB.NET
```
Public Sub New()
   ' code
End Sub
```

Through overloading (we'll talk about that shortly), you can even pass in parameters to your constructor. This gets back to the notion of setting some initial values for your class when it's instantiated. Say we wanted to make our car a certain color when we created it. We might write a constructor like this:

Listing 2.4 A constructor with a parameter

C#
```
public Car(string newColor)
{
  Color = newColor;
}
```

VB.NET
```
Public Sub New(newColor As String)
  Color = newColor
End Sub
```

Assuming for a moment that there is a property called Color, we take the parameter in the constructor, NewColor, and assign it to the Color property. Creating a Car object with a color, then, would look like this:

Listing 2.5 Instantiating an object with a parameter

C#
```
Car myCar = new Car("Red");
```

VB.NET
```
Dim myCar As New Car("Red")
```

Properties and Private Variables

Your classes will likely need to manipulate some kind of data. We can pass this data in through the constructors or other methods and get data back out by those methods. For classes that don't expose a lot of functionality, using return values from methods and parameters is fine, but for more complex classes, we'll need a place to store data.

Private members are members that fall into class scope, and the class can access them internally. They are not exposed as a part of the instantiated object. The simplest private members are variables used by other members in the class. They're straightforward to define, and you may optionally assign a value to them:

Listing 2.6 Declaring private variables

C#
```
private string _myString;
private int _myInt = 3;
```

VB.NET
```
Private _myString As String
Private _myInt As Integer = 3
```

Naming conventions for class members vary widely depending on other languages you've used, who you work with, your experience, your teammates' experience, and so on. There is no "right" way, but here are some suggestions you might want to consider. Most shops agree that private variables should begin with an underscore and use camel-case (first letter lower-case, each word thereafter capitalized). Use of Hungarian notation, where you prefix variables with something that indicates their type (i.e., `strMyString` or `intMyInt`), is discouraged because most development environments, and Visual Studio in particular, let you know what type a variable is when you mouse over it, though this often makes it harder to read the code in samples online or in books. Don't let developer snobbery dictate what you use, unless of course it's a convention in your shop.

For more information on Microsoft's suggested naming conventions, check out: http://msdn.microsoft.com/library/en-us/cpgenref/html/cpconnamingguidelines.asp

Although you can set the values for private variables right there in the class declaration, you shouldn't. Instead, assign the values in your constructors. This keeps all of your assignments in one place, so you won't have to search your code. Not only that, but if you have several different constructors, you also may want to assign different values depending on which constructor is called.

A private variable might be used in one method and then later be used by another method during the lifetime of an object. The calling code outside of the class can't access this variable as a member of the object instance. For example, if the previous example of _myString was used internally by a class that we've instantiated into an object called MyObject, we couldn't access it with MyObject._myString.

Properties really go hand-in-hand with using private variables. A property is the public face of data for an instantiated object. Going back to our car object, the Color property was something we could get and set from the object. Properties have a special structure that "get" and "set" their values, and we store those values in matching private variables. If our Color property is a string, we'll need to declare the private variable as well as the property used by code that instantiates the class into an object. Listing 2.7 shows this structure.

Listing 2.7 A basic property and a matching private variable

C#

```
private string _color;
public string Color
{
  get { return _color; }
  set { _color = value; }
}
```

VB.NET

```
Private _color As String
Public Property Color() As String
  Get
    Return _color
  End Get
  Set
    _color = value
  End Set
End Property
```

The special `value` keyword is used in the property structure to represent the value being assigned to the property. The code in `get` is called when the property is referenced, and the code in `set` is called when a new value is assigned to the property.

```
Trace.Warn(MyCar.Color); // get called
MyCar.Color = "Red"; // set called
```

This is not the place to write your code to manipulate data. Properties are intended only to hold your data, not to manipulate it. You'll manipulate data in methods.

Properties can be read-only. To implement this in C#, you drop the `set` method, and in VB, you need to add the `ReadOnly` keyword, as shown in Listing 2.8.

Listing 2.8 A read-only property

C#
```
private string _color;
public string Color
{
  get { return _color; }
}
```

VB.NET
```
Private _color As String
Public ReadOnly Property Color() As String
  Get
    Return _color
  End Get
End Property
```

Methods

Methods are the workhorses of your classes. When you call a method, it executes some code. It may, but doesn't have to, return some value directly. It may also take some parameters, but again, it doesn't have to.

In Visual Basic .NET, methods appear in the syntax with the name `Function` or `Sub`, as in "subroutine." This is largely a throwback to the old Basic days where the same piece of code was used several places throughout the program. "Subroutine" really isn't a good name for a method because it implies that it lives all by itself and is not critical to the design of the class. For example, if you call the `Unlock()` method of the `MyCar` object with `MyCar.Unlock()`, you aren't calling a subroutine at all—you're calling code to manipulate that instance of the object. It's not generally used by the application at-large.

You've already seen a number of different methods as they appear in your class code, as well as how to call them from an instantiated object. They may be declared not to return any kind of value, like the method in Listing 2.9.

Listing 2.9 Basic method with no return value

C#
```
public void MyMethod()
{
   // some code
}
```

VB.NET
```
Public Sub MyMethod()
   ' some code
End Sub
```

If you'd like the method to return some kind of value, you'll need to declare its type in the method declaration, and then at some point (or points) in the method, you'll need to return the value with the `return` keyword, as shown in Listing 2.10.

Listing 2.10 A method that returns a string

C#
```
public string MyMethod()
{
   return "some string";
}
```

VB.NET
```
Public Function MyMethod() As String
   Return "some string"
End Function
```

Notice the difference in syntax compared to Listing 2.8, where the method does not return a value, especially if you're using VB.NET. When you need to return a value, you use the `Function` syntax instead of the `Sub` syntax. In C#, when you don't intend to return any value, you use the pseudo-type `void`.

You probably have used methods that return a value, even if you haven't used that value. For example, if you've called the `ExecuteNonQuery()` method of a `SqlCommand` object, that method returns an integer indicating the number of rows in the database that were affected by your command (i.e., `myInteger = SomeSqlCommand.ExecuteNonQuery()`). If you don't capture that value, it's simply not used.

Methods can give you something back, but you also can put something into a method as well by feeding it parameters. A method can have any number of parameters of any types. Listing 2.11 shows a method that takes a `string` and an `int`.

Listing 2.11 Method with parameters

C#
```
public void MyMethod(string myName, int myAge)
{
   Trace.Warn(myName);
   Trace.Warn(myAge.ToString());
}
```

VB.NET
```
Public Sub MyMethod(myName As String, myAge As Integer)
   Trace.Warn(myName)
   Trace.Warn(myAge.ToString())
End Sub
```

You can now see that there are really two primary ways to get data in and out of your instantiated objects. You can use parameters and return values in your methods, or you can assign and read values from properties.

Alternatively, you can do both. We'll look closer at both approaches in Chapter 3, "Class Design."

Public methods can be called from any instance of the class. So what good are private methods? Suppose you have some common piece of code that other methods in the class need to call, but you don't want that common code to be called directly from an instance of the class. Marking the method private accomplishes this, and it's a handy way to avoid code duplication in your class.

Member Scope

When we talk about scope, we talk about which parts of your code can reach a member or variable. You may recall the use of private variables declared in Listing 2.6. As we revealed earlier, the strings declared in this class can be used by any other member in the class. This variable is said to have class scope. Although this is handy for sharing data across the class, sometimes you don't need to declare a variable that is used by the entire class. In these cases we declare the variable in the body of the method.

In Listing 2.12, we show a variable declared in a method, and we show that it can't be reached by other methods. It is said to be out of scope when you attempt to get to it from another method. Specifically, the code will throw an "object reference not set to an instance of an object" error because `TwoMethod()` has no idea that `MyString` exists.

Listing 2.12 Demonstrating variable scope

C#
```
public class MyClass
{
   public string OneMethod()
   {
     string MyString = "hello";
     return MyString;
   }
   public string TwoMethod()
   {
     return MyString; // throws an exception
   }
}
```

VB.NET
```
Public Class MyClass
  Public Function OneMethod() As String
    Dim MyString As String = "hello"
    Return MyString
  End Function
  Public Function TwoMethod() As String
    Return MyString ' throws an exception
  End Function
End Class
```

Overloading

Overloading is a great way to expose similar functionality in methods that all have the same name. The method signature, which is defined by the number, order, and type of parameters the method takes, determines which method is fired.

You've used overloaded methods before, probably with something simple such as the ToString() method of many different classes. The Int32 structure, which is the structure that holds your integer values, has four overloads:

```
Int32.ToString();
Int32.ToString(IFormatProvider);
Int32.ToString(string);
Int32.ToString(string, IFormatProvider);
```

The framework knows which version of the method to call based on the parameters you provide. If you provide no parameters, the first one is called. If you pass in a string such as "C" (to format the number as currency), it knows to call the third version of the method.

You can write your own overloaded methods as well. Going back to our car example, perhaps we want two Accelerate methods. In Listing 2.13, one method accelerates the car to a speed we give it, whereas the other method just provides momentary acceleration and doesn't need a parameter.

Listing 2.13 Overloaded methods in the Car class

C#
```
public class Car
{
  public void Accelerate(int speed)
  {
    // code to make the car reach the value speed
  }
  public void Accelerate()
  {
    // code to make the car momentarily accelerate
  }
}
```

VB.NET
```
Public Class Car
  Overloads Public Sub Accelerate(speed As Integer)
    ' code to make the car reach the value speed
  End Sub
  Overloads Public Sub Accelerate()
    ' code to make the car momentarily accelerate
  End Sub
End Class
```

Overloading makes your code a little easier to understand for others, especially if you're writing a class that will be used by other developers who won't see the compiled code. If you have three methods that essentially arrive at the same result with different parameters, there's less confusion if they're all named the same thing. Without overloading in the previous example, you might have methods like "AccelerateToASpeed" and "AccelerateMomentarily."

Static (Shared) Members

There are times when you don't need an entire class to perform some action. If you need a method that, for example, redirects a user to a specific URL, instantiating an entire class would be overkill. That's where static methods come in!

Marking a method `static` (or `Shared` in VB) means that you don't have to create an instance of the containing class in order to use it. A redirect method that you might use across your entire application might look like the method in Listing 2.14.

Listing 2.14 A static method

C#
```
public class MyMethods
{
  public static void SpecialRedirect()
  {
    Response.Redirect("somepage.aspx");
  }
}
```

VB.NET
```
Public Class MyMethods
  Public Shared Sub SpecialRedirect()
    Response.Redirect("somepage.aspx")
  End Sub
End Class
```

Calling this method is just a matter of specifying the class name itself, followed by the method name:

```
MyMethods.SpecialRedirect()
```

I find that in almost every large project, there are little pieces of functionality that don't really fit anywhere and that certainly don't merit their own class. Inevitably, I end up with a class called `Utility` with several static methods like the previous one.

Inheritance

We used our `Car` class in Chapter 1, "The Object Model," to demonstrate inheritance. We won't go over that again here, but it's an important aspect of object-oriented programming.

Interfaces

Interfaces provide a way to specify an entire class signature so that other classes can manipulate instances of a class that implements that interface. Got all that? It's actually really simple.

In Chapter 8, "HttpHandlers and HttpModules," we'll talk about HttpHandlers. An HttpHandler is a class that takes a Web request and does something with it. ASP.NET has a number of handlers. Requests for .aspx pages are handled by the System.Web.UI.PageHandlerFactory class, for example. Every handler implements the IHttpHandler interface so that the framework can manipulate the class and serve pages.

The easiest way to explain the interface is to show it to you. Listing 2.15 shows how the .NET Framework defines the IHttpHandler interface.

Listing 2.15 The IHttpHandler interface

C#
```csharp
public interface IHttpHandler
{
   void ProcessRequest(HttpContext context);
   bool IsReusable
   {
     get;
   }
}
```

VB.NET
```vbnet
Public Interface IHttpHandler
   Sub ProcessRequest(context As HttpContext)
   ReadOnly Property IsReusable() As Boolean
End Interface
```

If you think that the code in Listing 2.15 looks like a class without any implementation, then you're on the right track. An interface only defines the "signature" for the class, not the code that must be contained in its members. If we wanted to write a class that implemented the IHttpHandler interface (and we will in Chapter 8), it might look something like Listing 2.16.

Listing 2.16 An implementation of the IHttpHandler interface

C#
```csharp
public class MyHandler : IHttpHandler
{
  public void ProcessRequest(HttpContext context)
  {
    // do something here
  }
  public bool IsReusable
  {
    get { return true; }
  }
}
```

VB.NET
```vbnet
Public Class MyHandler
  Implements IHttpHandler
  Public Sub ProcessRequest(context As HttpContext)
    ' do something here
  End Sub
  Public ReadOnly Property IsReusable() As Boolean
    Get
      Return True
    End Get
  End Property
End Class
```

So why might you create an interface? One practical reason would be to define a data access layer for your application. Your interface might have dozens of method signatures that define how to get or save data to a database, while a class that implements the interface does the actual work. You could create several classes that all implement the same interface but interact with different databases (such as SQL Server or Access). If a developer comes along who wants to use yet another database, such as Oracle, she can write her own class that implements your interface and swap out the other class that uses SQL Server. The rest of your application won't break (assuming of course that the implementation is well tested and that the developer knows what she's doing).

Abstract Classes

An abstract class is a lot like an interface, except that an abstract class actually contains some code. Abstract classes may not be directly instantiated. They're designed to be used only as a base class to other classes. Listing 2.17 shows an example of an abstract class and another class that inherits it.

Listing 2.17 An abstract base class and a class that inherits it

C#

```csharp
abstract class ABaseClass
{
  public abstract void MyMethod()
  {
    // base method implementation
  }
}

public class SuperClass : ABaseClass
{
  public override void MyMethod()
  {
    // override implementation
  }
}
```

VB.NET

```vbnet
MustInherit Class ABaseClass
  Public MustOverride Sub MyMethod()
    ' base method implementation
  End Sub
End Class

Public Class SuperClass
  Inherits ABaseClass
  Public Overrides Sub MyMethod()
    ' override implementation
  End Sub
End Class
```

An example of an abstract class in the .NET Framework is the `Stream` class. The `Stream` class by itself can't be instantiated and used because it's not complete enough. Instead, it acts as the base class for a number of other classes, including `NetworkStream` and `MemoryStream`. The base `Stream` class has a number of useful members that are common to all of the derived classes, but the base members aren't useful without the specific implementation found in the derived classes. Check the documentation in the .NET Framework SDK for more information on these classes.

Enumerations

Back in the old days of computer mainframes, values were stored with alphanumeric codes that, without some kind of documentation, didn't mean much of anything to anyone but the person who programmed them. For example, an insurance company might rate a car with the code "CC." Any idea what that means? I don't know either.

Enumerations make it easier to specify a value that you can spot and understand. In our auto insurance example, `CarType.CompactCar` is a lot easier to understand than "CC." Listing 2.18 shows how we declare an enumeration.

Listing 2.18 A sample enumeration for car types

C#
```
enum CarType
{
  CompactCar,
  Truck,
  SportsCar,
  Suv
}
```

VB.NET
```
Enum CarType
  CompactCar
  Truck
  SportsCar
  Suv
End Enum
```

Let's apply this concept to something you've probably used before. Every `SqlConnection` object has a `State` property that returns a `ConnectionState` value. Among the more popular values for this property are `ConnectionState.Open` and `ConnectionState.Closed`. Beats the heck out of a number or alphanumeric code!

You can also specify numeric values for your enumeration values, but they are optional.

Summary

Although this is not an exhaustive list of code components in .NET (or in object-oriented platforms in general), we've presented you with a number of items you'll use in your code. In the next two chapters, you'll get a sense of how these fit into the bigger picture.

CHAPTER 3

Class Design

In the last chapter, we blazed through the basics of many of the components that can make up a class. With that overview in mind, let's consider the process of designing a class.

Again, I must stress that with regards to "best practices," different scenarios require different solutions. As you gain experience with ASP.NET, you'll become comfortable with modifying and making these practices your own.

Assessing Your Needs and Requirements

I hate writing documentation. To a certain degree, I don't like finding out what exactly it is that my customer wants either (because we all know exactly what customers need). Gathering requirements just isn't as fun as hacking out some code and making the little box do something.

Sadly, this guerilla coding technique creates all kinds of problems. The truth is that we don't know what our customers need, and without documenting your goals, you'll be stuck in an endless mode of revisions and tweaks, and you'll never get your product out the door. So important are requirements that many large books have been written on the subject, and many colleges require a course on requirements gathering in their computer science curriculum.

Once again, there is no universal truth. Among the core tenants of *extreme* or *agile* programming are that your code is the documentation and that short iterations of development lead to more efficient code that gets to market faster. Having worked in that environment, I agree that there are a lot of advantages to this approach to development, particularly with back-end components or systems that process huge amounts of data without user interaction.

> If you're interested in learning more about extreme and agile programming, visit http://www.xprogramming.com/ and http://agilemanifesto.org/.

Books have been written on class design too, and somewhere in the world, a class probably is being held on the subject right now. There are dozens of popular design patterns that are widely accepted to tackle common problems. If you really want to be a student of these patterns, I encourage you to read up on them. Many can be found that are specific to .NET (some in the .NET Framework SDK), and more general books can show you patterns that are more platform-neutral.

A class should encapsulate some kind of functionality into an easy-to-use package, and you shouldn't have to understand its underlying code in order to use it. Our car analogy demonstrated this idea—we don't care how the engine works, or even if it's a gasoline motor or a hybrid (assuming of course that you're not an environmentalist). All we care about is that a car does what we need—it gets us between points. When we design a class, we concentrate on what we want the class to do (i.e., its "behavior"), not how we want the class to do it.

Narrowing Your Focus

It's easy to get wrapped up in writing code and make a class do too much. If we started adding coffee makers and paper shredders to our car class, that would be silly. These functions are not essential to the basic functionality that we need from a car. Not only that, but if we wanted to make coffee in some other context, we would need the entire car. Can you imagine a car in your kitchen?

Speaking of kitchens, the point is that you shouldn't include the kitchen sink in your class design. A class should do one fairly simple thing. When we're designing a class and considering what it should include, we want it to be simple. Code reuse is certainly an important consideration, but keeping your code organized and easy to maintain is another reason to narrow the scope of the class.

This is not to say that classes should be limited to a few dozen lines of code that deal with the most primitive objects possible. A

`VendingMachine` class would serve one important function, namely dispensing soda, but it would do a great many things with different objects. It would dispense `SodaBottle` objects, accept `Coin` objects, give `Coin` objects back for change, scroll a promotional message across its `LedDisplay`, and so on.

That same `VendingMachine` should not, however, do things that aren't important to dispensing soda. It should not make phone calls to the distributor (actually, some machines might already do this, but don't start making exceptions!), it should not be an automated teller machine, it shouldn't be a bottle opener (that would be its own class because beer bottles need to be opened as well), and it shouldn't drink the soda for you.

> Maybe our vending machine doesn't call headquarters, but the beauty of object-oriented programming is that someone else could inherit our `VendingMachine` class and add that functionality.

If you look at the classes in the .NET Framework, you'll find that almost every class is fairly specific in its function, even if it has hundreds of methods and properties. The `Calendar` control is a great example—it can do many things regarding its display, but its core function is still just to display a calendar on a page. It doesn't take on responsibilities at the page level because those are things that the page and other controls need to do.

Getting Data In and Out

As fascinating as it might be to make a page display "Hello world," eventually your classes need to do something with data you provide and then return new data. You'll find that there are different ways to do the same thing.

As we demonstrated in the "Methods" section of Chapter 2, "Classes: The Code Behind the Objects," you can get data in and out through a combination of parameters passed into methods, method return values, and properties. Listing 3.1 shows a class that uses only properties, with no parameters or return values for the methods. Listing 3.2 shows how you would call this class.

Listing 3.1 Methods that don't take parameters or have return values

C#

```csharp
public class SomeClass
{
  public void MyMethod()
  {
    _myName = "new name";
    _myAge = 12;
  }

  private string _myName;
  public string MyName
  {
    get { return _myName; }
    set { _myName = value; }
  }

  private int _myAge;
  public int MyAge
  {
    get { return _myAge; }
    set { _myAge = value; }
  }
}
```

VB.NET

```vbnet
Public Class SomeClass
  Public Sub MyMethod()
    _myName = "new name"
    _myAge = 12
  End Sub

  Private _myName As String
  Public Property MyName() As String
    Get
      Return _myName
    End Get
    Set
      _myName = value
    End Set
  End Property
```

```
    Private _myAge As Integer
    Public Property MyAge() As Integer
      Get
        Return _myAge
      End Get
      Set
        _myAge = value
      End Set
    End Property
End Class
```

Listing 3.2 Calling the class from Listing 3.1

C#

```
SomeClass ThisClass = new SomeClass();
ThisClass.MyName = "Jeff";
ThisClass.MyAge = 30;
ThisClass.MyMethod();
Trace.Warn(ThisClass.MyName); // outputs "new name"
Trace.Warn(ThisClass.MyAge.ToString()); // outputs "12"
```

VB.NET

```
Dim ThisClass As New SomeClass()
ThisClass.MyName = "Jeff"
ThisClass.MyAge = 30
ThisClass.MyMethod()
Trace.Warn(ThisClass.MyName) ' outputs "new name"
Trace.Warn(ThisClass.MyAge.ToString()) ' outputs "12"
```

We can rewrite this code to a similar class that doesn't use properties at all but arrives at a similar result, as shown in Listing 3.3 and Listing 3.4.

Listing 3.3 The refactored class without properties

C#

```
public class SomeClass
{
  public string MyMethod(string oldName)
  {
    return "new name";
  }
```

(Continues)

Listing 3.3 The refactored class without properties *(Continued)*

```
  public int AnotherMethod(int oldAge)
  {
    return 12;
  }
}
```

VB.NET
```
Public Class SomeClass
   Public Function MyMethod(oldName As String) As String
     Return "new name"
   End Function

   Public Function AnotherMethod(oldAge As Integer) As Integer
     Return 12
   End Function
End Class
```

Listing 3.4 Manipulating the class without properties

C#
```
SomeClass ThisClass = new SomeClass();
Trace.Warn(ThisClass.MyMethod("Jeff")); // outputs "new name"
Trace.Warn(ThisClass.AnotherMethod(30).ToString()); // outputs "12"
```

VB.NET
```
Dim ThisClass As New SomeClass()
Trace.Warn(ThisClass.MyMethod("Jeff")) ' outputs "new name"
Trace.Warn(ThisClass.AnotherMethod(30).ToString()) ' outputs "12"
```

I know what you're thinking—"Wow, the second version sure looks easier. I'm going to do things that way!" Stop and think about it first because these classes don't do much of anything exciting. Imagine now that these classes have a dozen different methods that need to manipulate the same data. In the first example, you'd need to assign the data once to the properties and then execute your various methods. In the second example, you would need to pass in that data on every single method. Not a good use of your time! What's worse is that you can't get a number of different values out of the same method because the method can only return one value. That's why we have two separate methods to alter the name and age values in our example.

Another way to introduce data to the instantiated class right off the bat is to pass in values to the constructor of the class, as in Listing 3.5. Listing 3.6 shows how to pass in the data when you create a class instance. Your constructors can have parameters, just as a method can. You can also overload constructors, just as you would any other method.

Listing 3.5 Constructors with parameters

C#
```
public class SomeClass
{
  public SomeClass(string someString)
  {
    // do something here with someString
  }
}
```

VB.NET
```
Public Class SomeClass
  Public Sub New(someString As String)
    ' do something here with someString
  End Sub
End Class
```

Listing 3.6 Instantiating the class and passing in parameters

C#
```
SomeClass ThisClass = new SomeClass("my string");
```

VB.NET
```
Dim ThisClass As New SomeClass("my string")
```

Instantiated Classes Versus Static Methods

Up to this point, you've seen data go in and out of a class instance via properties and methods. In Chapter 2, we looked briefly at static (shared) methods. These are class methods that do not require an instance of the class to be called. The .NET Framework is filled with methods like this.

For example, you can call `Convert.ToInt32(myString)` to convert the value of a string to an integer without having to create an instance of the `Convert` class. Listing 2.13 from that chapter shows how you can declare static methods within a class.

The decision to use a static method over using a class instance really comes down to your data requirements. If you have a dozen pieces of data and need to get three or four different calculated values based on that data, a single static method is obviously not going to suit your needs. Having several static methods wouldn't be any good either because you would need to feed all that data in for every method. It's much easier to create an instance of a class, assign values to its properties, and then call its methods.

Starting with v2.0 of C# (Visual Studio 2005), you can declare an entire class as static. All of the methods in the class must also be declared static. Static classes have no constructors, so consuming code can't create an instance of the class.

Using Classes for Simple Data Structures

To this point, we've focused on making a class perform some kind of work. We can also use a class to represent some kind of data structure or to act as a bucket for pieces of data that should be grouped together.

Object/relational mapping is a technique where a programmer can manipulate a class instance's properties and persist the changes in data to a data store. This hides the database plumbing and implementation and enables the developer to concentrate on manipulating the data. A framework generally maps database fields to properties of a class. The forthcoming ObjectSpaces (originally intended to ship with .NET v2.0) is an example of this technology in action.

The part that you "develop" is just a shell of properties. Populated with data, instances of these objects can be grouped together in an `ArrayList` or other collection and can be bound to controls.

> We'll actually build a class like this in Chapter 5, "Object-Oriented Programming Applied: A Custom Data Class," except we'll add a number of methods to handle creation, retrieval, updating, and deletion of the data.

Test-Driven Development

What does testing have to do with class design? Everything! Test-driven development (TDD) is a methodology where you actually write tests before you write the classes. The goal is to write the classes so that they pass the tests. In Chapter 16, "Testing, Deployment, and Code Management," we'll cover TDD in more detail, but for the sake of design, we'll discuss it briefly here.

In test-driven development, you write tests that satisfy a business requirement. Going back to our car example, we would write a test to unlock the car before we've written a single line in our Car class. Naturally, this test won't even compile because the Car class doesn't yet exist. However, by writing the test in this manner, we can concentrate on how the class we're going to write should be structured. Our business requirement is that we want to be able to unlock the car, so it makes sense that we should have an Unlock() method. Listing 3.7 shows a fragment of test code that puts the emphasis on the design of our future Car class, not its implementation.

Listing 3.7 Test code fragment

```
Car myCar = new Car();
car.Unlock();
Assert.IsFalse(car.Locked);
```

This example is ridiculously simple, but imagine for a moment that you need to do something more complex. We had an earlier discussion about whether it makes more sense to have method-driven code or use a combination of properties and methods (or even use static methods). By writing a test that simulates some real use for a class, we take some of the guesswork out of the class definition process.

Another benefit of this development style is the avoidance of "scope creep" or "feature creep," where we write more than we need because it seems like a good idea at the time. By defining our class through the use of tests derived from business requirements, we don't have to guess what to include. We only need to develop the code that satisfies the tests.

After you've written your tests, you can "stub out" the class with just enough code to indicate the class's structure. At that point, your tests (and your class) will compile, but naturally your tests will still fail. You'll continue to write code until your tests pass. This methodology can give you great confidence that your code will work as you expect because hopefully you've created unbiased tests that account for most situations before you've even written the class itself.

Testing is performed using free tools like NUnit, which we'll cover in Chapter 16.

Summary

In this chapter, we explored the process of class design. Although many volumes exist on design and existing design patterns, we agree that design starts with the consideration of our requirements.

It's easy to get wrapped up in building a class that does a hundred incredible things, but narrowing the focus of your class provides several benefits. Most importantly, a narrow focus makes your code easier to maintain because your classes do simple things. You can also reuse these focused classes in different combinations with other code, so you lower the risk of duplication.

Getting data in and out of your classes can be achieved through a combination of properties and methods, methods with parameters, or static methods that don't require an instance of the class. Your requirements, and the volume of data and processes you need to deal with, will dictate which combinations make the most sense.

Classes can also act as shells for related data. These classes are perfectly suited for use in an object/relational framework, such as ObjectSpaces. These objects can be grouped together in various collections and can be bound to data controls.

Finally, test-driven development can help you focus on getting just what you need out of your class without overdoing it.

CHAPTER 4

Application Architecture

To this point in the book, we've explored the design and development of individual classes. These units of code enable you to encapsulate functionality into reusable components that perform some specific task. Naturally these parts will operate in the context of some bigger picture—some grand scheme that performs the greatest things ever. We refer to this scheme as the application architecture.

In this chapter we'll look at ways to split up your application into logical pieces and how your classes come together to do the greatest things ever.

> In this chapter, we talk about layering and tiers. Technically, these are not the same thing, though they're frequently used interchangeably. A tier is often defined as a single machine or group of machines that share the responsibility in a bigger system. In fact, the Web browser is considered a tier of an application because it ultimately acts as the user interface. A layer refers more to the conceptual unit of an application, such as a data layer that includes the database.

The Benefit of Splitting Applications into Layers

In large corporations that have large software applications, teams of developers and analysts concentrate on specific layers of the application. This is necessary because it would be difficult for developers to understand at a detailed level everything that's going on. The application is just too big.

Imagine all of the functions that an insurance company's application must perform. To really oversimplify the process, let's say that the company must be able to accept a new insurance policy, rate the risk involved with that policy, bill the insured, print out the policy and mail it, process claims against the policy, renew the policy, cancel the policy if it expires (or hasn't been paid for!), and so on. This huge process isn't handled by a single desktop application, obviously!

Web applications are easily split into layers as well, in some cases whether you want to or not. If you store data in a SQL Server database, the database is already its own layer, separate from the Web server (even if they're both physically on the same box).

One of the biggest complaints about the old Active Server Pages was that you had a mess of code intertwined in your HTML, and it was hard to maintain. Developers back then would frequently break out data access, and even the generation of HTML in some cases, into COM components that made the separation of code and presentation (i.e., the HTML) more clear.

ASP.NET, being an object-oriented platform, makes it even easier to break out these layers. Application layers make life easier because they encapsulate some higher purpose into a discrete unit that can be maintained or altered by itself, distributing the work of your application as well as the workload of maintaining it.

Your favorite online retailer probably has a number of application layers. Let's assume that a retailer has layers that work together in the manner described in Figure 4.1.

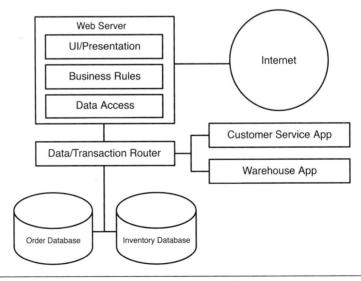

Figure 4.1 Application layers for an online retailer.

The diagram shows a combination of physical hardware layers and application layers. The Web server actually has three layers running on it. The first part generates the user interface for the Web user. It's fed by the business rules layer, which decides what data to send to the UI. The business rules layer talks with the data access layer, which works through a transaction router to get the data it needs. Other systems for the customer service representatives and the warehouse also get data as needed from the transaction router.

Each layer only cares about its function. The business rules layer doesn't need to know anything about the data store itself; it only needs to know about the interface offered by the data access layer. In fact, it doesn't care what kind of database is out there, or even if there's a database at all. It only cares that there's a data access layer that it can talk to, and that it will give and take data as needed via an agreed upon interface.

Although there should be some kind of integration testing for the entire system, we can change the innards of any one layer without having to disturb other layers, provided that the agreed upon interfaces are not changed.

The Classic n-tier

No discussion of application architecture is complete without mentioning the classic n-tier. The "n" stands for any number, as in three-tier, four-tier, or whatever is applicable to the application we're building. The number of tiers, or layers, in your application is dictated by the requirements and structure of your application pieces.

Generally speaking, even the most basic Web application can be broken into three layers: UI, business rules, and data. The user interface is the HTML and the Web controls that our users will see. The business rules are classes that do what you might call the "heavy lifting" of the application. The data layer is your database and, depending how you structure the application, perhaps some of the data access code.

You can divide up the layers even further if the application calls for it. You can have the UI (your .aspx page), your class or partial class that your page inherits (code-behind or code-beside, respectively) acting as the UI "glue," your business rules layer (heavy lifting and logic classes), the data access layer (data access classes), and then the data layer itself (your database).

Why bother? Let's say that you decide to replace your SQL Server database with an Oracle database for cost reasons (if you manage an IT budget, hold your laughter please). Imagine you didn't break out the application into layers, and you had data access actually right in the .aspx pages. You would need to go through all of those pages and risk breaking everything. This is not a very efficient way to manage your code. In fact, you might not even manipulate the data the same way from one page to the next.

If you had all of your data access code together in a single layer, probably a single class with methods for manipulating the database, you would have a single point at which you could alter the code without breaking the logic or UI in the process.

In a more common scenario, assume that your business has charged you with changing how tax is calculated in your e-commerce application. The database has not changed, and the site itself has not changed. Only the logic has changed, and that means you only need to change the classes in your business rules layer to make the change. Again, this would be difficult to do if the logic was built into your pages or consisted of some calculation in your database's stored procedures.

In a less extreme example, tax rates may change frequently. You wouldn't hard-code the values of these tax rates into your code. The natural solution is to store the rates in a database and create user-friendly tools that alter these rates.

A common stumbling block for some developers in thinking about application layers is equating them with physical files and servers, the nuts and bolts. The application layers could quite conceivably be all in one executable file (if you were clever enough to write your own Web server and database software), or it could be several layers in one file on your Web server, connecting to a separate database server. There are endless variations and combinations. We'll get into some of those nuts and bolts in Chapter 6, "The Nuts and Bolts of IIS and Web Applications," but for now, try to think about application architecture in a more abstract sense.

Case Study: The POP Forums Architecture

The POP Forums application, which is a Web forum app for ASP.NET (http://www.popforums.com), has an architecture that divides up responsibilities into a number of different layers that interact with the ASP.NET architecture and SQL Server. Figure 4.2 shows how these parts talk to each other.

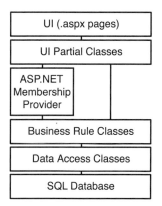

Figure 4.2 The POP Forums architecture.

The forum architecture is simple to understand, and makes altering the application easy. Writing a new data access layer for a Microsoft Access database would require only changing the one layer. Getting data in and out of the database from the UI is a matter of creating objects from the business rule classes. Creating a new post in the forum, for example, requires the creation of a `Post` object, populating its properties, and calling its `Create()` method. If you were tasked with creating a user interface, you wouldn't have to know anything about the database or the plumbing.

This application also takes advantage of the architecture provided in ASP.NET. Starting in ASP.NET v2.0, a provider model enables you to replace the data plumbing built into the framework with your own. The benefit for developers who use your code is that they can still use the well-known interfaces in the framework and not worry about the implementation underneath. In this case, the application has its own `Membership` provider. When the calling code manipulates ASP.NET's `Membership` class, the POP Forums provider handles the data plumbing. The developer doesn't care that it happens to be stored in the forum database instead of being used in the .NET Framework's built-in SQL Express database. We'll take a closer look at this provider model in Chapter 11, "Membership and Security."

Let's look at some code samples from each of the layers in the forum application. We'll start at the data end. We have a table in our SQL Server database called `Posts`. Not surprisingly, this is where we keep all of the thoughtful compositions made by the members of our forum. There isn't anything unusual about this table, and it has a typical primary key called `PostID` and a foreign key called `TopicID`, which tells us the topic in the `Topics` table with which the post is associated.

Let's concentrate on the insertion of new data into the `Posts` table. The first task is creating the code to do the dirty work of opening a connection, creating a command object, and executing the command, as in Listing 4.1. The listing includes the namespace and class declarations.

Listing 4.1 The simple act of inserting data into the database

C#

```
namespace PopForums.Data
{
  public class SqlClient : IPopForumsData
  {

    public int CreateNewPost(int TopicID, DateTime PostTime,
      string Name, int PeopleID, string IP, bool FirstInTopic,
      string FullText, bool ShowSig)
    {
      SqlConnection connection = new
SqlConnection(ConfigurationSettings.AppSettings["PopForumsDbConnect"]);
        connection.Open();
      string sql = "INSERT INTO pf_Posts (TopicID, PostTime, Name, "
        + "PeopleID, IP, FirstInTopic, FullText, ShowSig) VALUES ("
        + "@TopicID, @PostTime, @Name, @PeopleID, @IP, @FirstInTopic, "
        + "@FullText, @ShowSig)";
      SqlCommand command = new SqlCommand(sql, connection);
      command.Parameters.AddWithValue("@TopicID",TopicID);
      command.Parameters.AddWithValue("@PostTime",PostTime);
      command.Parameters.AddWithValue("@Name",Name);
      command.Parameters.AddWithValue("@PeopleID",PeopleID);
      command.Parameters.AddWithValue("@IP",IP);
      command.Parameters.AddWithValue("@FirstInTopic",FirstInTopic);
      command.Parameters.AddWithValue("@FullText",FullText);
      command.Parameters.AddWithValue("@ShowSig",ShowSig);
      command.ExecuteNonQuery();
      command.CommandText = "SELECT @@IDENTITY";
      int postID = Convert.ToInt32(command.ExecuteScalar());
      connection.Close();
      return postID;
    }

    ... more methods
  }
}
```

VB.NET

```
Namespace PopForums.Data
  Public Class SqlClient
    Implements IPopForumsData

    Public Function CreateNewPost(TopicID As Integer, _
      PostTime As DateTime, Name As String, PeopleID As Integer, _
      IP As String, FirstInTopic As Boolean, FullText As String, _
      ShowSig As Boolean) As Integer
      Dim connection As New _
SqlConnection(ConfigurationSettings.AppSettings("PopForumsDbConnect"))
      connection.Open()
      Dim sql As String = "INSERT INTO pf_Posts (TopicID, PostTime, "_
        & "Name, PeopleID, IP, FirstInTopic, FullText, ShowSig) "_
        & " VALUES (@TopicID,@PostTime,@Name,@PeopleID,@IP, "_
        & "@FirstInTopic,@FullText,@ShowSig)"
      Dim command As New SqlCommand(sql, connection)
      command.Parameters.AddWithValue("@TopicID", TopicID)
      command.Parameters.AddWithValue("@PostTime", PostTime)
      command.Parameters.AddWithValue("@Name", Name)
      command.Parameters.AddWithValue("@PeopleID", PeopleID)
      command.Parameters.AddWithValue("@IP", IP)
      command.Parameters.AddWithValue("@FirstInTopic", FirstInTopic)
      command.Parameters.AddWithValue("@FullText", FullText)
      command.Parameters.AddWithValue("@ShowSig", ShowSig)
      command.ExecuteNonQuery()
      command.CommandText = "SELECT @@IDENTITY"
      Dim postID As Integer = _
Convert.ToInt32(command.ExecuteScalar())
      connection.Close()
      Return postID
    End Function

    ... more methods
  End Class
End Namespace
```

The AddWithValue() method of the ParameterCollection is new to v2.0 of .NET. If you're using a previous version, you can use the same syntax with the Add() method (though it has been marked as obsolete in v2.0). The v2.0 compiler will warn you if you use the obsolete Add() method.

Even if you're fairly new to ASP.NET, you've probably written code like this many times. You should pay particular attention to the fact that the `SqlClient` class implements an interface called `IPopForumsData`. Recall that we wanted to make the data access layer easy to change so that we could support some other database. To do this, we use an interface that forces us to implement the entire class signature. This way, our business rules classes can predictably call a `CreateNewPost()` method regardless of the data access class we have installed.

That means that we need to define an interface. As mentioned in Chapter 2, "Classes: The Code Behind the Objects," an interface is little more than a signature that says what members a class must have. Listing 4.2 shows a little piece of our interface.

Listing 4.2 The IPopForumsData interface

C#

```
namespace PopForums.Data
{
  public interface IPopForumsData
  {
    int CreateNewPost(int TopicID, DateTime PostTime,
      string Name, int PeopleID, string IP,
      bool FirstInTopic, string FullText, bool ShowSig);

  ...more member definitions
  }
}
```

VB.NET

```
Namespace PopForums.Data
  Public Interface IPopForumsData
    Function CreateNewPost(TopicID As Integer, _
      PostTime As DateTime, Name As String, _
      PeopleID As Integer, IP As String, _
      FirstInTopic As Boolean, FullText As String, _
      ShowSig As Boolean) As Integer

    ... more member definitions
  End Interface
End Namespace
```

Our interface doesn't have any actual code in it. Its sole purpose is to let us know how our classes that implement it should look.

That's great, but our business rules classes are going to need to hit all these methods in our `SqlClient` class. To do this, we'll create a class that loads our data access class and caches it, according to values in our `web.config` file. A single static method called `Methods()` in the `ClientLoader` class will do this, as shown in Listing 4.3.

> This is a technique I blatantly used from the original forums on Microsoft's www.asp.net site. Don't worry if you don't understand what's going on in this code. In a nutshell, the method uses two keys from the config file indicating the assembly name and the class inside of it that we want to use for data access. It is then cached because loading a class in this manner on every single data call would be an expensive process and would slow the application down. The `Methods()` method returns an instance of the class with all of the methods for the data access. The idea is that we could just as well have it load a class meant to hit Access instead of SQL Server, provided the class also implements `IPopForumsData`.

Listing 4.3 Loading our data access layer

C#
```
namespace PopForums.Data
{
  public class ClientLoader
  {
    public static IPopForumsData Methods()
    {
      Cache cache = HttpContext.Current.Cache;
      if (cache["IPopForumsData"] == null)
      {
        if ((ConfigurationSettings.AppSettings["PopForumsDataClass"] ==
null) || (ConfigurationSettings.AppSettings["PopForumsDataDll"] == null))
          // no data layer specified, use the internal one
          cache.Insert("IPopForumsData",
typeof(PopForums.Data.Provider).Module.Assembly.GetType("PopForums.Data.
SqlClient").GetConstructor(new Type[0]));
```

(Continues)

Listing 4.3 Loading our data access layer   *(Continued)*

```
        else
        {
          // user has specified an external data layer
          string assemblyPath = "~\\bin\\" +
ConfigurationSettings.AppSettings["PopForumsDataDll"];
          string className =
ConfigurationSettings.AppSettings["PopForumsDataClass"];
          cache.Insert("IPopForumsData",
Assembly.LoadFrom(assemblyPath).GetType(className).GetConstructor(new
Type[0]));
        }
      }
      return (IPopForumsData)(
((ConstructorInfo)cache["IPopForumsData"]).Invoke(null) );
    }
  }
}
```

VB.NET

```
Namespace PopForums.Data
    Public Class ClientLoader

      Public Shared Function Methods() As IPopForumsData
          Dim cache As Cache = HttpContext.Current.Cache
          If cache("IPopForumsData") Is Nothing Then
            If ConfigurationSettings.AppSettings("PopForumsDataClass")
Is Nothing Or ConfigurationSettings.AppSettings("PopForumsDataDll") Is
Nothing Then
              ' no data layer specified, use the internal one
              cache.Insert("IPopForumsData",
GetType(PopForums.Data.Provider).Module.Assembly.GetType("PopForums.Data
.SqlClient").GetConstructor(New Type(0) {}))
            Else
              ' user has specified an external data layer
              Dim assemblyPath As String = "~\bin\" +
ConfigurationSettings.AppSettings("PopForumsDataDll")
              Dim className As String =
ConfigurationSettings.AppSettings("PopForumsDataClass")
              cache.Insert("IPopForumsData",
[Assembly].LoadFrom(assemblyPath).GetType(className).GetConstructor(New
Type(0) {}))
            End If
          End If
```

```
        Return CType(CType(cache("IPopForumsData"),
ConstructorInfo).Invoke(Nothing), IPopForumsData)
      End Function
   End Class
End Namespace
```

The important thing to understand about the class in Listing 4.3 is that it loads an instance of the class we choose, which happens to implement `IPopForumsData`. If one isn't specified, it loads the default, our `SqlClient` class (for the purpose of this project, the `SqlClient` class is compiled in the same assembly as the rest of this code). The result is that we can call any method in our `SqlClient` class by creating an instance of it via the `ClientLoader` class and its `Methods()` method:

```
IPopForumsData data = PopForums.Data.ClientLoader.Methods();
```

As you can see, you can actually create an object whose type is an interface! Then you might see that we can call our `CreateNewPost()` method like this:

```
data.CreateNewPost( [parameters here] );
```

The `IPopForumsData` interface, the `ClientLoader` class, and the `SqlClient` class collectively make up our data access layer. This code is solely responsible for getting data in and out of the SQL Server database. To pipe the data in and out of another data store, we need only write a class that implements `IPopForumsData` and set values in our `web.config` file to load that class instead.

Now that we've found a way to isolate all our data access methods, we can create business rules. We'll create a class called `Post` and give it properties that match each of the fields in our database table. We'll also give it a constructor to create a new instance of a `Post` object, as well as methods to `Create()`, `Update()`, and `Delete()` data.

> Our example class in Chapter 5, "Object-Oriented Programming Applied: A Custom Data Class," does something similar to this, only it makes database calls directly instead of calling the methods from a class dedicated to data access. That example combines the data access layer with the business rules.

To add a new post entry to the database, we want our class to call the method from our data access layer and pass in the values as parameters. The `Create()` method of the `Post` class can perform any calculations, caching, or validation that we require and then execute the method from the data access layer, as in Listing 4.4.

Listing 4.4 The Create() method of the Post class

C#

```csharp
public int Create()
{
  Cache cache = HttpContext.Current.Cache;
  if (cache["pftopic" + _TopicID.ToString()] != null)
cache.Remove("pftopic" + _TopicID.ToString());
  if (cache["pfpeopleposts" + _PeopleID.ToString()] != null)
cache.Remove("pfpeopleposts" + _PeopleID.ToString());
  IPopForumsData data = PopForums.Data.ClientLoader.Methods();
  int postID =
data.CreateNewPost(_TopicID,_PostTime,_Name,_PeopleID,_IP,_FirstInTopic,
_FullText,_ShowSig);
  _PostID = postID;
  Topic objTopic = new Topic(_TopicID);
  objTopic.Update(); // this also calls the forum's update, which will
refresh lastpostime
  return postID;
}
```

VB.NET

```vbnet
    Dim cache As Cache = HttpContext.Current.Cache
    If Not (cache(("pftopic" + _TopicID.ToString()))) Is Nothing) Then
        cache.Remove(("pftopic" + _TopicID.ToString()))
    End If
    If Not (cache(("pfpeopleposts" + _PeopleID.ToString()))) Is Nothing)
Then
        cache.Remove(("pfpeopleposts" + _PeopleID.ToString()))
    End If
    Dim data As IPopForumsData = PopForums.Data.ClientLoader.Methods()
    Dim postID As Integer = data.CreateNewPost(_TopicID, _PostTime,
_Name, _PeopleID, _IP, _FirstInTopic, _FullText, _ShowSig)
    _PostID = postID
    Dim objTopic As New Topic(_TopicID)
    objTopic.Update() ' this also calls the forum's update, which will
```

```
refresh lastpostime
    Return postID
End Function
```

This method does several things that fit squarely in the business rules layer of our application that we wouldn't want to leave to the user interface or the data access layer. You can see that it removes two cache entries—one that stores data on the parent topic and one that stores data on the user making the post. Those cached values are invalidated because the topic has changed, as well as information about the user with regards to the posts they've made. After that has been taken care of, it creates an instance of our data access class and calls the method to create a new post. The parameters that begin with an underscore are the private members of the class that correspond to properties, as we saw in Chapter 2 in Listing 2.7. Finally, the method creates a `Topic` object (another business rule class) and causes it to update its data, which forces the topic to calculate a new "last post" time.

It's not that critical that you understand all of those action items in the method, but it is important that you understand why they happen in this discrete business rules layer of the application. It isn't important to know how the data is stored or how the UI gets data into the class. Only the rules that deal with the data and how it's handled or calculated are important.

This gets us to what I call the user interface "glue." Despite having a great many declarative controls, ASP.NET still needs a bit of code to make the user interface work with your business rules layer. This glue code can appear in any of three places: in the page itself in a `<script>` block, in a partial class (unofficially known as "code-beside"), or in a class that the page inherits (known as "code-behind," the default place for code in versions of Visual Studio prior to 2005). Where you put this code is a matter of preference, but if you put it in the .aspx page file, some people may consider this an application design fault because it doesn't create that separation many programmers require. I put this code in with the rest of the page for convenience and to make it accessible for people not using Visual Studio. Considering you can't change the .aspx page without impacting the code-behind, or vice-versa, I don't feel that this separation is entirely necessary.

Partial classes are new as of v2.0 of .NET. In ASP.NET, they're merged on first-run with pages to form one complete class. We'll go into more detail in Chapter 6, "The Nuts and Bolts of IIS and Web Application."

Continuing up the chain, the code in this layer is ridiculously straight-forward, and you could probably understand it even if you didn't know anything about the rest of the application. Listing 4.5 shows how we simply create an instance of the `Post` class, assign some values to its properties, and then call its `Create()` method.

Listing 4.5 Using the Post class in our user interface glue

C#
```csharp
Post post = new Post();
post.TopicID = topic.TopicID;
post.PostTime = DateTime.UtcNow;
post.Name = user.Username;
post.PeopleID = (int)user.UserId;
post.IP = Request.UserHostAddress;
post.FirstInTopic = false;
post.FullText = ReplyBox.Text;
post.ShowSig = ShowSigCheckBox.Checked;
post.Create();
```

VB.NET
```vbnet
Dim post As New Post()
post.TopicID = topic.TopicID
post.PostTime = DateTime.UtcNow
post.Name = user.Username
post.PeopleID = CInt(user.UserId)
post.IP = Request.UserHostAddress
post.FirstInTopic = False
post.FullText = ReplyBox.Text
post.ShowSig = ShowSigCheckBox.Checked
post.Create()
```

Again, the important point to consider with this code is that it's very single-minded. Remember all of the things that the `Create()` method does with caching and updating the parent topic? This code doesn't need to worry about any of that. Its sole purpose is acquiring what's in the controls and the request and passing that to the business rules layer. Even further removed, it doesn't need to worry about the data store or how data is written to it.

That leaves only the actual user interface layer. This final layer consists only of the HTML that defines the page and its controls. It doesn't need to know anything about how to feed data into the business rules.

We've traversed five layers in the application, starting at the database itself and working our way back to the user interface. Each layer does its own thing, and it only has to know how to interact with the layers above and below it. The implementation in the adjacent layers is not important.

This architecture is friendly to developers who have certain areas of expertise. I'm not much of an Oracle programmer, but a friend or co-worker that has guru status could jump in there and make a great Oracle data access layer to work with the rest of the application. I'm also not much of a designer, but another person could create a killer user interface and have no problem using the business rules classes to process the data.

Talking to Other Applications

The POP Forums case study assumes that you are building your application from top to bottom in your own little universe. We know that the bigger the company, the less likely that is. In fact, in a large organization, different business units might draw on the same resources that are maintained by another unit.

The resulting scenario from this distribution of resources is frequently called a service oriented architecture, or SOA. Going back to the retail outfit we described in Figure 4.1, a number of different units (the Web site, customer service, and the warehouse) need to get product data. It wouldn't make much sense for each unit to create its own data access layer to retrieve that data, not to mention that the lack of coordination could cause conflicts in terms of data concurrency.

One solution to this problem is to have another unit that provides services for the other units. Both the Web site and the customer service department need to know if an item is in stock, so the unit maintaining the transaction router can provide an interface that they can both use to discover that information. At the same time, they can provide a service for the warehouse system to update inventory numbers.

A service-oriented architecture is most easily implemented in the .NET world using Web services and .NET remoting. There are also classes that help you work with message queue systems, where data is queued for processing across a network between systems. The topic of SOA and large-scale distributed applications is beyond the scope of this book.

Assessment of Needs and Requirements in the Real World

You'll often find that hard-core academics of programming science insist that an n-tier architecture is the only correct way to build an application. Although I can see that point pretty clearly (after all, I am writing this book), we all know that the real world has a lot of variations on correctness.

We've talked about a few of the benefits of the layered architecture— namely, that it's easier to maintain and understand. However, just as you shouldn't implement object-oriented programming for the sake of doing so, you shouldn't build these layered or tiered applications just for the sake of doing so.

Consider the scope of the application you're building and the business problem you're trying to solve. If you need to bang out a two-page application that collects contact information into an Access database, chances are you won't need to break out the application into four or more layers. Even the POP Forums application could have been consolidated by combining the data access layer and the business rules layer. (You'll see an example of this combination in the next chapter.)

It's not uncommon for your requirements to include the ability to process huge amounts of data. This kind of requirement will force you to divvy up the application because it will spread the workload across more than one machine. When the database server is on a physically separate machine, that means the database server CPU and the Web server CPU can be dedicated to doing their own tasks.

Summary

A layered application architecture breaks the application up into more manageable chunks that are more easily maintained, swapped out, and revised. It also enables people and teams to stick to areas of their expertise, which is an important consideration for Web applications that involve design, programming, data optimization, and so on.

CHAPTER 5

Object-Oriented Programming Applied: A Custom Data Class

In Chapter 1, "The Object Model," I gave you an analogy that compares the concept of a class to that of a car. A class encapsulates some kind of functionality into one neat and simple package.

Many Web coders who have used other platforms such as PHP or Cold Fusion are a little surprised at the number of steps required to get data in and out of a database in .NET. Just to get a few values out of the database, you need to create a connection object, a command object, and then at the very least a `DataReader`. (In all fairness, you get back much of your time when data binding!) Sounds like the perfect place to build a useful class!

If we put all of our database logic into one class, we can write the SQL statements once and manipulate the data with far less code throughout our application. You'll also benefit from having just one place to change code if you decide to use a different database (such as Oracle). Best of all, implementing a data-caching scheme is that much easier when all of your data code is in one place.

To help you see the benefit of this write-once, use-everywhere class, Listing 5.1 shows a code sample that creates a row in our database, reads the row, and then deletes it, all via a class that we'll build in this chapter.

Listing 5.1 A class in action

C#

```csharp
// Instantiate the Customer class using the default constructor
Customer customer = new Customer();
// Assign some of its properties
```

(Continues)

Listing 5.1 A class in action   *(Continued)*

```
customer.LastName = "Jones";
customer.FirstName = "Jeff";
// Call its Create() method to save the values in the database,
// and get its new primary key (CustomerID) value
int customerID = customer.Create();

// Instantiate the Customer class using the constructor that takes
// the CustomerID as a parameter
Customer customer2 = new Customer(customerID);
Trace.Write("LastName: " + customer2.LastName);
Trace.Write("FirstName: " + customer2.FirstName);

// Change the value of the first name then save the changes
// to the database
customer2.FirstName = "Stephanie";
customer2.Update();

// On second thought, let's just delete the record entirely
customer2.Delete();
```

VB.NET

```
' Instantiate the Customer class using the default constructor
Dim customer As New Customer()
' Assign some of its properties
customer.LastName = "Jones"
customer.FirstName = "Jeff"
' Call its Create() method to save the values in the database,
' and get its new primary key (CustomerID) value
Dim customerID As Integer = customer.Create()

' Instantiate the Customer class using the constructor that takes
' the CustomerID as a parameter
Dim customer2 As New Customer(customerID)
Trace.Write(("LastName: " + customer2.LastName))
Trace.Write(("FirstName: " + customer2.FirstName))

' Change the value of the first name then save the changes
' to the database
customer2.FirstName = "Stephanie"
customer2.Update()

' On second thought, let's just delete the record entirely
customer2.Delete()
```

You can see by these few lines of code that we didn't go through the entire process of creating connection, command, and other data objects. A few simple method calls are all we need to manipulate the data. Imagine how much time you'd save if you had to manipulate the data in dozens of places around your application!

> This is a good place to mention that, in terms of n-tier architecture (see Chapter 4, "Application Architecture"), this sample class we're about to build does not create the discrete layers often representative of such architectures. We're going to combine data container classes and data access into one package. That isn't wrong per se, and in fact it might be just what you need in your own application.

Analyzing Design Requirements

The first step in designing any class is to identify your needs in human terms before writing code. In our case, we want to make it easy to get, update, and delete data from a table called Customers in SQL Server. None of the columns in our table allows null values.

Table 5.1 The Customers table

CustomerID (primary key/identity)	int
LastName	nvarchar
FirstName	nvarchar
Address	nvarchar
City	nvarchar
State	nvarchar
Zip	nvarchar
Phone	nvarchar
SignUpDate	datetime

Why are we using nvarchar instead of varchar? The difference is that nvarchar uses Unicode, the generally accepted standard of character encoding that includes a much larger character set. Using Unicode in your Web application means there's less chance of getting weird characters generated by users in other countries. The tradeoff is that it takes up twice as much disk space, but in an age of giant inexpensive hard drives, this should hardly be a concern.

We know that the Customers table has nine columns that we can manipulate. We also know that we want to create, update, and delete records in this table. The most obvious need we'll have is to get data from the table. After we have the basics of our class nailed down, we'll revise the class to cache data and explore ways to get a number of records at one time.

Choosing Our Properties

Let's start writing our class by declaring it and creating the necessary references that we'll need in Listing 5.2. We'll also set up the properties and corresponding private variables.

Listing 5.2 The start of our data class

C#
```
using System;
using System.Data;
using System.Data.SqlClient;
using System.Web;

namespace UberAspNet
{
  public class Customer
  {
    private int _CustomerID;
    public int CustomerID
    {
      get {return _CustomerID;}
    }
```

```
private string _LastName;
public string LastName
{
   get {return _LastName;}
   set {_LastName = value;}
}

private string _FirstName;
public string FirstName
{
   get {return _FirstName;}
   set {_FirstName = value;}
}

private string _Address;
public string Address
{
   get {return _Address;}
   set {_Address = value;}
}

private string _City;
public string City
{
   get {return _City;}
   set {_City = value;}
}

private string _State;
public string State
{
   get {return State;}
   set {_State = value;}
}

private string _Zip;
public string Zip
{
   get {return _Zip;}
   set {_Zip = value;}
}
```

(Continues)

Listing 5.2 The start of our data class   *(Continued)*

```
  private string _Phone;
  public string Phone
  {
    get {return _Phone;}
    set {_Phone = value;}
  }

  private DateTime _SignUpDate;
  public DateTime SignUpDate
  {
    get {return _SignUpDate;}
    set {_SignUpDate = value;}
  }
 }
}
```

VB.NET

```
Imports System
Imports System.Data
Imports System.Data.SqlClient
Imports System.Web


Namespace UberAspNet

   Public Class Customer

      Private _CustomerID As Integer
      Public ReadOnly Property CustomerID() As Integer
         Get
             Return _CustomerID
         End Get
      End Property

      Private _LastName As String
      Public Property LastName() As String
         Get
             Return _LastName
         End Get
         Set
            _LastName = value
         End Set
      End Property
```

```
Private _FirstName As String
Public Property FirstName() As String
   Get
       Return _FirstName
   End Get
   Set
       _FirstName = value
   End Set
End Property

Private _Address As String
Public Property Address() As String
   Get
       Return _Address
   End Get
   Set
       _Address = value
   End Set
End Property

Private _City As String
Public Property City() As String
   Get
       Return _City
   End Get
   Set
       _City = value
   End Set
End Property

Private _State As String
Public Property State() As String
   Get
       Return State
   End Get
   Set
       _State = value
   End Set
End Property

Private _Zip As String
Public Property Zip() As String
   Get
```

(Continues)

Listing 5.2 The start of our data class   *(Continued)*

```
            Return _Zip
        End Get
        Set
            _Zip = value
        End Set
    End Property

    Private _Phone As String
    Public Property Phone() As String
        Get
            Return _Phone
        End Get
        Set
            _Phone = value
        End Set
    End Property

    Private _SignUpDate As DateTime
    Public Property SignUpDate() As DateTime
        Get
            Return _SignUpDate
        End Get
        Set
            _SignUpDate = value
        End Set
    End Property

End Class

End Namespace
```

The code is fairly straightforward. We've created a property to correspond to each of the columns in our database table, matching the data
types. We've also created a private variable for each column for internal
use in our class. The only unusual thing here is that we've made the
CustomerID property read-only. That's because our database table is
designed to make this a primary key and an identity field, meaning that
SQL Server will number the column automatically when we add new rows.
For that reason, we don't want the class to have the ability to alter this
property. This read-only strategy also protects other developers (or yourself if you can't remember every detail about what you've written) from
doing something that could break the program.

In our case we've named the private variables with the same name as the properties, only with an underscore character in front of them. There are a number of different ways to name these according to various academic standards and recommendations, but ultimately it's up to you. Be consistent in your naming conventions. If they confuse you, imagine what they might do to other developers who need to edit your code!

You could declare default values for each private variable, but we're going to defer those assignments to our constructors. We might want to assign different default values depending on the overload of the constructor called.

The Constructors

Now that we know what pieces of data our class should contain, it's time to set up that data when we instantiate the class. There are two scenarios: We'll populate the properties with default values, or we'll populate them with values from our database. To do this, we'll create two constructors by way of overloading.

In writing our constructors, we'll have to decide up front how we'll distinguish between default data and data we've entered or retrieved from the database. We could simply allow each property to return a null value, but that wouldn't correspond well to the fact that our database table doesn't allow null values. Instead, we'll make all of our string values equal empty strings, our `SignUpDate` value will equal January 1, 2000, and our `CustomerID` will be set to 0.

The `CustomerID` is perhaps the stickiest point in our class design. Although the chances are that we'll always know exactly what we're doing in our code (I know, you can stop laughing), we need to know and document how we're going to know if the instantiated `Customer` object actually corresponds to an existing database record or not. Again, we could just keep `CustomerID` null until we've created a record, but for our case, we'll decide right now that a value of 0 means that either no record exists or we've created a new object with default values. This leaves the potential for populating our object with default values from both constructors, so we'll create a private method just for this purpose in Listing 5.3.

Listing 5.3 The private `PopulateDefault()` method

C#

```csharp
private void PopulateDefault()
{
  _CustomerID = 0;
  _LastName = "";
  _FirstName = "";
  _Address = "";
  _City = "";
  _State = "";
  _Zip = "";
  _Phone = "";
  _SignUpDate = new DateTime(2000,1,1);
}
```

VB.NET

```vbnet
Private Sub PopulateDefault()
  _CustomerID = 0
  _LastName = ""
  _FirstName = ""
  _Address = ""
  _City = ""
  _State = ""
  _Zip = ""
  _Phone = ""
  _SignUpDate = New DateTime(2000, 1, 1)
End Sub
```

Now that we have that issue out of the way, our default constructor is a piece of cake, as shown in Listing 5.4.

Listing 5.4 The default constructor

C#

```csharp
public Customer()
{
  PopulateDefault();
}
```

VB.NET

```vbnet
Public Sub New()
  PopulateDefault()
End Sub
```

Within our calling code, creating the object and assigning values to its properties is as easy as the first fragment of code we showed you in this chapter.

Our second overload for the constructor, shown in Listing 5.5, has the familiar database code you've been waiting for. It takes a single parameter, the `CustomerID`, and populates our object's properties based on a match in the database.

> In our examples in this chapter, we're using the `AddWithValue()` method of the `SqlParameterCollection`. This method is new to v2.0 of the .NET Framework. Earlier versions can simply use `Add()` with the same two parameters.

Listing 5.5 The record-specific constructor

C#

```
private string _ConnectionString =
"server=(local);database=test;Integrated Security=SSPI";

public Customer(int CustomerID)
{
  SqlConnection connection = new SqlConnection(_ConnectionString);
  connection.Open();
  SqlCommand command = new SqlCommand("SELECT CustomerID, "
    + "LastName, FirstName, Address, City, State, Zip, Phone, "
    + "SignUpDate WHERE CustomerID = @CustomerID",
    connection);
  command.Parameters.AddWithValue("@CustomerID", CustomerID);
  SqlDataReader reader = command.ExecuteReader();
  if (reader.Read())
  {
    _CustomerID = reader.GetInt32(0);
    _LastName = reader.GetString(1);
    _FirstName = reader.GetString(2);
    _Address = reader.GetString(3);
    _City = reader.GetString(4);
    _State = reader.GetString(5);
    _Zip = reader.GetString(6);
    _Phone = reader.GetString(7);
    _SignUpDate = reader.GetDateTime(8);
  }
```

(Continues)

Listing 5.5 The record-specific constructor   *(Continued)*

```
    else PopulateDefault();
    reader.Close();
    connection.Close();
}
```

VB.NET

```
Private _ConnectionString As String = _
    "server=(local);database=test;Integrated Security=SSPI"

Public Sub New(CustomerID As Integer)
    Dim connection As New SqlConnection(_ConnectionString)
    connection.Open()
    Dim command As New SqlCommand("SELECT CustomerID, LastName, "_
        & "FirstName, Address, City, State, Zip, Phone, SignUpDate "_
        & "WHERE CustomerID = @CustomerID", connection)
    command.Parameters.AddWithValue("@CustomerID", CustomerID)
    Dim reader As SqlDataReader = command.ExecuteReader()
    If reader.Read() Then
        _CustomerID = reader.GetInt32(0)
        _LastName = reader.GetString(1)
        _FirstName = reader.GetString(2)
        _Address = reader.GetString(3)
        _City = reader.GetString(4)
        _State = reader.GetString(5)
        _Zip = reader.GetString(6)
        _Phone = reader.GetString(7)
        _SignUpDate = reader.GetDateTime(8)
    Else
        PopulateDefault()
    End If
    reader.Close()
    connection.Close()
End Sub
```

The methods we're using to populate our properties from the SqlDataReader might seem strange to you now, but we'll explain why this is the best way to do it in terms of performance in a later chapter (and because you're crafting this nifty data class, you only have to do it once).

First we create our connection object using a connection string we've added to the class. (In real life, you would probably store your connection string in web.config, but we include it here for simplicity.) When open, we create a command object that has our SQL query, including the parameter in the WHERE clause that we'll use to choose the record. In the next line, we add a parameter to our command object, setting its value from the parameter of the constructor. We create a `SqlDataReader`, and if it can read, we populate our properties with the values from the database. If no record is found, we populate our object with the default values, using the standalone method we created earlier.

So far, we've got all of our properties and a means to create a `Customer` object with default values or values from an existing database record. Next we need ways to create, update, and delete that data.

Create, Update, and Delete Methods

In the example we gave at the beginning of the chapter, we created a `Customer` object using the default constructor, assigned some properties, and then called a `Create()` method. This `Create()` method takes all of the current property values and inserts them into their corresponding columns in a new row in the `Customers` table. Again, the code in Listing 5.6 should be very familiar to you.

Listing 5.6 The `Create()` method

C#

```
public int Create()
{
  SqlConnection connection = new SqlConnection(_ConnectionString);
  connection.Open();
  SqlCommand command = new SqlCommand("INSERT INTO Customers "
    + "(LastName, FirstName, Address, City, State, Zip, Phone, "
    + "SignUpDate) VALUES (@LastName, @FirstName, @Address, "
    + "@City, @State, @Zip, @Phone, @SignUpDate)",
    connection);
  command.Parameters.AddWithValue("@LastName", _LastName);
  command.Parameters.AddWithValue("@FirstName", _FirstName);
  command.Parameters.AddWithValue("@Address", _Address);
  command.Parameters.AddWithValue("@City", _City);
  command.Parameters.AddWithValue("@State", _State);
  command.Parameters.AddWithValue("@Zip", _Zip);
  command.Parameters.AddWithValue("@Phone", _Phone);
  command.Parameters.AddWithValue("@SignUpDate", _SignUpDate);
  command.ExecuteNonQuery();
  command.Parameters.Clear();
  command.CommandText = "SELECT @@IDENTITY";
```

(Continues)

Listing 5.6 The `Create()` method   *(Continued)*

```
int newCustomerID = Convert.ToInt32(command.ExecuteScalar());
connection.Close();
_CustomerID = newCustomerID;
return newCustomerID;
}
```

VB.NET

```
Public Function Create() As Integer
  Dim connection As New SqlConnection(_ConnectionString)
  connection.Open()
  Dim command As New SqlCommand("INSERT INTO Customers " _
    & "(LastName, FirstName, Address, City, State, Zip, Phone, "_
    & "SignUpDate) VALUES (@LastName, @FirstName, @Address, @City, "_
    & "@State, @Zip, @Phone, @SignUpDate)", connection)
  command.Parameters.AddWithValue("@LastName", _LastName)
  command.Parameters.AddWithValue("@FirstName", _FirstName)
  command.Parameters.AddWithValue("@Address", _Address)
  command.Parameters.AddWithValue("@City", _City)
  command.Parameters.AddWithValue("@State", _State)
  command.Parameters.AddWithValue("@Zip", _Zip)
  command.Parameters.AddWithValue("@Phone", _Phone)
  command.Parameters.AddWithValue("@SignUpDate", _SignUpDate)
  command.ExecuteNonQuery()
  command.Parameters.Clear()
  command.CommandText = "SELECT @@IDENTITY"
  Dim newCustomerID As Integer = _
    Convert.ToInt32(command.ExecuteScalar())
  connection.Close()
  _CustomerID = newCustomerID
  Return newCustomerID
End Function
```

Generally when we create a record in the database, we're done with it, and we move on to other things. However, just in case, we've added an extra step to our `Create()` method. We're going back to the database to see what the value is in the `CustomerID` column of the new record we've created, using the SQL statement "`SELECT @@IDENTITY`." We're assigning that value to the `CustomerID` property of our class and sending it back as the return value of our method. Given the design parameter decision we made earlier, changing the `CustomerID` value to anything other than 0 means that it corresponds to an actual record in the database.

Going back again to the first code sample, we'll use a method called `Update()` to change the data in a specific row of our database table. That method is shown in Listing 5.7.

Listing 5.7 The `Update()` method

C#

```
public bool Update()
{
  if (_CustomerID == 0) throw new Exception("Record does not exist in
Customers table.");
  SqlConnection connection = new SqlConnection(_ConnectionString);
    connection.Open();
  SqlCommand command = new SqlCommand("UPDATE Customers SET "
    + "LastName = @LastName, FirstName = @FirstName, "
    + "Address = @Address, City = @City, State = @State, "
    + "Zip = @Zip, Phone = @Phone, SignUpDate = @SignUpDate "
    + "WHERE CustomerID = @CustomerID", connection);
  command.Parameters.AddWithValue("@LastName", _LastName);
  command.Parameters.AddWithValue("@FirstName", _FirstName);
  command.Parameters.AddWithValue("@Address", _Address);
  command.Parameters.AddWithValue("@City", _City);
  command.Parameters.AddWithValue("@State", _State);
  command.Parameters.AddWithValue("@Zip", _Zip);
  command.Parameters.AddWithValue("@Phone", _Phone);
  command.Parameters.AddWithValue("@SignUpDate", _SignUpDate);
  command.Parameters.AddWithValue("@CustomerID", _CustomerID);
  bool result = false;
  if (command.ExecuteNonQuery() > 0) result = true;
  connection.Close();
  return result;
}
```

VB.NET

```
Public Function Update() As Boolean
  If _CustomerID = 0 Then Throw New Exception("Record does not exist in
Customers table.")
  Dim connection As New SqlConnection(_ConnectionString)
  connection.Open()
  Dim command As New SqlCommand("UPDATE Customers SET "_
    & "LastName = @LastName, FirstName = @FirstName, "_
    & "Address = @Address, City = @City, State = @State, "_
```

(Continues)

Listing 5.7 The `Update()` method *(Continued)*

```
    & "Zip = @Zip, Phone = @Phone, SignUpDate = @SignUpDate "_
    & "WHERE CustomerID = @CustomerID", connection)
  command.Parameters.AddWithValue("@LastName", _LastName)
  command.Parameters.AddWithValue("@FirstName", _FirstName)
  command.Parameters.AddWithValue("@Address", _Address)
  command.Parameters.AddWithValue("@City", _City)
  command.Parameters.AddWithValue("@State", _State)
  command.Parameters.AddWithValue("@Zip", _Zip)
  command.Parameters.AddWithValue("@Phone", _Phone)
  command.Parameters.AddWithValue("@SignUpDate", _SignUpDate)
  command.Parameters.AddWithValue("@CustomerID", _CustomerID)
  Dim result As Boolean = False
  If command.ExecuteNonQuery() > 0 Then result = True
  connection.Close()
  Return result
End Function
```

We start our `Update()` method with a check of the `CustomerID` value. If it's 0, we know that the object does not correspond to an existing record in the database, so we throw an exception. If the code is allowed to continue, the rest includes the familiar connection and command objects, as well as parameters that take the current values of our properties and use them to update our database record.

The last few lines are used to check for a successful update of the database. The `ExecuteNonQuery()` method of the command object returns an integer indicating the number of rows affected by our command. Because our `WHERE` clause is matching the `CustomerID` column, a column that we know must have a unique value, the only thing we're interested in knowing is that at least one row was affected. If a value greater than 0 is returned from `ExecuteNonQuery()`, then we return a Boolean true value back to the calling code. This enables us to confirm that the data was indeed updated.

Where we can create and update data, we can also delete it. Enter our `Delete()` method in Listing 5.8, the simplest of the lot.

Listing 5.8 The `Delete()` method

C#
```
public void Delete()
{
  SqlConnection connection = new SqlConnection(_ConnectionString);
```

```
connection.Open();
SqlCommand command = new SqlCommand("DELETE FROM Customers "
    + "WHERE CustomerID = @CustomerID", connection);
command.Parameters.AddWithValue("@CustomerID", _CustomerID);
command.ExecuteNonQuery();
connection.Close();
_CustomerID = 0;
}
```

VB.NET
```
Public Sub Delete()
  Dim connection As New SqlConnection(_ConnectionString)
  connection.Open()
  Dim command As New SqlCommand("DELETE FROM Customers "_
    & "WHERE CustomerID = @CustomerID", connection)
  command.Parameters.AddWithValue("@CustomerID", _CustomerID)
  command.ExecuteNonQuery()
  connection.Close()
  _CustomerID = 0
End Sub
```

There isn't anything complex about this code. We create our connection object and command objects, use the current value of the CustomerID property to make our match in our SQL statement, and execute the command. Just in case the calling code decides it wants to do something with the data, such as call the object's Update() method against a record that no longer exists, we set the CustomerID property back to 0.

Caching the Data for Better Performance

Modern servers, even the cheap ones, generally have a ton of memory, much of which goes unused. The data that you're sucking out of the database and serving to hundreds or thousands of users over and over might not change much, but it does take a bit of time to search for it and extract it from the database. That means reading data off of a hard drive and dragging it through the database's process and then piping it through drivers to .NET so you can display it. Why not store it in memory? It's considerably faster to retrieve the data from memory.

The `System.Web.Caching.Cache` class provides us with a powerful means to keep objects in memory so that they can be quickly retrieved and used throughout our application.

Part of the power of this class is its ability to decide when the object in memory is no longer needed. It makes this decision based on the type of cache dependency that you choose. You can base the dependency on changes to a file or directory, which is great if you're using some file-based resource, but it's a problem for us because our data isn't coming from a file (not in the literal sense, anyway).

We can also kill off our cached items after a certain amount of time has passed or if the object hasn't been accessed for a certain amount of time.

All these methods make data caching difficult because our data might be changed in the meantime by another page or some other process. Obviously we want only the current data to be served to people visiting our site. The key to maintaining this data integrity while caching our data is to only access the database via our data class.

To cache the data, we'll add a few lines of code to our constructor and our `Update()` and `Delete()` methods. We don't have to add any code to the `Create()` method because at that point, we have no idea if the data will be retrieved by some other page or process.

Cached objects are organized and retrieved by a key, much in the same way that you find the right portion of a query string or access a column by name from a `DataReader`. We'll name our cached customer objects "UberCustomer" plus the primary key of the record we retrieve. So for example, if my customer record's `CustomerID` column has a value of 216, the cached object will be named "UberCustomer216."

We'll start by adding a single "if" statement to our constructor, checking to see if the cached object exists. If it does, we'll load those values into our properties. If it doesn't exist, we'll get the data from the database and insert it into the cache. The revised constructor looks like the code in Listing 5.9.

Listing 5.9 Revised constructor with caching

C#
```
public Customer(int CustomerID)
{
  HttpContext context = HttpContext.Current;
  if ((context.Cache["UberCustomer" + CustomerID.ToString()] == null))
  {
```

```
      SqlConnection connection = new SqlConnection(_ConnectionString);
      connection.Open();
      SqlCommand command = new SqlCommand("SELECT CustomerID, "
        + "LastName, FirstName, Address, City, State, Zip, "
        + "Phone, SignUpDate WHERE CustomerID = @CustomerID",
connection);
      command.Parameters.AddWithValue("@CustomerID", CustomerID);
      SqlDataReader reader = command.ExecuteReader();
      if (reader.Read())
      {
        _CustomerID = reader.GetInt32(0);
        _LastName = reader.GetString(1);
        _FirstName = reader.GetString(2);
        _Address = reader.GetString(3);
        _City = reader.GetString(4);
        _State = reader.GetString(5);
        _Zip = reader.GetString(6);
        _Phone = reader.GetString(7);
        _SignUpDate = reader.GetDateTime(8);
      }
      else PopulateDefault();
      reader.Close();
      connection.Close();
      context.Cache.Insert("UberCustomer" +
      _CustomerID.ToString(), this, null,
      DateTime.Now.AddSeconds(60), new TimeSpan.Zero);
    }
    else
    {
      Customer customer = (Customer)context.Cache["UberCustomer" +
        CustomerID.ToString()];
      _CustomerID = customer.CustomerID;
      _LastName = customer.LastName;
      _FirstName = customer.FirstName;
      _Address = customer.Address;
      _City = customer.City;
      _State = customer.State;
      _Zip = customer.Zip;
      _Phone = customer.Phone;
      _SignUpDate = customer.SignUpDate;
    }
}
```

(Continues)

Listing 5.9 Revised constructor with caching *(Continued)*

VB.NET

```
Public Sub New(CustomerID As Integer)
    Dim context As HttpContext = HttpContext.Current
    If context.Cache(("UberCustomer" + CustomerID.ToString())) Is Nothing
Then
        Dim connection As New SqlConnection(_ConnectionString)
        connection.Open()
        Dim command As New SqlCommand("SELECT CustomerID, LastName, "_
            & "FirstName, Address, City, State, Zip, Phone, "_
            & " SignUpDate WHERE CustomerID = @CustomerID", connection)
        command.Parameters.AddWithValue("@CustomerID", CustomerID)
        Dim reader As SqlDataReader = command.ExecuteReader()
        If reader.Read() Then
            _CustomerID = reader.GetInt32(0)
            _LastName = reader.GetString(1)
            _FirstName = reader.GetString(2)
            _Address = reader.GetString(3)
            _City = reader.GetString(4)
            _State = reader.GetString(5)
            _Zip = reader.GetString(6)
            _Phone = reader.GetString(7)
            _SignUpDate = reader.GetDateTime(8)
        Else
            PopulateDefault()
        End If
        reader.Close()
        connection.Close()
        context.Cache.Insert("UberCustomer" + _CustomerID.ToString(), _
            Me, Nothing, DateTime.Now.AddSeconds(60), TimeSpan.Zero)
    Else
        Dim customer As Customer = _
            CType(context.Cache(("UberCustomer" + CustomerID.ToString())), _
Customer)
        _CustomerID = customer.CustomerID
        _LastName = customer.LastName
        _FirstName = customer.FirstName
        _Address = customer.Address
        _City = customer.City
        _State = customer.State
        _Zip = customer.Zip
        _Phone = customer.Phone
        _SignUpDate = customer.SignUpDate
    End If
End Sub
```

We start the new version of the constructor by checking to see if an existing cache object corresponds to the record we're looking for. Because our class has absolutely no clue that it's being used in a Web application, we first create an `HttpContext` object to reference, in this case, `HttpContext.Current`, which provides a reference to the current request.

If there is no cached object, everything proceeds as before, except for the very last line. We call the `Insert()` method of the cache object, which takes a number of parameters. (There are a number of overloads for the Insert method, but this one offers the most control for our purposes. Consult the .NET documentation for more information.)

```
context.Cache.Insert("UberCustomer" + _CustomerID.ToString(),
this, null, DateTime.Now.AddSeconds(60), TimeSpan.Zero);
```

The first parameter is a string to name the cache entry. As we mentioned earlier, it's a combination of the `"UberCustomer"` and the `CustomerID` value. The second parameter is `this` (or `Me` in VB), which is the instance of the class itself. That means that all of the values assigned to the class' properties are stored in memory. The third parameter is for a `CacheDependency` object, and in our case we're using `null` (`Nothing` in VB) because we're not tying any dependency to the cached object.

The fourth parameter is the time at which we want the cached object to be removed from memory, which is an absolute expiration time. The fifth parameter is a sliding expiration time expressed as the `TimeSpan` that passes without the cached object being accessed. That means an object could live indefinitely if it's accessed over and over. Because we've already set an absolute expiration, we must set this to a `TimeSpan` object that indicates zero time.

You must experiment with these values to decide how much memory you want to use (see Chapter 15, "Performance, Scalability, and Metrics"). If you write a number of different data classes similar to this one, you may want to store a value in `web.config` that indicates the number of seconds (or minutes, hours, or whatever you want) so that you can change the setting all from one place.

If the object has been cached, it's easy enough to retrieve those values and assign them to our private class members. We create a new `Customer` object and fill it with the cached version. We have to cast the object to the `Customer` type because the type returned by the `Cache` object is `System.Object`.

This is a point of confusion for some developers because we're creating an instance of the class from within the class and then assigning its properties to the private members of the class in which we're working.

Getting this cached data will save many trips to the database, but we need to devise a way to make sure that we always have current data. If another user loads the data and changes it by calling Update() or deletes it with the Delete() method, we must remove the cached data so that it is sought from the database instead of being loaded from memory. This is easy enough with a private method that uses the cache's Remove() method. Listing 5.10 demonstrates the cache removal.

Listing 5.10 Private DeleteCache() method

C#
```
private void DeleteCache()
{
    if (HttpContext.Current.Cache["UberCustomer"
        + _CustomerID.ToString()] != null)
        HttpContext.Current.Cache.Remove("UberCustomer"
            + _CustomerID.ToString());
}
```

VB.NET
```
Private Sub DeleteCache()
    If Not (HttpContext.Current.Cache(("UberCustomer" & _
        _CustomerID.ToString())) Is Nothing) Then
        HttpContext.Current.Cache.Remove(("UberCustomer" & _
            _CustomerID.ToString()))
    End If
End Sub
```

Again, we reference the HttpContext.Current object. First we see if the object exists, and if it does, we call the Remove() method, which looks for the object by its key name.

We'll need to call the DeleteCache() method from both the Update() and Delete() methods. It's as simple as adding one line to both of the methods: DeleteCache().

As long as we access the database through this class only, we will always have current data.

Getting More than One Record at a Time

This model for a data class might be great for getting one record, but what happens when you need to get a group of records? Fortunately we can group these data objects together in an `ArrayList`, a structure that is often less complicated and less work for .NET to create and maintain than a `DataTable`.

Continuing with our example, let's say that we frequently need to look up groups of customers by their Zip code. We'll add a `static` (`shared`) method to the class that takes a single parameter, the Zip code, and searches the database for matching records. The method will return an `ArrayList` of `Customer` objects. The `ArrayList` class is in the `System.Collections` namespace, so we need to add a `using` statement (`Imports` in VB) to the top of our class file. Listing 5.11 shows our new method.

> Why are we using a static method? Simply put, this method doesn't require any of the class's structure to function. We don't need any of its properties or functions to run, and we don't want the calling code to have to create an instance of the class first. We include the method within the class anyway because its functionality is closely related to the class.

Listing 5.11 The static method to get an `ArrayList` full of `Customer` objects

C#
```
public static ArrayList GetCustomersByZip(string Zip)
{
   SqlConnection connection = new
   SqlConnection("server=(local);database=test;Integrated
Security=SSPI");
   connection.Open();
   SqlCommand command = new SqlCommand("SELECT CustomerID, "
      + "LastName, FirstName, Address, City, State, Zip, Phone, "
      + "SignUpDate WHERE Zip = @Zip ORDER BY LastName, "
      + "FirstName ", connection);
```

(Continues)

Listing 5.11 The static method to get an `ArrayList` full of `Customer` objects
(*Continued*)

```
command.Parameters.AddWithValue("@Zip", Zip);
SqlDataReader reader = command.ExecuteReader();
// create the ArrayList that the method will return
ArrayList objList = new ArrayList();
while (reader.Read())
{
  // create a new customer object
  Customer customer = new Customer();
  // assign the database values to the object's properties
  customer.CustomerID = reader.GetInt32(0);
  customer.LastName = reader.GetString(1);
  customer.FirstName = reader.GetString(2);
  customer.Address = reader.GetString(3);
  customer.City = reader.GetString(4);
  customer.State = reader.GetString(5);
  customer.Zip = reader.GetString(6);
  customer.Phone = reader.GetString(7);
  customer.SignUpDate = reader.GetDateTime(8);
  // add the customer object to the ArrayList
  objList.Add(customer);
}
reader.Close();
connection.Close();
// return the finished ArrayList with customer objects
return objList;
}
```

VB.NET

```
Public Shared Function GetCustomersByZip(Zip As String) As ArrayList
   Dim connection As New _
SqlConnection("server=(local);database=test;Integrated Security=SSPI")
   connection.Open()
   Dim command As New SqlCommand("SELECT CustomerID, LastName, "_
     & "FirstName, Address, City, State, Zip, Phone, SignUpDate "_
     & "WHERE Zip = @Zip ORDER BY LastName, FirstName", connection)
   command.Parameters.AddWithValue("@Zip", Zip)
   Dim reader As SqlDataReader = command.ExecuteReader()
   ' create the ArrayList that the method will return
   Dim objList As New ArrayList()
   While reader.Read()
      ' create a new customer object
      Dim customer As New Customer()
```

```
     ' assign the database values to the object's properties
     customer.CustomerID = reader.GetInt32(0)
     customer.LastName = reader.GetString(1)
     customer.FirstName = reader.GetString(2)
     customer.Address = reader.GetString(3)
     customer.City = reader.GetString(4)
     customer.State = reader.GetString(5)
     customer.Zip = reader.GetString(6)
     customer.Phone = reader.GetString(7)
     customer.SignUpDate = reader.GetDateTime(8)
     ' add the customer object to the ArrayList
     objList.Add(customer)
   End While
   reader.Close()
   connection.Close()
   ' return the finished ArrayList with customer objects
   Return objList
End Function
```

At first glance, this new method looks a lot like our constructor. The first difference is that we're using a static method that returns an `ArrayList` object populated with `Customer` objects by looping through more than one record of data. We can call static methods without instantiating the class. To look up customers in the 44114 Zip code, for example, we'd need only one line:

```
ArrayList objList44114 = Customer.GetCustomersByZip("44114");
```

The next difference is in our SQL statement. This time we're looking for records where the Zip is matched to the parameter we've passed in. Because the `Zip` column of the database is not our primary key and may not be unique, we may get several records.

Just after we execute the `SqlDataReader`, we create an `ArrayList` object. This will be the container for our `Customer` objects. Using a `while` loop, we go through each record returned by the database, creating a `Customer` object each time, assigning the database values to the object's properties, and then adding that `Customer` object to the `ArrayList`. When we're done and we've cleaned up our connection, we return the `ArrayList` populated with `Customer` objects.

There are a few other changes we need to make. First, our `CustomerID` property can't be read-only because we need to assign data to it when we execute these searches from static methods. We revise it to include the "set" portion of the property in Listing 5.12

Listing 5.12 The revised `CustomerID` property

C#
```csharp
public int CustomerID
{
  get {return _CustomerID;}
  set {_CustomerID = value;}
}
```

VB.NET
```vbnet
Public Property CustomerID() As Integer
    Get
        Return _CustomerID
    End Get
    Set
        _CustomerID = value
    End Set
End Property
```

The other change is that our static method doesn't know anything about the string `_ConnectionString` because the rest of the class hasn't been instantiated. We've included the string here right in the code, but a better practice is to store it elsewhere, perhaps in `web.config`, instead of hard-coding it.

The big surprise for many people is that your wonderful new `ArrayList` can be bound to a `Repeater` control, and you can access the properties of the `Customer` objects just as if you bound a `SqlDataReader` or `DataTable`. That's because the `ArrayList` implements the `IEnumerable` interface, just like `SqlDataReader` and `DataTable`. As long as your `ArrayList` contains all the same objects, in this case `Customer` objects, there's nothing more to do. Your `Repeater`'s `ItemTemplate` might look something like this:

```
<ItemTemplate>
  <p><%# DataBinder.Eval(Container.DataItem,"LastName") %>,
<%# DataBinder.Eval(Container.DataItem,"FirstName") %></p>
</ItemTemplate>
```

You can cache these result sets as well by putting the finished `ArrayList` into the cache using a name such as "UberCustomerList44114" in this case. However, you'll have to add more plumbing to the `Update()`

and `Delete()` methods, as well as the `Create()` method to remove any customer `ArrayLists` being cached if the Zip matches. Otherwise, the cached `ArrayList` wouldn't have a new record (or would include a deleted record) of a customer with a 44114 Zip code.

Summary

Our custom data class represents a block of code that manipulates data in our database. If you look back to the code samples at the beginning of the chapter, you can see that a few simple properties and methods replace the blocks of data access code that we would otherwise need to write over and over again in our application, in any place that we would need to change data in our database.

This encapsulation of common functionality gets to the core of writing object-oriented code. We achieve code reuse, and we manipulate an object with names we understand. The purpose of our `Update()` method is not immediately apparent, based on the appearance of the code. Compare that to the first code sample, where we create a `Customer` object, assign new values to its properties, and then call its `Update()` method. This code is much easier to deal with, and its purpose is almost immediately obvious. Again, we can view the code from a "user" view and a "programmer" view, the former concentrating on how it's used, and the latter worrying about the underlying implementation.

> This is a good time to mention that you can implement a provider design pattern similar to the one used for Membership and Profile, which we'll cover in Chapter 11, "Membership and Security," and Chapter 12, "Profiles, Themes, and Skins."

Data access is just one problem you can address with your own classes. If you start to think in abstract terms of a tool that solves a problem, you can apply similar concepts to virtually anything. For example, if you needed a tool that checked loan balances for a bank customer service representative, you might create a balance checking class that takes some parameters or properties that represent the customer and some method or property that indicates the balance due. You might also include methods that verify the customer's information or that check to see whether they've paid on time or whether the customer service representative has permission to look up the balance. This tool might be used by a Web site or a Windows application, or it might be used by another system, such as a system that takes new loan applications and makes decisions based on the customer's payment history from your balance checking tool.

Microsoft has solved hundreds or thousands of problems like this. Take our friend the `TextBox` control. Here Microsoft has created a tool, a class just like one you might build, that renders HTML to the browser, stores data in the control's viewstate, and generates style information if it's needed, among other things. It's a lot easier than having to do all that work over and over again in the context of every page!

PART II

The ASP.NET Architecture

CHAPTER 6

The Nuts and Bolts of IIS and Web Applications

In the first part of the book, we discussed a lot of code in rather abstract terms. The reason for this approach is that code can live in a number of different places, and those locations aren't that important in the bigger concept of object-oriented programming.

However, after you get comfortable with OOP, it's important to understand what is going on from the time a request is made to your site to the time a response lands on the Web browser. This knowledge will allow you to push your application development well beyond just creating pages.

IIS: The First Step

Internet Information Services is the part of the Windows operating system that services requests to your Web site. The IIS Manager shows a tree of sites grouped under the Web Sites group, as shown in Figure 6.1. Each site is set to take requests by IP address, port (normally port 80), and a host header value, which allows one IP to be used for several sites.

When an HTTP request arrives at the machine, IIS determines which application will handle the request based on the file extension of the request. If no matching extension is found, the requested file is served straight, the file is served without any processing. These applications that handle the various file types are known as ISAPI applications (Internet Server Application Program Interface). Back in the old days, you needed these applications to do fancy processing of HTTP requests on your own, though in the .NET world we can do this with `HttpModules` (coming in Chapter 8, "HttpHandlers and HttpModules").

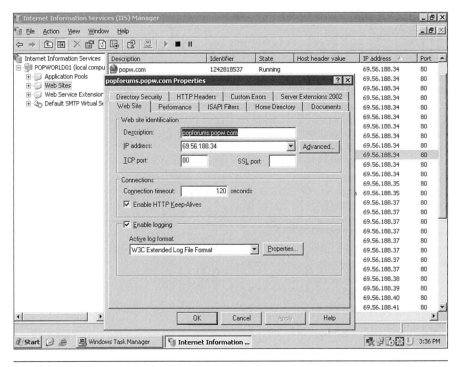

Figure 6.1 IIS with open site property sheet.

The preceding description isn't technically the whole story. A driver called `http.sys` actually gets the request first in Windows Server 2003 (IIS v6.0). It passes off the processing to one worker process instance (`w3wp.exe`) for each application pool. In IIS v5.x in Windows 2000 and Windows XP, the request is first received by `inetinfo.exe`, which sends it to `aspnet_isapi.dll` and then to the ASP.NET worker process, `aspnet_wp.exe`. IIS6 has a shorter pipeline, so ASP.NET requests are generally handled more quickly.

Your server already has some of this mapping set up for you, provided you have enabled ASP.NET (it is not turned on by default as a security precaution in Windows Server 2003, though it is easily turned on via the "Web Service Extensions" node in the IIS control panel). Figure 6.2 shows the IIS dialog used to map these extensions, whereas Figure 6.3 shows the dialog that appears when you click Edit in Figure 6.2. (The application configuration dialog in Figure 6.2 can be found by clicking the "configuration" button on the Home Directory tab of the site properties.) In plain English, this tells the server, "If you get a request for a file ending in '.aspx,' send it to the program `aspnet_isapi.dll` to execute." The "Verify that file exists" checkbox will cause IIS to check to see if an actual file by that name exists, and if not, IIS will return a 404 "not found" error. As you'll see later, we don't necessarily need to have an existing file to handle a request.

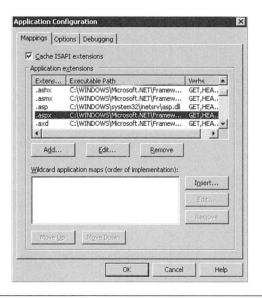

Figure 6.2 Application configuration dialog in IIS.

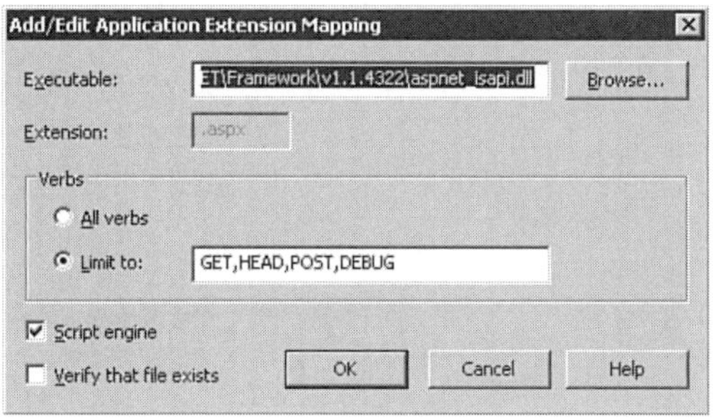

Figure 6.3 Editing the mapping of a file extension to an application.

You might be wondering what happens when the request does not include any particular file name, and therefore no file extension (such as a request for http://www.microsoft.com or http://www.microsoft.com/sql). In those cases, IIS will try to load default pages, in the order specified on the Documents tab of the site's properties. Figure 6.4 shows this tab, indicating that default.aspx is the first one to try.

You can also force every request to be handled by a particular ISAPI program. This is handy when you want to build a site that interprets the request's URL and executes some other page. It's also useful when you need to process certain files, such as images, before sending them back to the user's browser. To have ASP.NET process all requests, you must add a wildcard map, which is also shown in Figure 6.2. It opens up a dialog almost exactly like the one in Figure 6.3, except that it doesn't apply to any one particular file extension. The application you specify for the wildcard is the same `aspnet_isapi.dll` that handles .aspx, .asax, .asmx, and other requests.

> Prior to IIS 6, wildcards were accomplished by adding an additional entry to the application extensions part of the dialog by specifying ".*" as an extension.

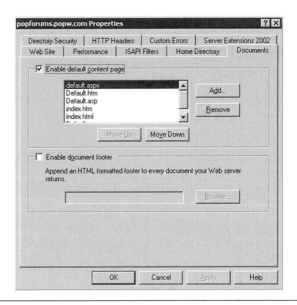

Figure 6.4 Specifying default documents.

In the event that your mappings to ASP.NET somehow are removed or altered in a way that prevents ASP.NET from getting normal requests, a command line utility is included to fix these all at once. If you navigate to `C:\WINDOWS\Microsoft.NET\Framework\v2.x.xxxx` (where the last part indicates the version of the framework you want to use, with v1.1.4322 being the production release of v1.1 of the .NET Framework), you'll find a program called `aspnet_regiis.exe`. Execute this file at a command prompt, and you'll get a list of switches that will restore these maps and install the client-side JavaScript for certain Web controls in the root of each site.

Deciding What ASP.NET Will Handle

As we mentioned earlier, enabling ASP.NET on the server will map some file extensions to be handled by ASP.NET. The most important and obvious of these are requests ending in .aspx, the default extension for an ASP.NET page. If you open up the application configuration dialog, you'll find a number of file extensions that IIS will send to `aspnet_isapi.dll`. After the hand-off is made, IIS doesn't care about what happens to the request. As we'll see in Chapter 8, some file extensions are handled by built-in classes that simply return a response indicating that the user isn't allowed to see the file (.cs and .vb code files, for example).

This is the place where we'll add .jpg files to the list of those handled by ASP.NET for our example in Chapter 8.

Where the Code Lives

The .NET Framework, as you may already know, is not an interpreted script platform. In the old days of Active Server Pages, Perl, and PHP, each page was interpreted line-by-line every time the page was executed. The script engine had to go through and figure out what every line was supposed to do every time.

In the .NET world, everything is compiled. Your page, as well as the C# or VB.NET code, is compiled at some point to Microsoft Intermediate Language (MSIL). MSIL is compiled just in time to code that the CPU understands. Assemblies are already in MSIL form, but your pages are not compiled until they're needed. Page compilation occurs once, and the resulting temporary assemblies are cached. That's the high-level view, but the actual text that makes up your code can come from a number of places. The following sections describe some of those places that the code can live. We'll show you the older code-behind models to be complete, but you should understand that with Visual Studio 2005 and ASP.NET v2.0, the inline and code-beside models are considered the two preferred schemes to handle page code. Classes intended for general use throughout the application either may be compiled to an assembly for the /bin folder, or the raw uncompiled class files can be placed in the /App_Code folder.

Inline Code

The closest thing to the old script days is the inline code model, where your methods appear in <script runat="server"></script> blocks, right in the .aspx page. Listing 6.1 shows an example of this technique.

Listing 6.1 Inline code

C#

```
<%@ Page Language="C#" %>
<script runat="server">
  void Page_Load(object sender, EventArgs e)
  {
    FirstLabel.Text = "Hello world!";
  }
</script>
<html>
<body>
  <form id="form1" runat="server">
    <asp:Label ID="FirstLabel" Runat="Server" />
  </form>
</body>
</html>
```

VB.NET

```
<%@ Page Language="VB" %>
<script runat="server">
  Sub Page_Load(sender As Object, e As EventArgs)
    FirstLabel.Text = "Hello world!"
  End Sub
```

```
</script>
<html>
<body>
  <form id="form1" runat="server">
    <asp:Label ID="FirstLabel" Runat="Server" />
  </form>
</body>
</html>
```

The first time this page loads, it is compiled into a class that resides in an assembly stored in a subfolder of the `C:\WINDOWS\Microsoft.NET\Framework\v2.x.xxxx\Temporary ASP.NET Files` folder. That compiled version of the page is good until the .aspx file changes or the application is restarted, at which time it will have to be recompiled.

With ASP.NET v2.0, this way of writing code has come back into favor, provided it is being used solely for gluing together the UI and the classes that make up your business rules. This gets back into the application architecture we talked about in Chapter 4, "Application Architecture," where we separated the heavy lifting from the UI.

If you're tempted to drop script blocks all over the .aspx page, don't do it. One script block at the top of the page is all you should have. That block will have the typical set of event handlers, including `Page_Load` and event handlers that deal with button clicks, for example.

It's worth mentioning that your page inherits from the `System.Web.UI.Page` class, even though we haven't expressly indicated this. If you want the page to inherit from some other class (which must in turn eventually inherit from `Page`), you can indicate this by adding the `Inherits` attribute to the `Page` directive (you'll see this in the code-behind model).

Code-Behind: Non-Compiled

This technique of code separation was most commonly used by people who wanted to change code on-the-fly without having to "build" their projects, or by people who wanted to separate code from HTML but didn't have a tool like Visual Studio to automate the process. Generally speaking, using the inline or code-beside methods is more popular. Listing 6.2 shows a page using code-behind, without compiling the class.

Listing 6.2 Code-behind, non-compiled

default.aspx

```
<%@ Page Language="C#" Src="default.aspx.cs" Inherits="CodeBehindClass" %>
<html>
<body>
  <form id="form1" runat="server">
    <asp:Label ID="FirstLabel" Runat="Server" />
  </form>
</body>
</html>
```

C# (default.aspx.cs)

```csharp
using System;
using System.Web;

public class CodeBehindClass : System.Web.UI.Page
{
  protected System.Web.UI.WebControls.Label FirstLabel;

  public void Page_Load(object sender, EventArgs e)
  {
    FirstLabel.Text = "Hello world!";
  }
}
```

VB.NET (default.aspx.vb)

```vbnet
Imports System
Imports System.Web

Public Class CodeBehindClass
  Inherits System.Web.UI.Page
  Protected FirstLabel As System.Web.UI.WebControls.Label
  Public Sub Page_Load(sender As Object, e As EventArgs)
    FirstLabel.Text = "Hello world!"
  End Sub
End Class
```

This example uses two files (we've created two code-behind files, one for C# and one for VB.NET). The actual .aspx page looks just like the inline page, except that the code has been moved to the code-behind file.

The first line, the `Page` directive, has two attributes that weren't there before. The `Src` attribute points to the physical file where the code-behind class is located (substitute this with `default.aspx.vb` if you're using the VB.NET version). The `Inherits` attribute tells us which class in that code-behind file the page should inherit because there technically could be any number of classes in that file.

The code-behind class must do two more things. First, it must inherit from `System.Web.UI.Page`, the base class for all ASP.NET pages. Second, it must declare all of the controls we'll access on the page as `protected` members of the class. That's why you'll notice that `FirstLabel` is declared in the structure of the class.

The first time this page is requested, it will be compiled and cached only as the inline code version, using the code-behind file as the source for its base class. It will remain cached until the .aspx or code-behind files have been changed or the application has been restarted.

Code-Behind: Compiled

For the developer, this works almost exactly like the non-compiled code-behind method. The important distinction is in the `Page` directive:

```
<%@ Page Language="C#" Codebehind="default.aspx.cs"
Inherits="CodeBehindClass" %>
```

The `Codebehind` attribute was used only by Visual Studio 2002 and 2003 to let the designer know where the code was being kept. Because no `Src` was specified, the class indicated in the `Inherits` attribute had to be compiled in an assembly located in the `/bin` folder. In the older versions of Visual Studio, selecting Build -> Build Project from the menu would take all of the `.cs` (or `.vb`) files in the project and compile them to one assembly. The first time the page was requested, it would be compiled in much the same way as the previous methods, except that it would inherit from a class compiled in an assembly found in the `/bin` folder.

This scheme is obsolete and is not supported in Visual Studio 2005. It required constant synchronization between the pages and code files, generated a ton of code, and meant that you had to do a build every time you wanted to test the page. It's probably the reason that people new to the platform gave up on trying to use Visual Studio and went to WebMatrix, Dreamweaver, or even Notepad.

Code-Beside/Partial Classes

Although Visual Studio 2005 supports inline code better than any other development environment ever written, some developers might very well prefer to separate their code from the HTML in the .aspx file. There are advantages to doing this, including code reuse and the separation of design duties between a page designer and coder (anyone that hates designing HTML pages knows what I'm talking about). To accomplish this, we use partial classes, a new feature of the .NET Framework starting with v2.0.

Listing 6.3 shows the layout of the HTML in the .aspx page, as well as the separate code files. This is known as code-behind in the .NET documentation, but it is also frequently called code-beside.

Listing 6.3 Code-beside files

default.aspx

```
<%@ Page Language="C#" Codefile="default.aspx.cs"
  Inherits="Default_aspx" %>
<html>
<body>
  <form id="form1" runat="server">
    <asp:Label ID="FirstLabel" Runat="Server" />
  </form>
</body>
</html>
```

C#

```
using System;
using System.Web;

public partial class Default_aspx : System.Web.UI.Page
{
  public void Page_Load(object sender, EventArgs e)
  {
    FirstLabel.Text = "Hello world!";
  }
}
```

VB.NET

```
Imports System
Imports System.Web

Partial Class Default_aspx
  Inherits System.Web.UI.Page
```

```
Public Sub Page_Load(sender As Object, e As EventArgs)
    FirstLabel.Text = "Hello world!"
End Sub
End Class
```

Notice how much cleaner this is compared to the old code-behind model. Gone are the references to every control on the page, as well as all the generated code in the older versions of Visual Studio. When a request for the page is made for the first time, the page combines itself with the partial class to become the functional equivalent of the inline code example in Listing 6.1. Just as with the others, the compiled class remains valid until one of the involved files is changed.

Even setting up a new page in your Visual Studio 2005 project is easier because the new Web form dialog has a checkbox indicating you want to separate your code, as shown in Figure 6.5. If you check the box Place Code in Separate File, a partial class file will be generated for you.

The /App_Code Folder

There is one additional place you can put code, and given this book's emphasis on object-oriented programming, it's an important one. You can place class files (.cs or .vb) in the /App_Code folder of the application.

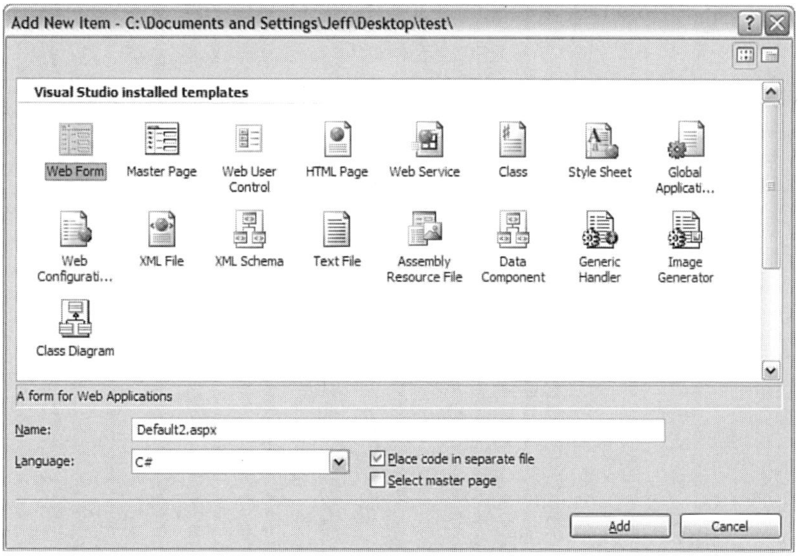

Figure 6.5 Add New Item dialog for Web form.

Think of the /App_Code folder as an uncompiled /bin. Class files stored here are compiled when the application is run, and they can be accessed from any page or class in the application. This is especially handy in the Visual Web Developer 2005 Express Edition because that product doesn't "build" (compile all class files to an assembly) the way that Visual Studio does, and you can't reference a separate class library project.

The development environment is smart enough to know where to place code. For example, if you added a LinkButton to the page in Listing 6.1 using the visual designer, double-clicking that control will create an event handler method inline, in the script block. If you did the same thing to our example in Listing 6.3, the event handler method would be added to the code-beside file.

> To be complete, we should mention that there is another place that a compiled class can be reached other than the /bin folder of the Web application. The global assembly cache (GAC) is a collection of classes that can be accessed by any .NET application on the computer. The command line utility gacutil.exe, found in Visual Studio's SDK\bin folder, is used to add the classes found in an assembly to the GAC. This might be useful to you if there are classes that several applications on the box need to access without having to maintain separate copies of them for each application. Keep in mind, though, that the design of .NET is such that it should eliminate "DLL hell," the phenomenon from the COM days where several versions of a library existed on the same computer, causing confusion for consuming applications. With this in mind, it's a good idea to deploy assemblies with the applications they were meant for.
>
> You can get more information on using the GAC here:
> http://www.gotdotnet.com/team/clr/when_to_use_the_gac.aspx

A fairly common technique is to build a class library outside of the site project itself, where you keep all of your business objects and do the "heavy lifting." By adding a class library project to a solution in Visual Studio 2005, you create some of the code separation we talked about in Chapter 4.

You'll need to do two things to use a class library in your solution. First, right-click the Web project in the solution explorer and choose Add Reference. On the Projects tab of the resulting dialog, choose the project in the solution that contains your class library. Visual Studio will automatically copy the compiled assembly of that project into the /bin folder of the Web project whenever it's changed.

The second thing you'll need to do in your class library is to create references to ASP.NET's objects. In addition to `importing` (`using` in C#) the `System.Web` namespace, you'll need to get some kind of context to the application and page's lifecycle. You can do this by creating a new `HttpContext` object and assigning `HttpContext.Current` to it. In your code, typing the name of the object followed by a period will cause Intellisense to pop up all of the familiar objects you'd normally find when coding in the page, such as `Request`, `Response`, `Cache`, and so on. You got to see this technique in action in Chapter 5, "Object-Oriented Programming Applied: A Custom Data Class," when we added caching to our custom data class.

Pre-Compiled Deployment

It's usually considered bad form to deploy uncompiled code to your production site. If an attacker was able to gain access to your site, he or she could read the .cs, .vb or .aspx files to see what exactly you're doing, which could lead to even more damage. In other cases, you simply might not want a client poking around and messing with your stuff. Pre-compiling your site addresses these issues.

You can publish your site by clicking Website -> Publish Website… in Visual Studio 2005 to perform pre-compilation. Figure 6.6 shows the simple dialog to perform this action. You can also use the `aspnet_compiler.exe` command line tool.

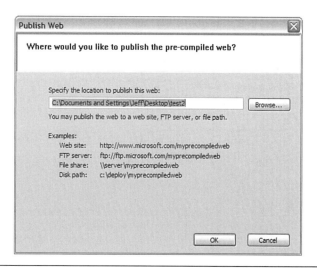

Figure 6.6 The pre-compilation dialog in Visual Studio 2005.

This function does some interesting things to your code. First, in the "published" version of your pages, you can open them up to find that they contain only one line of text: "This is a marker file generated by the precompilation tool, and should not be deleted!" In the /bin folder, you'll find some XML configuration files with a .compiled file extension, and of course you'll also find an actual assembly with some random name. Together, these files function just as your application would have if you had simply copied it all to the server. Remember that your pages would be compiled into assemblies anyway, stored in ASP.NET's temporary files folder. Pre-compilation skips that step.

The benefit of compilation is that any possible compilation errors in your site are found before the site is deployed. The source code, including the HTML, is not visible to anyone that can view the files. Although this is not generally a big deal, you also won't get that brief delay the first time you access a page while it's compiled.

Summary

In this chapter, we've explored the process of getting a Web request into the machine, and we followed it from IIS through the various stages of page compilation.

IIS first gets the request and figures out which ISAPI program will process the page. In the case of ASP.NET, it makes its way to `aspnet_isapi.dll` and is processed.

ASP.NET compiles pages in one of several different physical file schemes and caches that code for execution in other requests. Of the different schemes possible, inline code and code-beside are the easiest and most practical means of writing and maintaining code.

The pre-compilation performed by the publishing utility can ease deployment by hiding your code, checking for errors, and avoiding the first-run compilation process on the first request.

CHAPTER 7

The ASP.NET Event Model

Everything in ASP.NET happens because some trigger caused it to happen. In many scripting languages, a script is executed only because a request was made for that script. ASP.NET goes well beyond the simple HTTP request to make things happen. This rich event model comes from a long tradition of visual desktop application development.

Events are what the name implies, occurrences or actions. Events have to occur in order for us to know it's time to do something. When your toast pops up out of the toaster, you know it's time to butter the toast and eat it. When the "feed me" light comes on in your car, you know it's time to get gas. When your credit card statement comes in the mail and the balance isn't zero, you know it's time to pay it. Our Web applications have all kinds of events to let us know it's time to fire off some code!

History

One of the things that made the visual development environments so popular was the fact that they enabled you to drag and drop controls onto a form, and then the program would write code that would react to action on that control. For example, in a Visual Basic application, you could drag a button onto a form and then double-click that button in the development environment to create method code that would handle the clicking of that button.

This method of dealing with events on a form in a Windows application is, by comparison to a Web app, easy to implement. The application, at any given time, is in a known state in memory. The application knows what the mouse is doing, knows what's on the screen, can access resources such as the computer's hard drive, and so on.

You can understand, then, that trying to duplicate this type of event handling on the Web poses certain challenges. The Web, by its very nature, is stateless. A request comes to the server from a user's browser, and the server does some processing and then responds by sending HTML back to the browser. After the server has finished sending the response, it "forgets" about the request. It doesn't really know or care about the state of controls in the user's browser, and if there are 10,000 simultaneous users, it can't be bothered with all that data.

> You'll notice that we frequently talk about "rendered HTML." Rendering is simply the process of the ASP.NET framework and its controls turning all the objects into HTML to send to the browser. In fact, you'll see that these objects have a render event near the end of their lifecycle when actual HTML is generated.

ASP.NET addresses the need to develop visually and simulate state on the stateless Web with some clever tricks that enable you to develop applications in a similar manner to a Windows application developer. The first part of this is the hidden __VIEWSTATE input tag in the rendered HTML of the form. Listing 7.1 shows a fairly large sample from a rendered page.

Listing 7.1 Viewstate rendered to the finished page

```
<input type="hidden" name="__VIEWSTATE"
value="dDwtMTcwMzMxMDE2NDt0PDtsPGk8MT47aTwzPjs+O2w8dDxwPGw8aW5uZXXJodG1sO
z47bDxDb2FzdGVyQnV6eiAtIEhvbWU7Pj47Oz47dDw7bDxpPPDU+Oz47bDx0PDtsPGk8MD47P
jtsPHQ8O2w8aTwxPjs+O2w8dDw7bDxpPPDI+Oz47bDx0PHA8cDxsPFZpc2l2bGU7PjtsPG88Z
j47Pj47Pjs7Pjs+Pjs+PjtsPF9jdGwwOl9jdGwwOlNpdGVsYXR1cjpfY3RsY2ljp4Y
3RsMDpfY3RsMDtfY3RsMDpfY3RsMDpTaXRlUmVwZWF0ZXI6X2N0bDI6X2N0bDA7X2N0bDA6X
2N0bDA6U2l0ZVJlcGVhdGVyOl9jdGw0Ol9jdGww0l9jdGww0l9jdGww0lNpdGVsYXR1cjpfY3Rc
jpfY3RsNjpfY3RsMDtfY3RsMDpfY3RsMDpTaXRlUmVwZWF0ZXI6X2N0bDg6X2N0bDA7X2N0b
DA6X2N0bDA6U2l0ZVJlcGVhdGVyOl9jdGwxMDpfY3RsMDtfY3RsMDpfY3RsMDpTaXRlUmVwZ
WF0ZXI6X2N0bDEyOl9jdGww0l9jdGww0l9jdGww0lNpdGVsYXR1cjpfY3RsMTQ6X2N0b
DA7X2N0bDA6X2N0bDA6U2l0ZVJlcGVhdGVyOl9jdGwxNjpfY3RsMDtfY3RsMDpfY3RsMDpTa
XRlUmVwZWF0ZXI6X2N0bDE4Ol9jdGww0z4+BW1dvuXwoUhYlCbVaKY2H4hNGgg=" />
```

The viewstate is an encoded representation of the state of the controls on the page. It lets the server "remember" what it sent to the browser. For example, it might indicate that a drop-down has certain values and a certain item selected, or it might contain the entire contents of data in a DataGrid.

All this information hidden in the HTML does come at a price. Each time the page is loaded, or a request is received from the same page, that data has to be encoded and/or decoded. Multiply that by thousands of users, and you can see where this process might become a problem. We'll look at the implication of this in Chapter 15, "Performance, Scalability, and Metrics."

The other part of this simulated form state is of course *postback*. ASP.NET's postback mechanism causes the entire contents of a page's form to be "posted back" to the server for processing. These form element values, combined with the information in the viewstate, can be compared so that changes can be sensed and some kind of processing can take place.

You might compare this arrangement to a traditional Windows application. In Windows, when an event is triggered, the application checks the state of things in memory and does something. In the ASP.NET application, the browser posts back to the server, the old and new form states are compared, and the server sends back HTML to reflect the changes.

The truth is, as a developer, you probably don't really need to know what's going on in the background during this process. In fact, many people might find it easier that way. For example, say you have a button on your form. When the user clicks the button, it fires off an event handler on the server that you wrote, which in turn saves some data to a database. You could just as easily leave it at that and not be concerned with the fact that a postback occurs. That's a leap of faith for developers who come from script backgrounds because you have to trust that all of the plumbing provided by ASP.NET works correctly.

However, after you're comfortable with this postback model, it's helpful to know what's going on because it can help you diagnose performance problems later on.

The Postback Process

Let's look at the postback process in detail so you can see how ASP.NET makes the stateless Web appear to have state, similar to the way a Windows application works.

The basic way to send any data from a Web page is via the HTML `form` element. Every ASP.NET Web form has a `form` element. When you write the page, you include the `runat="server"` attribute. It's rendered in the final page, as shown in Listing 7.2.

Listing 7.2 The rendered `form` tag in a Web form

```
<form method="post" action="Default.aspx" onsubmit="javascript:return
WebForm_OnSubmit();" id="form1">
```

You're familiar with most of these attributes from your HTML 101 days. The `post` method is the HTTP way of sending form data, the `action` attribute says where to post the data to (the same page we're viewing, including any query string information), and the `ID` identifies the form by name. There's also a JavaScript `onsubmit` attribute, which will contain different things depending on what kind of controls you have loaded on the page. It may call any number of functions embedded in the page or external scripts that perform form validation or other control-specific actions.

Next you'll find several hidden form fields used to store data that we'll send back to the server on postback, as shown in Listing 7.3. You already know about the `__VIEWSTATE` field. The other two are used to pass along two pieces of data: `__EVENTTARGET` and `__EVENTARGUMENT`. You'll notice that these values are empty, but they won't be for long.

Listing 7.3 The hidden form fields

```
<input type="hidden" name="__EVENTTARGET" value="" />
<input type="hidden" name="__EVENTARGUMENT" value="" />
<input type="hidden" name="__VIEWSTATE"
value="/wEPDwUKMTE2MjI0Mzc0MQ9kFgICAw9kFgICAw8UKwANDxYIHghEYXRhS2V5cxYAH
gtfIUl0ZW1Db3VudAL/////Dx4JUGFnZUNvdW50AgEeFV8hRGF0YVNvdXJjZUl0ZW1Db3Vud
AL/////D2RkZGRkZGRkZGRkZGRkGAEFH19fQ29udHJvbHNNSZXF1aXJlUG9zdEJhY2tLZXlfX
xYCBRFMb2dpbjEkUmVtZW1iZXJNZQUSTG9naW4xJEltYWdlQnV0dG9uKI3dzTLbZM2g4Pn/Z
FiCcm7ffag=" />
```

The three hidden fields act as messengers to the server to help it understand what to do. With our Windows application analogy, it's just a matter of checking memory to see what action took place and how to deal with it. With our ASP.NET application, we can determine this with three pieces of information. The first is the state of the controls when we first sent the page to the browser. We already covered the fact that __VIEWSTATE contains this information. The second bit of information we need is the event target of the postback, which is generally the name of the control that caused it. The last piece of data is the argument of the event, which might indicate some other information to aid in the processing of the postback.

Naturally we'll need some way to get values into the __EVENTTARGET and __EVENTARGUMENT fields before sending the form data back to the server. This is accomplished through a short JavaScript function rendered automatically in the page, as shown in Listing 7.4.

Listing 7.4 The doPostBack client-side script

```
<script type="text/javascript">
<!--
var theForm = document.forms['form1'];
function __doPostBack(eventTarget, eventArgument) {
  if (theForm.onsubmit == null || theForm.onsubmit()) {
    theForm.__EVENTTARGET.value = eventTarget;
    theForm.__EVENTARGUMENT.value = eventArgument;
    theForm.submit();
  }
}
// -->
</script>
```

The script is fairly straightforward; it takes two parameters and assigns their values to the hidden __EVENTTARGET and __EVENTARGUMENT fields and then submits the form. The server now has all the information it needs to determine what happened on the client and what corresponding action to take. You don't have to worry about what exactly is going on in the round trip; you only must ensure that you have appropriate event handlers to respond to the changes in the form's state.

Different server controls do different things, and as such, you'll find a variety of different data items that need to be passed back to the server. Some controls render additional client-side script to handle validation or other functions before posting back. To keep it simple, let's take a LinkButton as an example. Listing 7.5 shows how you would write the control in the page, as well as how it would render in the browser.

Listing 7.5 A `LinkButton` in your page and in the rendered output

The `LinkButton` in the .aspx page
```
<asp:LinkButton ID="LinkButton1" Runat="server"
OnClick="SomeHandler">LinkButton</asp:LinkButton>
```

The `LinkButton` in the rendered HTML sent to the browser
```
<a id="LinkButton1"
href="javascript:__doPostBack('LinkButton1','')">LinkButton</a>
```

In your page, you've declared the `LinkButton` with a name and specified the `OnClick` attribute to fire a method in your code called `SomeHandler`. When the user clicks on this button, you can see that the `href` attribute calls the automatically generated `__doPostBack` JavaScript function (from Listing 7.4), passing the button's name (`LinkButton1`) and a blank value to the function. The function copies the name of the button to the hidden `__EVENTTARGET` field and a blank string to the hidden `__EVENTARGUMENT` field. As the final step, the function submits the form to the server.

When the server gets the request from the browser, it sees that the `__EVENTTARGET` field has a value of `LinkButton1`. That can only mean that the `__doPostBack` Javascript function was called by `LinkButton1`, and the server should.check to see what that control is supposed to do. It sees that the button was clicked (because that's all you can really do to a `LinkButton`) and that our code says we should run the `SomeHandler` method in response. The event handler is fired, as well as the other page events, and the updated page is sent back to the browser. That's the end of the postback cycle.

Server Controls, Their Events and Event Handlers

Before we get into the many events that the application and your pages will encounter, it's helpful to look at events on a smaller scale. Server controls such as our `LinkButton` (or Web controls, as they are sometimes called) can have events that let us determine that something happened on a form, and we can write code to handle these events.

Server controls have, at the very least, five events: `Init`, `Load`, `PreRender`, `Unload`, and `Disposed`. (Some controls also have a

`DataBinding` event.) These events indicate pretty obvious occurrences in the control's lifecycle, and they're all a part of the `System.Web.UI.Control` class, the base class for many controls you use all of the time. Some controls also have their own events to respond to changes in the control's state. The `Calendar` control, for example, has a `SelectionChanged` event that happens when the user chooses a new date.

When events occur, we may want some kind of code to fire. These blocks of code are event handlers. It's important to understand that events and event handlers are not the same thing. For example, the `Page` class (which also ultimately inherits from `Control`) has a `Load` event and an event handler called `OnLoad`. Event handlers typically are named by prefacing the event name with "On." Event handlers are "wired" or assigned to an event when the control is created. We'll get to event wiring shortly. Additionally, a number of methods are fired throughout the life of a control that can be overridden by your own derived controls.

These events and event handlers are called on every request for the page, for every control (unless of course the entire page is cached). We'll spend a chapter on this process, but for now, just be aware that these events and event handlers are there.

> You're probably wondering at this point how you can write your own events for your own controls. Fear not, we'll get to that in Chapter 9, "Server Controls." For now, let's just stick to handling events.

The Application and Page Events

You may recall that an "application" in ASP.NET is essentially all of the physical parts that sit in an IIS application, either from the site root or a subfolder marked as an application in its IIS property sheet. This application, running as an instance of `HttpApplication`, has a number of events that occur throughout the life of a request. These are intermingled with events that happen in the life of the `Page` object, created every time a request for a page is made. A number of methods also fire in the life of a `Page`. Some of the more relevant events and methods in the life of a page request are shown in Table 7.1.

Table 7.1 A Partial List of Control, Page, and Application Events and Methods

HttpApplication	Page	Control
BeginRequest		
AuthenticateRequest		
AuthorizeRequest		
ResolveRequestCache		
	Page Constructor fires	
AcquireRequestState		
PreRquestHandlerExecute		
	CreateControlCollection method	
		Init
		TrackViewState method
	Init	
	TrackViewState method	
		LoadViewState method
	Load	
		DataBind
		Load
	Postback event handler methods	
	PreRender	
	SaveViewState method	
		SaveViewState method
	Render method	
		RenderControl method
		Unload
		Dispose
	Unload	
	Dispose	
ReleaseRequestSate		
UpdateRequestCache		
EndRequest		

You can see from this table that a lot is going on from the time a request comes in to the server to the time a response is sent back to the browser. This doesn't even count many of the less frequently used events, especially at the application level.

Some events are more useful than others. You already know all about the Page's Load event because ASP.NET looks for a method in your code called `Page_Load()`. This event is wired up for you to facilitate your basic interaction with the event sequence.

Postback Events

Postback events are your chance to make something happen when a user interacts with the form. A postback occurs when a button is clicked or in cases where some other control's state is changed and forced to postback automatically (a `DropDownList`'s `AutoPostBack` property, for example, might be set to `true`, forcing a postback when the user changes the selection in the control).

Event handler methods all follow the same signature. They have no return value (`void` in C#) and require two parameters. The first is an `object` parameter, generally called `sender`, to provide a reference back to the control that raised the event. The second parameter is of type `EventArgs`, which is a collection of arguments. Not all controls return arguments, but the method still must include them.

> The reason for this method signature is that event handlers are actually calling a *delegate* called `System.EventHandler`. We skipped over delegates and events in Chapter 2, "Classes: The Code Behind the Objects," because a lot of people have a really hard time understanding them at first, and we were already throwing a lot of information at you in that chapter. Delegates frequently get lengthy chapters in C# and VB.NET books. Let's just keep it simple for now and say that delegates define a method signature so that some piece of code (the ASP.NET plumbing) can call a method with a known return value and parameters (your event handler).

If you take another look at Table 7.1, you'll notice that there's a place in the Page column for postback event handlers to fire. Notice its position compared to the page's `Load` and `PreRender` events. This might give you a hint on how best to handle the display of data on your form. For example, it wouldn't make sense to bind data to a `DataGrid` if that data was somehow changed by your postback event handler. The data returned to the user would end up being stale! Instead, you could bind this data in the `Page_PreRender` event, ensuring that queries to your database receive the current data.

Wiring Events

If a method is set to execute when an event occurs, it's said to be "wired." Event wire-up can be accomplished declaratively in most cases when it comes to control events or programmatically in any case.

Listing 7.5 showed an example of wiring up an event declaratively by assigning a method name to the `OnClick` attribute. This is the easiest and most straightforward way to wire up events.

You can also do this programmatically, and in fact you must wire up events programmatically at the application level. We'll demonstrate the application-level events when we talk about `HttpModules` in Chapter 8, "HttpHandlers and HttpModules."

To programmatically wire up events in a page, you must override the `Page` class's `OnInit` method. To best demonstrate this, we'll show the code generated by versions of Visual Studio prior to the 2005 version. The `Page` directive in the .aspx file includes the attribute `AutoEventWireup="false"` so that no events, not even `Page_Load`, are fired automatically. Listing 7.6 shows the code generated in the code-behind file, assuming that there's a button on the form called `SendMessageButton`.

Listing 7.6 Programmatically wiring up events in a page

```
private void Page_Load(object sender, System.EventArgs e)
{
   // Put user code to initialize the page here
}

#region Web Form Designer generated code
override protected void OnInit(EventArgs e)
{
   //
   // CODEGEN: This call is required by the ASP.NET Web Form Designer.
   //
```

```
  InitializeComponent();
  base.OnInit(e);
}

/// <summary>
/// Required method for Designer support - do not modify
/// the contents of this method with the code editor.
/// </summary>
private void InitializeComponent()
{
  this.Load += new System.EventHandler(this.Page_Load);
  this.SendMessageButton.Click += new
System.EventHandler(this.SendMessageButton_Click);
}
#endregion

private void SendMessageButton_Click(object sender, System.EventArgs e)
{
...
}
```

The first thing to notice is the method called OnInit. Because we're overriding the method from the Page base class, this method will execute in the normal execution of the page. The method calls the generated InitializeComponent() method, where the actual event wiring takes place. The this keyword refers to the instance of the class itself, and because the page is derived from the Page class, there is a Load event. We add a new event handler, Page_Load, to the Load event. Remember that because the Page directive in the .aspx file has AutoEventWireup= "false" in it, no event automatically fires. Finally, the next line wires up our SendMessageButton_Click method to the button's Click event.

> If this seems like a lot of work, it is. However, it's inspired by the way a Windows application works and therefore is probably familiar to someone who develops Windows apps. The InitializeComponent() method generates all kinds of code to establish, set properties (like control size and position) of, and wire up controls on a Windows form.

We'll show you how to wire up events to the application in the next chapter.

Summary

Incoming requests to ASP.NET trigger a series of events that begins and ends with the application. The page postback system simulates statefulness in a Web form through a combination of hidden form fields and JavaScript on the browser, while the code executing on the server works in a similar manner to a desktop application.

Events are wired up to event handlers, which are the actual methods that execute when an event occurs. In the context of a page, event handlers may be wired up declaratively in the page or programmatically.

If you want to get deeper into the specifics of server controls and events in ASP.NET, I highly recommend *Developing Microsoft ASP.NET Server Controls and Components* by Nikhil Kothari and Vandana Datye (Microsoft Press, 2002).

You might also want to consider Chris Sells' *Windows Forms Programming* (Addison-Wesley, 2003), which is available in both C# and VB.NET versions. Although it's not an ASP.NET book, it does teach events and delegates in one of the most easily digestible methods I've seen. You also might be surprised at how much you can learn by developing a Windows application and applying that knowledge to ASP.NET.

CHAPTER 8

HttpHandlers
and HttpModules

Web developers frequently think in terms of pages, but ASP.NET offers a framework that enables you to do virtually anything with an incoming HTTP request. Two special kinds of classes can extend the functionality of ASP.NET to do things other than serve pages.

HttpHandlers are special classes that do something with a request for a specific file type. You could in fact replace the entire page processing system by writing your own handler to process requests for .aspx pages.

HttpModules go to an even higher level by introducing code execution into the events of an `HttpApplication` object. Several built-in classes of the .NET Framework implement this to handle security details, as we'll do in our example.

The Built-in Handlers

You've been dealing with HttpHandlers all along, even if you didn't realize it. In Chapter 6, "The Nuts and Bolts of IIS and Web Applications," we explained that a number of different file extensions are mapped in the IIS control panel to be handled by ASP.NET. What the control panel doesn't show is how ASP.NET deals with the requests that land in its lap. To understand that, we'll have to take a look at the `machine.config` file, normally located in the `C:\WINDOWS\Microsoft.NET\Framework\v2.0.xxxx\CONFIG` folder.

> You're probably already familiar with the `web.config` file found in your applications, which sets up the configuration for the application. The `machine.config` file can store much of the same configuration data, except that it applies to the entire machine.

Listing 8.1 The `httpHandlers` section of `machine.config`

```
<httpHandlers>
    <clear />
    <add verb="*" path="trace.axd" type="System.Web.Handlers.TraceHandler" />
    <add verb="GET" path="WebAdmin.axd"
type="System.Web.Handlers.WebAdminHandler" />
    <add verb="GET" path="WebResource.axd"
type="System.Web.Handlers.AssemblyResourceLoader" />
    <add verb="GET" path="CachedImageService.axd"
type="System.Web.UI.Imaging.CachedImageServiceHandler" />
    <add verb="GET" path="counters.axd"
type="System.Web.Handlers.SiteCountersHandler" />
    <add verb="GET" path="precompile.axd"
type="System.Web.Handlers.PrecompHandler" />
    <add verb="GET" path="WebPartExport.axd"
type="System.Web.Handlers.WebPartExportHandler" />
    <add verb="*" path="*.aspx" type="System.Web.UI.PageHandlerFactory" />
    <add verb="*" path="*.ashx" type="System.Web.UI.SimpleHandlerFactory" />
    <add verb="*" path="*.asix" type="System.Web.UI.ImageGeneratorFactory" />
    <add verb="*" path="*.asmx"
type="System.Web.Services.Protocols.WebServiceHandlerFactory,
System.Web.Services, Version=2.0.3600.0, Culture=neutral,
PublicKeyToken=b03f5f7f11d50a3a" validate="false" />
    <add verb="*" path="*.rem"
type="System.Runtime.Remoting.Channels.Http.HttpRemotingHandlerFactory,
System.Runtime.Remoting, Version=2.0.3600.0, Culture=neutral,
PublicKeyToken=b77a5c561934e089" validate="false" />
    <add verb="*" path="*.soap"
type="System.Runtime.Remoting.Channels.Http.HttpRemotingHandlerFactory,
System.Runtime.Remoting, Version=2.0.3600.0, Culture=neutral,
PublicKeyToken=b77a5c561934e089" validate="false" />
    <add verb="*" path="*.asax" type="System.Web.HttpForbiddenHandler" />
    <add verb="*" path="*.ascx" type="System.Web.HttpForbiddenHandler" />
    <add verb="*" path="*.master" type="System.Web.HttpForbiddenHandler" />
    <add verb="*" path="*.skin" type="System.Web.HttpForbiddenHandler" />
    <add verb="*" path="*.browser" type="System.Web.HttpForbiddenHandler" />
    <add verb="*" path="*.sitemap" type="System.Web.HttpForbiddenHandler" />
    <add verb="GET,HEAD" path="*.dll.config"
type="System.Web.StaticFileHandler" />
    <add verb="GET,HEAD" path="*.exe.config"
type="System.Web.StaticFileHandler" />
```

```
<add verb="*" path="*.config" type="System.Web.HttpForbiddenHandler" />
<add verb="*" path="*.cs" type="System.Web.HttpForbiddenHandler" />
<add verb="*" path="*.csproj" type="System.Web.HttpForbiddenHandler" />
<add verb="*" path="*.vb" type="System.Web.HttpForbiddenHandler" />
<add verb="*" path="*.vbproj" type="System.Web.HttpForbiddenHandler" />
<add verb="*" path="*.webinfo" type="System.Web.HttpForbiddenHandler" />
<add verb="*" path="*.licx" type="System.Web.HttpForbiddenHandler" />
<add verb="*" path="*.resx" type="System.Web.HttpForbiddenHandler" />
<add verb="*" path="*.resources" type="System.Web.HttpForbiddenHandler" />
<add verb="*" path="*.mdb" type="System.Web.HttpForbiddenHandler" />
<add verb="*" path="*.vjsproj" type="System.Web.HttpForbiddenHandler" />
<add verb="*" path="*.java" type="System.Web.HttpForbiddenHandler" />
<add verb="*" path="*.jsl" type="System.Web.HttpForbiddenHandler" />
<add verb="*" path="*.ldb" type="System.Web.HttpForbiddenHandler" />
<add verb="*" path="*.mdw" type="System.Web.HttpForbiddenHandler" />
<add verb="GET,HEAD,POST" path="*" type="System.Web.DefaultHttpHandler" />
<add verb="*" path="*" type="System.Web.HttpMethodNotAllowedHandler" />
</httpHandlers>
```

Listing 8.1 shows the `httpHandlers` section of `machine.config`, and many of the file extensions there should seem familiar to you. This section of the configuration file maps file extensions to a particular handler for processing. Our good friend the .aspx extension is handled by a class called `System.Web.UI.PageHandlerFactory`. Files that the average Internet user should not be allowed to touch, such as `.cs` and `.vb` files, are handled by `System.Web.HttpForbiddenHandler`, which generates an error message for the user. We certainly wouldn't want users seeing our code!

Handling File Types of Your Own

To write an HttpHandler, you create a class that implements the `IHttpHandler` interface. All of the handlers in Listing 8.1 do this. You might recall from Chapter 2, "Classes: The Code Behind the Objects," that an interface is used to ensure that a well-known means of communicating with some other code is available. For ASP.NET to communicate with an HttpHandler, it must have a couple members defined by the interface. Listing 8.2 shows the basic interface.

Listing 8.2 A class implementing `IHttpHandler`

C#

```csharp
public class MyHttpHandler : IHttpHandler
{
  public void ProcessRequest(HttpContext context)
  {
    // do something here
  }

  public bool IsReusable
  {
    get { return true; }
  }
}
```

VB.NET

```vbnet
Public Class MyHttpHandler
  Implements IHttpHandler

  Public Sub ProcessRequest(context As HttpContext)
    ' do something here
  End Sub

  Public ReadOnly Property IsReusable() As Boolean
    Get
      Return True
    End Get
  End Property
End Class
```

The `ProcessRequest()` method is where we do work in response to the request. ASP.NET passes in a reference to the `HttpContext` object associated with the request. You'll notice in Visual Studio that as soon as you type a period following the `context` parameter, Intellisense will show you properties that correspond to all the familiar objects you might use in a page (see Figure 8.1).

You can get information about the request via the `Request` property, and you can send almost any kind of data you want back down the pipe with the `Response` property. This is very powerful because you can essentially do anything. If you wanted to divert .aspx file requests to a handler of your own (and had way too much time on your hands), you could implement the entire ASP.NET page factory yourself!

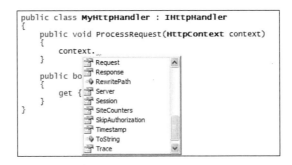

Figure 8.1 The properties of the `HttpContext` object in an HttpHandler.

The `IsReusable` property is the other member you'll have to implement in your HttpHandler. It's there to tell ASP.NET whether the instance of the handler can be reused from one request to the next, or if it should create a new instance each time. Generally it's best for this property to return true, especially if the HttpHandler will service many requests. However, if some user-specific action is occurring in the handler that you don't want the next user to use, you should cause the property to return false.

In order for ASP.NET to process any request at all, it must receive the request via IIS. This was covered in Chapter 6. After ASP.NET gets the request, it must designate which HttpHandler will process the request. Listing 8.1 showed the defaults listed in the `machine.config` file. Listing 8.3 shows the relevant parts of a `web.config` file to add the HttpHandler to your application.

Listing 8.3 Adding an HttpHandler to your `web.config`

```
<?xml version="1.0" encoding="utf-8" ?>
<configuration>
  <system.web>
    <httpHandlers>
      <add verb="*" path="*.jpg" type="MyClass, MyDll" />
    </httpHandlers>
  </system.web>
</configuration>
```

The element that does the actual work is the `<add />` element. The verb attribute indicates the types of requests that are covered (GET or POST), and you can use an asterisk as a wildcard. The path attribute describes the file path of the request. In this example we're using a wild-card with ".jpg" to indicate that we want to handle all requests for .jpg files, but you could just as easily specify anything else, such as "mypage.aspx." The `<add />` elements are considered in the order that they appear, so a request that fits the path of two elements will be serviced by the class in the last entry. Finally, the `type` attribute indicates the name of the class implementing `IHttpHandler` and the assembly name in which it resides, looking in the `/bin` folder. Keep in mind that the class name should be fully qualified, meaning that the namespace should be included.

Example: Protecting Your Images from Bandwidth Leeching

Let's apply the use of an HttpHandler to a real-world example. Imagine that you're analyzing your server logs, and you find that you have an enormous number of referrals from some site that you don't recognize. You check out the URL of the referrer and discover that some jerk is deep-linking to one of your prize photos of the Grand Canyon. The high-resolution photo is costing you 150kb toward your bandwidth limit on every request. It also demonstrates a high disregard for copyright.

To combat the problem, we'll develop an HttpHandler that checks to see if incoming requests for .jpg files came from your own site, not someone else's. If the referrer is either blank (the URL of the image was entered into a new browser window directly) or from someone else's site (your leeching friend), we'll serve an alternate image indicating that the user should visit your site directly for the photograph.

Listing 8.4 shows the finished class, as well as the `web.config` settings to make it work.

Listing 8.4 Anti-image leeching HttpHandler

C#
```
using System;
using System.Web;

public class JpgHandler : IHttpHandler
{
  public void ProcessRequest(HttpContext context)
```

```csharp
{
    string FileName = context.Server.MapPath(context.Request.FilePath);
    if (context.Request.UrlReferrer.Host == null)
    {
        context.Response.ContentType = "image/JPEG";
        context.Response.WriteFile("/no.jpg");
    }
    else
    {
        if (context.Request.UrlReferrer.Host.IndexOf("mydomain.com") > 0)
        {
            context.Response.ContentType = "image/JPEG";
            context.Response.WriteFile(FileName);
        }
        else
        {
            context.Response.ContentType = "image/JPEG";
            context.Response.WriteFile("/no.jpg");
        }
    }
}

public bool IsReusable
{
    get
    { return true; }
}
}
```

VB.NET

```vbnet
Imports System
Imports System.Web

Public Class JpgHandler
    Implements IHttpHandler

    Public Sub ProcessRequest(context As HttpContext)
        Dim FileName As String = _
context.Server.MapPath(context.Request.FilePath)
        If context.Request.UrlReferrer.Host Is Nothing Then
            context.Response.ContentType = "image/JPEG"
            context.Response.WriteFile("/no.jpg")
```

(Continues)

Listing 8.4 Anti-image leeching HttpHandler   *(Continued)*

```
      Else
        If context.Request.UrlReferrer.Host.IndexOf("mydomain.com")_
> 0 Then
          context.Response.ContentType = "image/JPEG"
          context.Response.WriteFile(FileName)
        Else
          context.Response.ContentType = "image/JPEG"
          context.Response.WriteFile("/no.jpg")
        End If
      End If
  End Sub


  Public ReadOnly Property IsReusable() As Boolean
    Get
      Return True
    End Get
  End Property
End Class
```

web.config

```xml
<?xml version="1.0" encoding="utf-8" ?>
<configuration>
  <system.web>
    <httpHandlers>
      <add verb="*" path="*.jpg" type="JpgHandler, MyDll" />
    </httpHandlers>
  </system.web>
</configuration>
```

The first step in our `ProcessRequest()` method is to identify the file name of the requested image. After we know that, we determine whether the `UrlReferrer` property of the `Response` object is null. If it is, that means the request isn't referred by a page on our site, so we set the content type of the response and use the `Response` object's `WriteFile()` method to send an image called "/no.jpg."

If there is a referrer, the next step is to determine whether it contains our domain name. If it does, the referral comes from our own site, and it's acceptable for the image to be served. If the referrer doesn't have our domain name, the request came from another site, so we should serve the alternative image.

Regardless, we set the `IsReusable` property to true because there's no reason why the class instance can't be reused for every request.

This class must be compiled to an assembly, and that assembly should be placed in the `/bin` folder of the application. You can compile with the command line compilers or in Visual Studio by building the project.

HttpHandlers can also be written in an .ashx file without being compiled, as shown in Listing 8.5, where we construct an image generator used to create a visual security code that helps prevent automated sign-ups in your Web application. The text generated by the images is stored in `Session` to be used for comparison to the user's input. Figure 8.2 shows the image generated when the page a user is viewing requests the handler.

Listing 8.5 Image generation HttpHandler image.ashx

C#

```
<%@ WebHandler Language="C#" Class="RegisterImageHandler" %>

using System;
using System.Drawing;
using System.Drawing.Imaging;
using System.Text;
using System.Web;
using System.Web.SessionState;

public class RegisterImageHandler : IHttpHandler, IRequiresSessionState
{
   public void ProcessRequest (HttpContext context) {
     context.Response.ContentType = "image/gif";
     Bitmap b = new Bitmap(200, 60);
     Graphics g = Graphics.FromImage(b);
     g.FillRectangle(new SolidBrush(Color.White), 0, 0, 200, 60);
     Font font = new Font(FontFamily.GenericSerif, 48, FontStyle.Bold,
GraphicsUnit.Pixel);
     Random r = new Random();
     string letters = "ABCDEFGHIJKLMNPQRSTUVWXYZ";
     string letter;
     StringBuilder s = new StringBuilder();
     for (int x = 0; x < 5; x++)
     {
        letter = letters.Substring(r.Next(0, letters.Length - 1), 1);
        s.Append(letter);
```

(Continues)

Listing 8.5 Image generation HttpHandler image.ashx   *(Continued)*

```
        g.DrawString(letter, font, new SolidBrush(Color.Black), x * 38,
r.Next(0, 15));
    }
    Pen linePen = new Pen(new SolidBrush(Color.Black), 2);
    for (int x = 0; x < 6; x++)
        g.DrawLine(linePen, new Point(r.Next(0, 199), r.Next(0, 59)), new
Point(r.Next(0, 199), r.Next(0, 59)));
    b.Save(context.Response.OutputStream, ImageFormat.Gif);
    context.Session["pfregisterimage"] = s.ToString();
    context.Response.End();
  }

  public bool IsReusable {
    get { return true; }
  }
}
```

VB.NET

```
<%@ WebHandler Language="VB.NET" Class="RegisterImageHandler" %>

Imports System
Imports System.Drawing
Imports System.Drawing.Imaging
Imports System.Text
Imports System.Web
Imports System.Web.SessionState

Public Class RegisterImageHandler
    Implements IHttpHandler
    Implements IRequiresSessionState

    Public Sub ProcessRequest(context As HttpContext)
        context.Response.ContentType = "image/gif"
        Dim b As New Bitmap(200, 60)
        Dim g As Graphics = Graphics.FromImage(b)
        g.FillRectangle(New SolidBrush(Color.White), 0, 0, 200, 60)
        Dim font As New Font(FontFamily.GenericSerif, 48, FontStyle.Bold,
GraphicsUnit.Pixel)
        Dim r As New Random()
        Dim letters As String = "ABCDEFGHIJKLMNPQRSTUVWXYZ"
        Dim letter As String
```

```
      Dim s As New StringBuilder()
      Dim x As Integer
      For x = 0 To 4
          letter = letters.Substring(r.Next(0, letters.Length - 1), 1)
          s.Append(letter)
          g.DrawString(letter, font, New SolidBrush(Color.Black), x *
38, r.Next(0, 15))
      Next x
      Dim linePen As New Pen(New SolidBrush(Color.Black), 2)
      Dim x As Integer
      For x = 0 To 5
          g.DrawLine(linePen, New Point(r.Next(0, 199), r.Next(0, 59)),
New Point(r.Next(0, 199), r.Next(0, 59)))
      Next x
      b.Save(context.Response.OutputStream, ImageFormat.Gif)
      context.Session("pfregisterimage") = s.ToString()
      context.Response.End()
   End Sub

   Public ReadOnly Property IsReusable() As Boolean
      Get
          Return True
      End Get
   End Property
End Class
```

HTML in a page calling the handler

```
<img src="image.ashx" alt="Security Code" />
```

Figure 8.2 Image generated by our image.ashx handler.

To place the image generated by this handler in a page, we use good old-fashioned HTML, as shown in the code listing. We start this simple text file with a @WebHandler directive, similar to the way we declare a @Page or @Control directive. We tell ASP.NET the language that we'll use and the name of our class, which must match the name we're about to give it. As with our previous handler, most of the action happens in the

`ProcessRequest()` method. First, the code randomly generates a five-letter string. Then it uses various classes from the `Drawing` namespace to generate a bitmap based on those letters, randomly staggering the characters and drawing some lines over it to make it less machine readable.

The slightly more tricky part is that we save the final image in GIF form to the `Response` object's `OutputStream`. We'll cover streams in more detail in Chapter 17, "More Advanced Topics." After we've sent the image to the requesting user, we save the string of random letters to the `Session` object.

If we were to use this in an application, we might put a text box right below the graphic generated by the handler for the user to type in the letters. On postback of the form, we would compare the user's input with the value saved in `Session` to confirm that the user is indeed human and not some machine signing up on our site to spam our forums, for example.

HttpHandlers are a sort of endpoint for a request. Sometimes you may want to execute code from other points in an application's lifecycle. For these instances, you may use HttpModules.

HttpModules: The Replacement for ISAPI

In Chapter 6, we mentioned how IIS can pass requests to an ISAPI program, which can then interpret the request according to how it was programmed. ASP.NET itself runs as an ISAPI program. The old version of Active Server Pages ran this way as well. Although this is certainly a powerful interface, it's not easy to implement.

To make this request processing easy, ASP.NET offers HttpModules as a way to hook into the request and response. Although HttpHandlers handle a request for a particular file extension or path specific to the request and get a reference to the `HttpContext` object, an HttpModule gets involved at the application level, first to touch the request on the way into the server, and then to touch it on the response's return to the browser. An HttpModule gets a reference to the `HttpApplication` object and is capable of assigning event handlers to the application events.

ASP.NET already has several HttpModules that may be in play by default in your application. For example, if you're using Forms Authentication, a class called `System.Web.Security.FormsAuthenticationModule` sets up the authentication information for the request. A class called `System.Web.Caching.OutputCacheModule` processes requests for cached pages and user controls. Listing 8.6 shows the `httpModules` section of `machine.config`. An HttpModule must be listed in `web.config` or `machine.config` to be used.

Listing 8.6 The `httpModules` section of `machine.config`

```
<httpModules>
  <clear />
  <add name="OutputCache" type="System.Web.Caching.OutputCacheModule" />
  <add name="Session" type="System.Web.SessionState.SessionStateModule" />
  <add name="SessionID" type="System.Web.SessionState.SessionIDModule" />
  <add name="WindowsAuthentication"
type="System.Web.Security.WindowsAuthenticationModule" />
  <add name="FormsAuthentication"
type="System.Web.Security.FormsAuthenticationModule" />
  <add name="PassportAuthentication"
type="System.Web.Security.PassportAuthenticationModule" />
  <add name="RoleManager" type="System.Web.Security.RoleManagerModule" />
  <add name="UrlAuthorization"
type="System.Web.Security.UrlAuthorizationModule" />
  <add name="FileAuthorization"
type="System.Web.Security.FileAuthorizationModule" />
  <add name="AnonymousIdentification"
type="System.Web.Security.AnonymousIdentificationModule" />
  <add name="Profile" type="System.Web.Profile.ProfileModule" />
  <add name="PageCountersModule" type="System.Web.PageCountersModule" />
  <add name="SqlBatchModule" type="System.Web.DataAccess.SqlBatchModule" />
</httpModules>
```

You can further distinguish the difference between HttpHandlers and HttpModules just by looking at the name of these components and thinking about the scope of their activity. For example, we saw earlier that the HttpHandler `PageHandlerFactory` handled requests specifically for ASP.NET pages, but it had nothing to do with the execution of application-level code. Here we have an HttpModule called `SessionIDModule`. Based on its name, you can infer that this module keeps track of session activity and that this process is not limited to a page request—it also calls for Web services or any other ASP.NET resource, even the .jpg requests in our previous HttpHandler.

The `IHttpModule` interface is similarly easy to implement, having only two members, as shown in Listing 8.7.

Listing 8.7 A class implementing `IHttpModule`

C#
```csharp
public class MyHttpModule : IHttpModule
{
  public void Init(HttpApplication application)
  {
    // do something here
  }

  public void Dispose()
  {
  }
}
```

VB.NET
```vbnet
Public Class MyHttpModule
  Implements IHttpModule

  Public Sub Init(application As HttpApplication)
    ' do something here
  End Sub

  Public Sub Dispose()
  End Sub
End Class
```

The `Init()` method of the interface provides our hook to the application. Through this reference to the application, we can wire up event handlers to application events, similarly to the manner in which we wired up control and page events in Listing 7.6. We'll wire up some new event handlers in our next code listing.

If there is some kind of clean up work to do when the application terminates, we can do it in the `Dispose()` method. You might delete temporary files or database records in this method, for example.

Example: Adding Users to Roles

Microsoft offers a couple of knowledge base articles on its Web site explaining how to add role-based security to your ASP.NET application. The Microsoft examples show how to add code to the `global.asax` file to make this happen. In retrospect, this technique surprises me, because I think that global.asax was ported from the old ASP days to make it familiar. It's advantageous to do the same thing in an HttpModule because you can add any number of event handlers to application events through any number of HttpModules.

The point of our custom HttpModule is to enable the pages in our application to simply call `User.IsInRole("somerole")` to determine if a user is in a role. Our custom HttpModule also enables us to use a `LoginView` control in our pages to display content templates based on the roles of the user. You could of course specify users' roles in `web.config`, but isn't it a lot easier to get that data from a database?

Listing 8.8 gets a logged in user's roles and assigns them to the user's `Principal` object. We've left the actual data access out of the example to keep it simple, so imagine that we have a class called `DataFetcherClass` with a static method called `GetRoles()` that takes the user's `Name` as a parameter and returns an `ArrayList` of role names.

> A `Principal` object is a container that is used to identify the user; it stores the user name and roles that the user belongs to. FormsAuthentication and Membership (in v2.0 of ASP.NET) do a lot of this work for you under normal circumstances, but the module we're using here provides more direct control.

Listing 8.8 An HttpModule to determine user roles

C#

```csharp
using System;
using System.Collections;
using System.ComponentModel;
using System.Web;
using System.Web.SessionState;
using System.Web.Security;
using System.Configuration;
using System.Security.Principal;

public class UserHttpModule : IHttpModule
{
```

(Continues)

Listing 8.8 An HttpModule to determine user roles *(Continued)*

```csharp
public void Init(HttpApplication application)
{
   application.AuthenticateRequest += new
EventHandler(Application_AuthenticateRequest);
}

public void Dispose()
{
}

private void Application_AuthenticateRequest(object sender, EventArgs e)
{
   HttpApplication application = (HttpApplication)sender;
   HttpContext context = application.Context;
   if (context.Request.IsAuthenticated)
   {
     // check for a cached lookup first
     if (context.Cache["uid" + context.User.Identity.Name] == null)
     {
       // create a new identity, based on the login name
       GenericIdentity identity = new
GenericIdentity(context.User.Identity.Name);
       // get the roles from the database
       ArrayList listRoles =
DataFetcherClass.GetRoles(context.User.Identity.Name);
       string[] roles = new string[listRoles.Count];
       for (int i=0; i<listRoles.Count; i++) roles[i] =
listRoles[i].ToString();
       // put the identity and roles in a new principal
       GenericPrincipal principal = new
GenericPrincipal(identity,roles);
       // cache it
       context.Cache.Insert("uid" + context.User.Identity.Name,
principal, null, DateTime.Now.AddSeconds(60), new TimeSpan(0));
       // assign the new principal to the user
       context.User = principal;
     }
     else
     {
       // get the user's new Principal object from cache
```

```
          context.User = (GenericPrincipal)context.Cache["uid" +
context.User.Identity.Name];
        }
      }
    }
}
```

VB.NET

```vbnet
Imports System
Imports System.Collections
Imports System.ComponentModel
Imports System.Web
Imports System.Web.SessionState
Imports System.Web.Security
Imports System.Configuration
Imports System.Security.Principal
Imports PopForums.Data

Public Class UserHttpModule
  Implements IHttpModule

  Public Sub Init(application As HttpApplication)
    AddHandler application.AuthenticateRequest, AddressOf _
Application_AuthenticateRequest
  End Sub

  Public Sub Dispose()
  End Sub

  Private Sub Application_AuthenticateRequest(sender As Object, _
e As EventArgs)
    Dim application As HttpApplication = CType(sender, _
HttpApplication)
    Dim context As HttpContext = application.Context
    If context.Request.IsAuthenticated Then
      ' check for a cached lookup first
      If context.Cache(("uid" + context.User.Identity.Name)) _
Is Nothing Then
        ' create a new identity, based on the login name
        Dim identity As New GenericIdentity(context.User.Identity.Name)
        ' get the roles from the database
        Dim listRoles As ArrayList = _
```

(Continues)

Listing 8.8 An HttpModule to determine user roles *(Continued)*

```
DataFetcherClass.GetRoles(context.User.Identity.Name)
        Dim roles(listRoles.Count) As String
        Dim i As Integer
        For i = 0 To listRoles.Count - 1
          roles(i) = listRoles(i).ToString()
        Next i
        ' put the identity and roles in a new principal
        Dim principal As New GenericPrincipal(identity, roles)
        ' cache it
        context.Cache.Insert("uid" + context.User.Identity.Name, _
principal, Nothing, DateTime.Now.AddSeconds(60), New TimeSpan(0))
        ' assign the new principal to the user
        context.User = principal
      Else
        ' get the user's new Principal object from cache
        context.User = CType(context.Cache(("uid" + _
context.User.Identity.Name)), GenericPrincipal)
      End If
    End If
  End Sub
End Class
```

web.config
```
<?xml version="1.0" encoding="utf-8" ?>
<configuration>
  <system.web>
    <httpModules>
      <add name="UserHttpModule" type="UserHttpModule, MyDll" />
    </httpModules>
  </system.web>
</configuration>
```

Our HttpModule is added to the processing stream just like an HttpHandler, via entries in web.config. The class must be compiled to an assembly and placed in the /bin folder.

The module's Init() method sets up the module for us by passing in a reference to the Application object. After we have that reference, we can wire up new event handlers to the application, just as we did in the programmatic wiring up of control and page events in Listing 7.6. In this case, we're going to add a new event handler that we're calling Application_AuthenticateRequest (we can call it anything) to the application's `AuthenticateRequest` event. Note that the event handler method has the signature you're used to seeing now, passing in object and `EventArgs` parameters. We could add any number of event handlers to application events here.

The `Dispose()` method doesn't do anything in our case, but because it's part of the `IHttpModule` interface, we must define it here.

Now we can fill out our actual event handler to do something. We start by defining an `HttpApplication` object. We need a reference to the application to interact with it, and this is where that well-defined method signature for event handlers comes in handy. The object we call `sender` is actually the application object running the show, but because event handlers have a generic object in the method signature, we need to cast `sender` into an `HttpApplication` object.

For our purposes, we need a reference to the current `HttpContext` of the request and response, including the user's `Principal` object and the `Cache` object. This is no problem now that we have a reference to the application. We'll create an `HttpContext` object that references the application object's `Context` property.

Now that we have the `HttpContext`, we have access to many of the objects we're used to having in pages. We first check the `Cache` to see if the user's `Principal` object is stored in memory, using a key that combines the string "uid" and the user's name. If it's not there, we'll get the roles from the database and build a new `Principal` from scratch. That part of the code is fairly well commented, so I'll let you decipher the rest on your own.

Why does this work? Recall Figure 7.1, which outlines some of the more critical events in the application, page, and control life cycles. You'll see that the application's `AuthenticateRequest` event happens fairly early in the sequence and that the forthcoming `Page` object isn't even a twinkle in the server's eye at that point. By the time all that code fires, we can use `User.IsInRole("somerole")` or a `LoginView` control to determine the user's role because it was established earlier.

Although this is a very practical example of an HttpModule in action, you technically wouldn't need it in ASP.NET v2.0. This version of the framework has a built-in role manager, which we'll explore in Chapter 11, "Membership and Security." However, if you're using v1.x of ASP.NET, this module solves a very common problem and is easy to implement.

For an additional HttpModule example, check out Listing 17.6 in Chapter 17. In a discussion about threading, you can see how easy it is to execute code on a regular interval without being tied to the request/response life cycle.

The application has other events you can wire into, some of which are not listed in Figure 7.1 to keep it simple. In fact, if you eliminated all HttpHandlers from executing in your application, you could create some kind of output right there in the HttpModule (rendering all of that HTML would be a lot of work, but you could do it if you had that kind of time).

Now that you have a grasp on HttpHandlers and HttpModules, let's look at the big picture. Figure 8.3 shows how these fit into the ASP.NET page lifecycle.

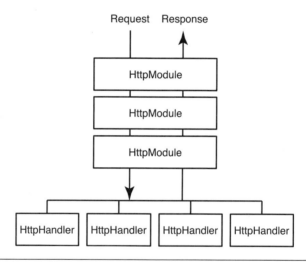

Figure 8.3 The role of HttpHandlers and HttpModules in the page lifecycle.

The diagram shows an incoming request to ASP.NET. The request first passes through HttpModules listed in `web.config` or `machine.config`. Recall the events listed in the HttpApplication column of Figure 7.1. If our module has added any event handlers to the application that correspond to events prior to the creation of the page (or other HttpHandler), they are fired here. Going back to our example in this chapter where we assign roles to the user, we added an event handler to the application's

`AuthenticateRequest` event. Other modules may add their own event handlers as well.

After the request has passed through all of the modules and fired off event handlers wired up in each of these modules, the request ends at an HttpHandler. As we learned earlier, .aspx pages by default are handled by `System.Web.UI.PageHandlerFactory`. In our example where we protect images from bandwidth leeching, our `JpgHandler` class gets requests for .jpg files. The important thing to realize here is that any number of modules can work on the request and response, but only one handler may actually process the request.

Continuing on, for the response to the user, an HTML page is sent back for .aspx pages, and an image is sent back for .jpg requests. The response must pass back through the modules at this point, where any events wired up that occur after the handler has generated the response are handled.

Summary

HttpHandlers and HttpModules provide two ways to process requests and responses by extending the typical page framework. An HttpHandler targets specific kinds of files or requests that conform to certain file paths in the URL, whereas an HttpModule is intended to be first in line to process a request and last to process a response.

HttpHandlers are classes that implement the `IHttpHandler` interface. They get a reference to the current `HttpContext` object in the `ProcessRequest()` method and can execute code against all of the `HttpContext`'s properties. Typically, the HttpHandler analyzes the data that comes in from the `Request` and then sends something back via the `Response` object. HttpHandlers also implement an `IsReusable` property, telling ASP.NET whether the same instance of the class can be used to process subsequent requests.

HttpModules enable code to interact with the application by adding event handlers to its events. These classes must implement the `IHttpModule` interface. The `Init()` method gives us a reference to the application, at which point we can wire up event handlers to the application's events. The event handlers can then interact with the application by implementing the standard event handler signature. The HttpModule also implements a `Dispose()` method, which is used to perform any necessary cleanup work if the application ends.

CHAPTER 9

Server Controls

Server controls are the heart of everything that makes developing a Web form easy. These classes give us a programmatic way to manipulate HTML and its interaction with users. Server controls more than anything differentiate ASP.NET from many other development platforms for the Web.

At its most basic level, a server control renders HTML to the page sent to a user. In more complex situations, a server control may render a ton of HTML and provide form elements that it can interpret on postback.

Although many server controls are built-in to ASP.NET for your use, you can also build your own. The implementation can be entirely your own, or it can be derived from existing controls.

Simple Derived Controls

You know what they say about reinventing the wheel—it's a waste of time! Because the .NET Framework is object-oriented, your time might better be spent using existing server controls instead of building your own.

Let's take a common task as the basis of making our own derived control. Your application has a drop-down list filled with familiar choices loaded from a database, and this list will appear all over your application. You could accomplish this by putting the control in every page where you need it and then writing some code to populate it on every page. Another way you could do it is to write a class with a static method that returns a data source. The best way, though, is to create your own server control, derived from an existing control.

Let's ignore for a moment all of the inner workings of a typical server control because you don't need to know anything about them to accomplish your assignment. If we look up `System.Web.UI.WebControls.DropDownList` in the .NET documentation, we can see a list of the control's members. It has a property called `Items`, which is of type

ListItemCollection. By following the links in the documentation, we can see that this type contains, cleverly enough, ListItem objects, which make up the selections in the final HTML that is sent to the browser.

That's enough to get started, so we can quickly whip up a shell of a class for now. We'll add to it as we go. Listing 9.1 shows our starting point. In it, we create a class that derives from DropDownList and has a constructor. Because this control will be a list of different content categories on our site, we'll call the class ContentCategoryDropDown. In this listing, we also show how the control will be declared in our page.

Listing 9.1 The start of our basic derived class and its declaration in a page

C#
```
namespace Testing
{
  public class ContentCategoryDropDown : DropDownList
  {
    public ContentCategoryDropDown()
    {
    }
  }
}
```

VB.NET
```
Namespace Testing
  Public Class ContentCategoryDropDown
    Inherits DropDownList

    Public Sub New()
    End Sub
  End Class
End Namespace
```

.aspx Page
```
<%@ Page Language="C#" %>
<%@ Register Namespace="Testing" TagPrefix="MyControl" %>
<html>
<body>
  <form id="form1" runat="server">
    <MyControl:TestControl runat="server" />
...
```

That's easy enough! In fact, the page in Listing 9.1 would generate a drop-down list just as if we used `<asp:DropDownList />` control.

> Note that the `Register` directive in the Listing 9.1 page sample assumes that our class is uncompiled in a `.cs` or `.vb` file in the `/App_Code` folder of our application. If that's not the case, and instead it's in an assembly, we must also specify its name, without the .dll on the end:
>
> ```
> <%@ Register Namespace="Testing" TagPrefix="MyControl"
> Assembly="MyDll" %>
> ```
>
> It's also important to note that your control, derived or original, must be contained in a namespace.

Now that we've proven that we can create a derived control, let's make it do something. We'll add code to the constructor of our class to add `ListItems` to the `Item` property of the underlying `DropDownList` class. Listing 9.2 shows our new constructor with data access code.

Listing 9.2 The constructor that populates the DropDownList with data

C#
```csharp
public ContentCategoryDropDown()
{
   this.Items.Add(new ListItem("Select a topic...","0"));
   SqlConnection connection = new SqlConnection("myconnectionstring");
   connection.Open();
   SqlCommand command = new SqlCommand("SELECT ContentCategoryID, Name
FROM ContentCategories ORDER BY Name", connection);
   SqlDataReader reader = command.ExecuteReader();
   while (reader.Read())
   {
     this.Items.Add(new ListItem(reader.GetString(1),
reader.GetInt32(0).ToString()));
   }
   reader.Close();
   connection.Close();
}
```

(Continues)

Listing 9.2 The constructor that populates the DropDownList with data   (*Continued*)

VB.NET
```
Public Sub New()
  Me.Items.Add(New ListItem("Select a topic...", "0"))
  Dim connection As New SqlConnection("myconnectionstring")
  connection.Open()
  Dim command As New SqlCommand("SELECT ContentCategoryID, Name " & _
"FROM ContentCategories ORDER BY Name", connection)
  Dim reader As SqlDataReader = command.ExecuteReader()
  While reader.Read()
    Me.Items.Add(New ListItem(reader.GetString(1), _
reader.GetInt32(0).ToString()))
  End While
  reader.Close()
  connection.Close()
End Sub
```

Just as we did in Chapter 5, "Object-Oriented Programming Applied: A Custom Data Class," we're getting values out of our reader by using one of the `DataReader`'s many `Get...` methods. This is a solid way to boost performance a little because it doesn't have to work as hard as it does when you specify a database column by name (i.e., `reader["ColumnName"]`). Most collections in .NET may be addressed by name or by index, as these reader methods do, and the index is faster because the framework doesn't need to compare the string you're specifying to each item in the collection.

In some of the code samples you've seen so far in this book, we've called other members of a class from various methods by name. You can do the same thing in a derived class, even though you can't "see" the existing members of the base class. For example, if you typed `Items` followed by a period in Visual Studio for this example, Intellisense would give you a list of all of the members available to you. In our example, all of the members of `DropDownList` are available. To make it somewhat easier to read, we can also use the keywords `this` (C#) or `Me` (VB.NET) to reference the class we're working in.

Visual Studio may hide some members from you. To see them, open the Options dialog and deselect Hide Advanced Members from the Text Editor -> Basic -> General Options.

The first line of our constructor uses the Add() method of the ListItemCollection (the type of the Item property) to add an item in the drop-down that says, Select a Topic. We're using this drop-down to tell the user that he or she can select something, so this will be the first item in our list.

Next we use a typical data access scenario, and we loop through the results of a SqlDataReader to add additional items to the collection. Listing 9.3 shows the HTML rendered to the browser.

Listing 9.3 Our control rendered to HTML at runtime

```
<select name="_ctl0">
  <option selected="selected" value="0">Select a topic...</option>
  <option value="19">Application</option>
  <option value="12">Basics</option>
  <option value="13">C#</option>
  <option value="10">Configuration</option>
  <option value="5">Controls</option>
  <option value="3">Data</option>
  <option value="18">HttpHandlers/Modules</option>
  <option value="9">Mobile</option>
  <option value="21">Pages/User Controls</option>
  <option value="6">Security</option>
  <option value="20">Session</option>
  <option value="15">SQL Server</option>
  <option value="8">Validation</option>
  <option value="14">Visual Basic .Net</option>
  <option value="7">Visual Studio</option>
  <option value="4">Web Services</option>
  <option value="23">Whidbey</option>
  <option value="1">XML</option>
</select>
```

As we mentioned before, you could add a normal `DropDownList` to your page and then use the same data access code to `DataBind()` the results to the control. Although that's certainly acceptable, doing that in every single page would get tedious. This method makes it portable and easier to maintain.

Now our derived drop-down list has data in it, but it doesn't do anything. Let's extend the functionality of the control to redirect to a new page when its selected index is changed. As you may already know, the `DropDownList` has a Boolean property called `AutoPostBack`. Let's add `AutoPostBack = true` to the constructor so that the property is true. That means when the user changes the selection, the page will postback.

If we go back to the documentation, we can see that `DropDownList` has a protected method called `OnSelectedIndexChanged()`, which is wired up to the `SelectedIndexChanged` event. This seems like a logical place to introduce our own logic, which would forward the user to another page, based on the user's selection.

Remember our discussion about inheritance? Because we're inheriting `DropDownList` as our base class, we can override it here and add our own code, as shown in Listing 9.4.

Listing 9.4 Overriding the `OnSelectedIndexChanged()` method

C#
```
protected override void OnSelectedIndexChanged(EventArgs e)
{
  this.Page.Response.Redirect("newswire.aspx?filter=" +
SelectedItem.Value);
}
```

VB.NET
```
Protected Overrides Sub OnSelectedIndexChanged(e As EventArgs)
  Me.Page.Response.Redirect("newswire.aspx?filter=" & _
SelectedItem.Value)
End Sub
```

The documentation shows that the method returns nothing and takes an `EventArgs` parameter, so we'll have to do the same thing in our derived method. All that's left to do is to add a redirect to the page that we want, based on the value of the new selected item.

That's all there is to it. If we need to insert this new derived control into a dozen different pages, we only have to write the code once. Using the

`Register` directive in Listing 9.1 and the tag between the `form` elements, this same control will appear, populated and ready to redirect users, on every page.

Building Your Own Server Control from Scratch

Let's build a simple text box control to demonstrate at a basic level how you might build your own control.

Using Visual Studio 2005, start a new class library project and call it SimpleTextBox. In the solution explorer of the new project, you'll need to add a reference to the `System.Web.dll` assembly because it's not included by default. To do this, right-click References and click Add Reference. Figure 9.1 shows the Add Reference dialog with the correct assembly selected. If you are planning to compile the class with the command line, be sure to use the reference switch and include `System.Web.dll`.

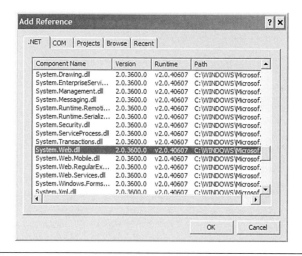

Figure 9.1 The Add Reference dialog.

Now we can begin writing the class. Start by adding a `using` (`Imports` in VB.NET) statement to include `System.Web` and any other namespaces you think you might need. Your class has to be in a namespace, so be sure to choose one that is unique. Finally, your class declaration should indicate that the class will inherit from one of three choices.

The first two choices are to inherit from `System.Web.UI.Control` or `System.Web.UI.WebControls.WebControl`. The primary difference between the two is that `WebControl` offers many visual properties, such as `Width`, `Height`, and `Font`. The third choice is to inherit from an existing class, as we did in our `DropDownList` example previously. We're keeping it really simple here, so we'll inherit from `Control`.

Because we're also planning to process postback data, we also need to implement the `IPostBackDataHandler` interface. That leaves our class looking something like Listing 9.5.

> This simple example is similar to one in the SDK documentation that ships with the .NET Framework, listed under the overview for the `IPostBackDataHandler` interface. Our example has a few changes to reflect what one might consider to be best practices.

Listing 9.5 The start of our custom server control

C#
```
using System;
using System.Collections.Specialized;
using System.Text;
using System.Web;
using System.Web.UI;

namespace SimpleTextBox
{
  public class MyTextBox : System.Web.UI.Control, IPostBackDataHandler
  {
    public MyTextBox()
    {

    }
  }
}
```

VB.NET
```
Imports System
Imports System.Collections.Specialized
Imports System.Text
```

```
Imports System.Web
Imports System.Web.UI

Namespace SimpleTextBox
   Public Class MyTextBox
      Inherits System.Web.UI.Control
      Implements IPostBackDataHandler

      Public Sub New()
      End Sub
   End Class
End Namespace
```

Let's start with the parts we'll need to get text in and out and to render the HTML in the page. We need a property that can hold the text to be displayed in the text box, so we'll create one called, cleverly enough, `Text`. This property differs from those you've seen in other class examples because we will save its value in the `ViewState` collection instead of saving it to a private variable. Note that the `get` part of our property requires that we cast the value from `ViewState` into a `string`, just as we would when fetching a value from `Session` or `Cache`.

We also override `Control`'s `Render()` method with our own in order to render the HTML to the browser. We're using a `StringBuilder` object to assemble a string that builds the HTML, including the control's name (which comes from the `UniqueID` property, a part of the `Control` base class) and the value of our text box, using `HttpUtility.HtmlEncode()` to escape characters that would otherwise break the HTML in the browser (such as quotes and "greater than" signs). Our two new members are shown in Listing 9.6.

Where the heck does this `Render()` method come from, and why do you have to use it? Remember that we're inheriting from `Control` as our base class. The documentation for `Control` says that the `Render()` method is where the code renders the actual HTML and inserts it into the page. Because we want to control that rendering, we override the method and do it ourselves because we're not satisfied with whatever the original `Control` class had in mind. As we mentioned earlier in the book, it doesn't matter that we don't know the specific implementation under the hood. We only care that the `Control` class is intended for rendering HTML to the browser.

Listing 9.6 Adding a property and overriding the Render() method in our control

C#

```csharp
public string Text
{
  get { return (string)ViewState["Text"]; }
  set { ViewState["Text"] = value; }
}

protected override void Render(HtmlTextWriter writer)
{
  StringBuilder builder = new StringBuilder();
  builder.Append("<input type=\"text\" name=\"");
  builder.Append(this.UniqueID);
  builder.Append("\" value=\"");
  builder.Append(HttpUtility.HtmlEncode(Text));
  builder.Append("\" />");
  writer.Write(builder.ToString());
}
```

VB.NET

```vbnet
Public Property Text() As String
  Get
    Return CStr(ViewState("Text"))
  End Get
  Set
    ViewState("Text") = value
  End Set
End Property

Protected Overrides Sub Render(writer As HtmlTextWriter)
  Dim builder As New StringBuilder()
  builder.Append("<input type=""text"" name=""")
  builder.Append(Me.UniqueID)
  builder.Append(""" value=""")
  builder.Append(HttpUtility.HtmlEncode(Text))
  builder.Append(""" />")
  writer.Write(builder.ToString())
End Sub
```

If we temporarily removed the IPostBackDataHandler from the class declaration, it would compile, and we could put it in a page. We could even assign a value to the Text property, and it would appear in the text box. However, it wouldn't be very useful because so far, we have no way of reading the data it will contain on postback.

Implementing `IPostBackDataHandler` requires that we add two methods: `LoadPostData(string, NameValueCollection)` and `RaisePostDataChangedEvent()`. The first is used to process the data on postback by accessing its value from the returned form data, returning a Boolean value that indicates whether or not the data has changed, while the second is used to execute code if the control's state has been altered.

> Confused yet? Don't be! There are a lot of interfaces that help you, as a server control author, to define the way a control will behave in the context of a Web form and its postback mechanism. Under no circumstance are we trying to cover every possibility here; we're only trying to give you a solid overview of how the entire process works.

Let's start with `LoadPostData()`. Its purpose is to compare the old value of the control's properties to those sent on postback. If the values have changed, we should assign the new values to our properties and make the method return true, signaling to ASP.NET that there has indeed been a change. This is easy because we only have one value to worry about. The two parameters, the `string` and `NameValueCollection`, give us access to the posted form data. We'll get the old value from the `Text` property and the new value from the form data posted back to us. If it changed, we'll update the `Text` property and return true; otherwise we'll do nothing and return false. Listing 9.7 shows the method added to our class.

Listing 9.7 The `LoadPostData()` implemented in our class

C#
```
public virtual bool LoadPostData(string postDataKey, NameValueCollection
postCollection)
{
  string oldValue = Text;
  string newValue = postCollection[this.UniqueID];
  if (oldValue == null || !oldValue.Equals(newValue))
  {
    Text = newValue;
    return true;
  }
}
```

(Continues)

Listing 9.7 The `LoadPostData()` implemented in our class   *(Continued)*

```
    return false;
}
```

VB.NET

```
Public Overridable Function LoadPostData(postDataKey As String, _
postCollection As NameValueCollection) As Boolean
  Dim oldValue As String = Text
  Dim newValue As String = postCollection(Me.UniqueID)
  If oldValue Is Nothing Or Not oldValue.Equals(newValue) Then
    Text = newValue
    Return True
  End If
  Return False
End Function
```

Under the hood, ASP.NET will call `RaisePostDataChangedEvent()` if your `LoadPostData()` method returns true. `RaisePostData ChangedEvent()` doesn't actually need to do anything for the purpose of our demonstration. However, if we wanted to do things right and release a commercial-grade control, we would implement our own event and event handler, called `TextChanged` and `OnTextChanged`, respectively (using the appropriate naming conventions). Listing 9.8 shows how we would write our event handler and event; otherwise we would leave `RaisePostDataChangedEvent()` empty.

Listing 9.8 Implementing our own event and event handler

C#

```
public virtual void RaisePostDataChangedEvent()
{
  OnTextChanged(EventArgs.Empty);
}

public event EventHandler TextChanged;

protected virtual void OnTextChanged(EventArgs e)
{
  if (TextChanged != null) TextChanged(this, e);
}
```

VB.NET

```
Public Overridable Sub RaisePostDataChangedEvent()
```

```
    OnTextChanged(EventArgs.Empty)
End Sub

Public Event TextChanged As EventHandler

Protected Overridable Sub OnTextChanged(e As EventArgs)
    If Not (TextChanged Is Nothing) Then
        TextChanged(Me, e)
    End If
End Sub
```

What does it mean "to do it right?" Think back to our HttpModule example where we added an event handler to application events. We could do that because the authors of ASP.NET programmed those events and made them available to us. By adding the code in Listing 9.8, we're doing the same thing for anyone who wants to tie into our server control.

Our control is finished! Listing 9.9 shows the finished class as well as its use in a page that, on postback, copies the text from the text box to a LinkButton's text value. We removed the constructor because it's not used. Figure 9.2 shows what it looks like in the browser after a postback.

Listing 9.9 The finished control, showing its use in a page

C#
```csharp
using System;
using System.Collections.Specialized;
using System.Text;
using System.Web;
using System.Web.UI;

namespace SimpleTextBox
{
    public class MyTextBox : System.Web.UI.Control, IPostBackDataHandler
    {
        public string Text
        {
            get { return (string)ViewState["Text"]; }
            set { ViewState["Text"] = value; }
```

(Continues)

Listing 9.9 The finished control, showing its use in a page   *(Continued)*

```
    }

    protected override void Render(HtmlTextWriter writer)
    {
      StringBuilder builder = new StringBuilder();
      builder.Append("<input type=\"text\" name=\"");
      builder.Append(this.UniqueID);
      builder.Append("\" value=\"");
      builder.Append(HttpUtility.HtmlEncode(Text));
      builder.Append("\" />");
      writer.Write(builder.ToString());
    }

    public virtual bool LoadPostData(string postDataKey,
NameValueCollection postCollection)
    {
      string oldValue = Text;
      string newValue = postCollection[this.UniqueID];
      if (oldValue == null || !oldValue.Equals(newValue))
      {
        Text = newValue;
        return true;
      }
      return false;
    }

    public virtual void RaisePostDataChangedEvent()
    {
      OnTextChanged(EventArgs.Empty);
    }

    public event EventHandler TextChanged;

    protected virtual void OnTextChanged(EventArgs e)
    {
      if (TextChanged != null) TextChanged(this, e);
    }
  }
}
```

VB.NET

```
Imports System
Imports System.Collections.Specialized
```

```vbnet
Imports System.Text
Imports System.Web
Imports System.Web.UI

Namespace SimpleTextBox
  Public Class MyTextBox
    Inherits System.Web.UI.Control
    Implements IPostBackDataHandler

    Public Property Text() As String
      Get
        Return CStr(ViewState("Text"))
      End Get
      Set
        ViewState("Text") = value
      End Set
    End Property

    Protected Overrides Sub Render(writer As HtmlTextWriter)
      Dim builder As New StringBuilder()
      builder.Append("<input type=""text"" name=""")
      builder.Append(Me.UniqueID)
      builder.Append(""" value=""")
      builder.Append(HttpUtility.HtmlEncode([Text]))
      builder.Append(""" />")
      writer.Write(builder.ToString())
    End Sub

    Public Overridable Function LoadPostData(postDataKey As String, _
postCollection As NameValueCollection) As Boolean
      Dim oldValue As String = Text
      Dim newValue As String = postCollection(Me.UniqueID)
      If oldValue Is Nothing Or Not oldValue.Equals(newValue) Then
        Text = newValue
        Return True
      End If
      Return False
    End Function

    Public Overridable Sub RaisePostDataChangedEvent()
      OnTextChanged(EventArgs.Empty)
    End Sub

    Public Event TextChanged As EventHandler
```

(Continues)

Listing 9.9 The finished control, showing its use in a page   *(Continued)*

```
      Protected Overridable Sub OnTextChanged(e As EventArgs)
        If Not (TextChanged Is Nothing) Then
          TextChanged(Me, e)
        End If
      End Sub
    End Class
End Namespace
```

.aspx page

```
<%@ Page Language="C#" Codefile="Default.aspx.cs" Inherits="Default_aspx" %>
<%@ Register Assembly="SimpleTextBox" Namespace="SimpleTextBox"
TagPrefix="Sample" %>
<script runat="server">
  void Page_Load(object sender, EventArgs e)
  {
    LinkButton1.Text = TextBoxTest.Text + " Click to postback!";
  }
</script>
<html>
<body>
  <form id="form1" runat="server">
    <Sample:MyTextBox ID="TextBoxTest" Runat="Server" /><br />
    <asp:LinkButton ID="LinkButton1"
Runat="server">LinkButton</asp:LinkButton>
  </form>
</body>
</html>
```

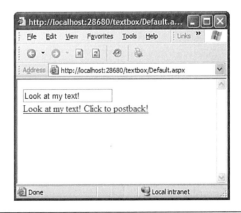

Figure 9.2 Our server control as seen in a browser.

Using Viewstate

Viewstate is of course the "bucket" that saves the state of all of the controls on the page so that the server can determine what the form looked like before the postback. You might recall from Chapter 7, "The ASP.NET Event Model," that it's transmitted as part of the page in a hidden HTML input field, and it can get quite large.

The size of the encoded viewstate is significantly better in ASP.NET v2.0, but it's still a good idea to think carefully about how it's used. After all, that data has to be sent to the browser and back on every request to the server. Not only does that consume bandwidth and the perceived time it takes for the page to load, but it also means that the server has to do more work encoding and decoding it.

For that reason, all good control authors think hard about how and when they'll save data in the `ViewState` object. If the control you're developing doesn't need to retain data on postback, you don't need to keep it in viewstate. For example, if you have a control that displays data from `Cache`, you don't need to save it in viewstate because, on postback, the control can read it from `Cache` again. There's no reason to encode it, send it to the client, send it back to the server, and then decode it!

Efficient Rendering of Your HTML

You may have noticed that we didn't simply concatenate a string in the `Render()` method of our custom server control and then send it to the `HtmlWriter`. The reason is that string concatenation is a fairly expensive process in terms of performance, especially if you need to assemble huge strings and do it multiple times in the same page, once for each instance of a control. Using a `StringBuilder` object to piece together a string is much faster by several orders of magnitude. We'll go into more depth in Chapter 15, "Performance, Scalability, and Metrics."

You can also output strings directly to the `HtmlWriter` because this is also faster than string concatenation.

Composite Controls

Because ASP.NET has so many useful controls, you might rightfully feel that there's no reason to reinvent the wheel with your own control implementation. Instead, a combination of controls might accomplish what you're after. Fortunately you can build composite controls to do just that. If you've ever ventured into the world of Windows forms, building a composite control will seem very familiar to you.

Building a composite control is simply a matter of instantiating existing controls and adding them to the `Controls` property of the base `CompositeControl` class. In fact, the first requirement to build a composite control is that your class must inherit from `CompositeControl`. You don't need to choose between the three choices we mentioned for our from-scratch server control.

The second requirement is to override `CompositeControl`'s `CreateChildControls()` method. This is where the real magic happens—it's where we create, name, and add controls to the `Controls` property of the base `CompositeControl` class (the property happens to be of the type `ControlCollection`).

Let's build a simple composite control that has little to no real use but that shows how easy it is to build a composite control. Let's say we need a `TextBox`, a `Label`, and a `Button` control. Clicking on the button should cause the text in the `TextBox` to display in the label.

Using what we know about class design and event handlers, we can quickly build the class. We'll need private variables to hold each of our three controls. We'll need an event handler that will copy the text of the `TextBox` to the `Text` property of the label. Finally, we'll need a place to create all of these controls, and that place is of course the `CreateChildControls()` method we mentioned earlier. Listing 9.10 shows the entire class (as well as its use in a page), while Figure 9.3 shows how the controls will be rendered in the browser.

Listing 9.10 A simple composite control

C#

```
using System;
using System.Collections.Specialized;
using System.Text;
using System.Web;
```

```csharp
using System.Web.UI;
using System.Web.UI.WebControls;

namespace SimpleComposite
{
  public class MyCompositeControl : CompositeControl
  {
    private TextBox _textBox;
    private Label _label;
    private Button _button;

    protected override void CreateChildControls()
    {
      _textBox = new TextBox();
      _textBox.ID = "MyTextBox";
      this.Controls.Add(_textBox);
      _label = new Label();
      _label.ID = "MyLabel";
      this.Controls.Add(_label);
      _button = new Button();
      _button.ID = "MyButton";
      _button.Text = "Click me!";
      _button.Click += new EventHandler(this.ButtonClickHandler);
      this.Controls.Add(_button);
    }

    private void ButtonClickHandler(object sender, EventArgs e)
    {
      _label.Text = _textBox.Text;
    }
  }
}
```

VB.NET

```vbnet
Imports System
Imports System.Collections.Specialized
Imports System.Text
Imports System.Web
Imports System.Web.UI
Imports System.Web.UI.WebControls

Namespace SimpleComposite
```

(Continues)

Listing 9.10 A simple composite control   *(Continued)*

```
Public Class MyCompositeControl
    Inherits CompositeControl
    Private _textBox As TextBox
    Private _label As Label
    Private _button As Button

    Protected Overrides Sub CreateChildControls()
        _textBox = New TextBox()
        _textBox.ID = "MyTextBox"
        Me.Controls.Add(_textBox)
        _label = New Label()
        _label.ID = "MyLabel"
        Me.Controls.Add(_label)
        _button = New Button()
        _button.ID = "MyButton"
        _button.Text = "Click me!"
        _button.Click += New EventHandler(Me.ButtonClickHandler)
        Me.Controls.Add(_button)
    End Sub

    Private Sub ButtonClickHandler(sender As Object, e As EventArgs)
        _label.Text = _textBox.Text
    End Sub
    End Class
End Namespace
```

.aspx page

```
<%@ Page Language="C#" Codefile="Default.aspx.cs" Inherits="Default_aspx" %>
<%@ Register Assembly="SimpleComposite" Namespace="SimpleComposite"
TagPrefix="Sample" %>
<html>
<body>
  <form id="form1" runat="server">
    <Sample:MyCompositeControl ID="CompositeTest" Runat="Server" />
  </form>
</body>
</html>
```

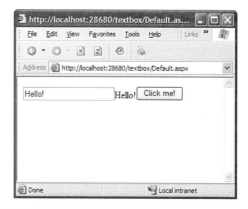

Figure 9.3 Our composite control rendered in the browser.

Could it be any easier? The CreateChildControls() method creates the controls one by one, assigning values to some of their properties and then adding them to the control collection. The button control gets one extra step, where we add an event handler to its Click method. The syntax for this is the same as what we used in Chapter 8, "HttpHandlers and HttpModules," for our sample HttpModule.

The event handler itself, which we're calling ButtonClick Handler(), has the familiar parameters of every other event handler: an object and an EventArgs object. When we type "Hello!" in the text box and click the button, it fires off our event handler and copies the value in the text box to the label.

Of course, you can see in Figure 9.3 that the formatting of our composite control leaves a lot to be desired. The controls are rendered in the order that they were added to the collection. There's something we can do about this, of course, and if you guessed that it involves overriding the Render() method of the base class, you were right!

As with our custom server control, we'll override Render() and create our own implementation. To write one of our controls, we call its RenderControl() method and pass in the HtmlTextWriter parameter of the Render() method. This might feel a little backward because in our custom control we were calling methods of the HtmlTextWriter.

This act of overriding Render() enables us to render the controls in the order that we'd like, but we also need to generate some HTML in between them to format them nicely. Fortunately, the HtmlTextWriter has a number of methods that enable us to cleanly create a tree of XHTMLcompliant tags. There's also an enumeration called `HtmlTextWriterTag` that enables us to pass in values to the writer that correspond to common HTML elements. The result of this, our overridden `Render()` method, is shown in Listing 9.11. The listing also shows the HTML rendered and sent to the browser. Figure 9.4 shows the display in the browser.

Listing 9.11 The `Render()` method and the HTML rendered for the browser

C#

```
protected override void Render(HtmlTextWriter writer)
{
  writer.RenderBeginTag(HtmlTextWriterTag.Table);
  writer.RenderBeginTag(HtmlTextWriterTag.Tr);
  writer.RenderBeginTag(HtmlTextWriterTag.Td);
  _textBox.RenderControl(writer);
  writer.RenderEndTag();
  writer.RenderEndTag();
  writer.RenderBeginTag(HtmlTextWriterTag.Tr);
  writer.RenderBeginTag(HtmlTextWriterTag.Td);
  _button.RenderControl(writer);
  writer.RenderEndTag();
  writer.RenderEndTag();
  writer.RenderBeginTag(HtmlTextWriterTag.Tr);
  writer.RenderBeginTag(HtmlTextWriterTag.Td);
  _label.RenderControl(writer);
  writer.RenderEndTag();
  writer.RenderEndTag();
  writer.RenderEndTag();
}
```

VB.NET

```
Protected Overrides Sub Render(writer As HtmlTextWriter)
   writer.RenderBeginTag(HtmlTextWriterTag.Table)
   writer.RenderBeginTag(HtmlTextWriterTag.Tr)
   writer.RenderBeginTag(HtmlTextWriterTag.Td)
   _textBox.RenderControl(writer)
   writer.RenderEndTag()
   writer.RenderEndTag()
   writer.RenderBeginTag(HtmlTextWriterTag.Tr)
   writer.RenderBeginTag(HtmlTextWriterTag.Td)
   _button.RenderControl(writer)
   writer.RenderEndTag()
   writer.RenderEndTag()
```

```
   writer.RenderBeginTag(HtmlTextWriterTag.Tr)
   writer.RenderBeginTag(HtmlTextWriterTag.Td)
   _label.RenderControl(writer)
   writer.RenderEndTag()
   writer.RenderEndTag()
   writer.RenderEndTag()
End Sub
```

HTML source sent to browser

```
<table>
  <tr>
    <td><input name="CompositeTest$MyTextBox" type="text" value="Hello!"
id="CompositeTest_MyTextBox" /></td>
  </tr><tr>
    <td><input type="submit" name="CompositeTest$MyButton" value="Click
me!" id="CompositeTest_MyButton" /></td>
  </tr><tr>
    <td><span id="CompositeTest_MyLabel">Hello!</span></td>
  </tr>
</table>
```

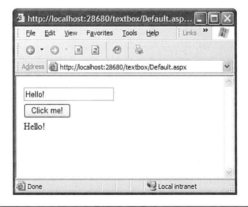

Figure 9.4 Our formatted composite control as seen in the browser.

The methods used should be straightforward. We build a tree of tags, starting with a table tag by calling the HtmlTextWriter's Render BeginTag() method. We do the same for table row and cell, and then we finally render our TextBox as we described. To close the last tag we opened, we simply call the RenderEndTag() method. We don't need to pass in any parameters because this method knows to close the last tag that hasn't yet been closed.

> If you need to work with XML, similar methods are found in the `XmlTextWriter` class, except that they're called `WriteStartElement()` and `WriteEndElement()`. They make the creation of well-formed XML a breeze.

Although our composite control does some fabulous things as a self-contained unit, it doesn't have any means to communicate with your own code. As with our custom server control example, you can add properties and events to give your calling code something to interact with. One advantage of the composite control is that each individual control already has an array of events and event handlers for you to interact with, so you don't have to write your own for each component of the user interface.

> You might be wondering why we marked our methods "protected." Recall from Chapter 2, "Classes: The Code Behind the Objects," that a protected member can only be called from within the class or from within the derived class. If someone were to derive from our class to make their own implementation, we don't want users of the derived control calling the member of the base class (our class) because it would cause confusion between the original member and the derived member. Therefore, we "protect" the original version.

Composite Controls Versus User Controls

Composite controls aren't the only way to bundle pieces of UI together. You can do the very same thing in user controls, which act as "mini pages" of sorts. As with many aspects of ASP.NET programming, the same task can be accomplished in a declarative way or a programmatic way. User controls are significantly more declarative because you can load up an .ascx file with markup, write a little "glue" code, and be on your way. Composite controls, on the other hand, require a programmatic approach, where you create each individual object and manipulate it, as well as the surrounding markup.

One disadvantage to composite controls is that you are, for the most part, tied into a particular "look" for the UI (though you can obviously create all kinds of style properties and even skin the individual controls). I would venture that the `Login` control's fairly rigid layout may deter a lot of people from using it (the control is essentially a composite control).

The big advantage of server controls is the very precise control you have over every aspect of the rendered HTML. You can decide how much to render, the order in which to render it, and so on, and therefore you can be in complete control of its performance. It's also very easy to distribute your work when compiled to an assembly. When other coders get the assembly, they drop it in their `/bin` folder, add two lines of code to their page, and it's done (and you look like a hero).

Summary

Server controls render HTML to the page programmatically by inheriting from existing controls, such as the `Control` base class or the `WebControls` base class. Composite controls combine existing controls into neat and easy-to-manage packages that can be added to a page with a simple `Register` directive and one declarative tag.

The topic of building your own server controls is huge, and we've only given you enough knowledge to be dangerous. If you want to pursue more detail, again I strongly suggest *Developing Microsoft ASP.NET Server Controls and Components* by Nikhil Kothari and Vandana Datye (Microsoft Press, 2003). Kothari wrote many of the controls in the framework and Datye wrote much of the documentation in the SDK and on MSDN.

CHAPTER 10

Web Services as Objects

Starting in 2001, Web services seemed to be the focus of every other technology story, as experts promised they would change the world or maybe cure cancer. Although the importance of Web services initially might have been overstated, they're incredibly useful for the purpose of enabling machines to communicate.

Web services transmit data in the same way that a Web browser and a Web server do, via HTTP (Hypertext Transfer Protocol). Instead of swapping HTML and form data, XML is sent. Furthermore, the Simple Object Access Protocol (SOAP) is an XML standard frequently used to send messages in a consistent format between systems.

The funny thing about Web services and ASP.NET is that you don't really need to know much about XML or SOAP to make Web services work. That's a real blessing, too, because trying to dig into the SOAP standard is enough to make some developers go running for the hills. Fortunately, the tools found in ASP.NET and Visual Studio make it easy to create and consume Web services.

When learning about Web services, you need to think of them in terms of having remote access to code, not just a means to send messages back and forth between systems. When you consume a Web service, it's like having a class locally, in your own code. The difference is that the execution happens on the remote system, not on your own. The application data is serialized between the two systems as XML.

What is serialization? It's the conversion of objects into a format that can be transmitted, in this case using XML.

In this chapter we'll look at using Web services in a more abstract way, trying to avoid the details about XML and SOAP. Many developers find it easier to see the purpose of Web services when they think of them in terms

165

of objects that interact with other objects on a remote server (instead of local memory).

> This is probably a good time to mention that although you can simulate object-oriented programming with Web services, it's far from ideal. Remember that because data must be serialized and calls must be made to the server any time that data must be processed, this could result in many potentially large messages being sent back and forth to the server. This kind of activity could cause a busy server to buckle under pressure and not scale or perform well. Thus, Web services should be as simple as possible, and they should act more as end-points for the exchange of data and less like remote objects.

Converting Your Code to a Web Service

Converting a business class to a Web service is ridiculously easy. The class can inherit from System.Web.Services.WebService in order to use the ASP.NET objects you've come to know and love (Application, Context, etc.), though this inheritance is *not* required. Beyond that, you simply need to add the WebMethod attribute to methods that you want to call remotely. Listing 10.1 shows a classic "Hello world" Web service.

> Visual Studio 2005 will automatically set up a new class for a Web service to inherit from WebService. Therefore, if you don't want it to do this, you'll need to manually remove it from the class declaration.

Listing 10.1 "Hello world" Web service (.asmx file)

C#

```
<%@ WebService Language="C#" Class="Hello" %>
using System;
using System.Web;
```

```
using System.Web.Services;
using System.Web.Services.Protocols;

public class Hello
{
    [WebMethod]
    public string World()
    {
        return "Hello world!";
    }
}
```

VB.NET

```
<%@ WebService Language="VB" Class="Hello" %>
Imports System
Imports System.Web
Imports System.Web.Services
Imports System.Web.Services.Protocols

Public Class Hello
  <WebMethod()> Public Function World() As String
    Return "Hello world!"
  End Function
End Class
```

Web service code can live inline in an `.asmx` file, in a code-behind file (non-compiled), or in an assembly in the `/bin` folder. The variations of the `WebService` directive in the `.asmx` file are:

- **Inline**: Language and a class name must be specified, and code immediately follows.

  ```
  <%@ WebService Language="C#" Class="Hello" %>
  ```

- **Code-behind**: Additionally, the name of the file containing the code must be specified.

  ```
  <%@ WebService Language="C#" CodeBehind="mycode.cs"
  Class="Hello" %>
  ```

- **Compiled**: The class specified must be the name of a compiled class in an assembly in the `/bin` folder.

  ```
  <%@ WebService Language="C#" Class="Hello" %>
  ```

ASP.NET has a built-in, though somewhat simple, means of testing Web services from a browser. If we pull up the Web service in a browser, we get the page shown in Figure 10.1. At the moment, the page shows some suggestions on how to change the namespace of the Web service (more on that in a minute) and has a link to the one Web method we've specified called "World."

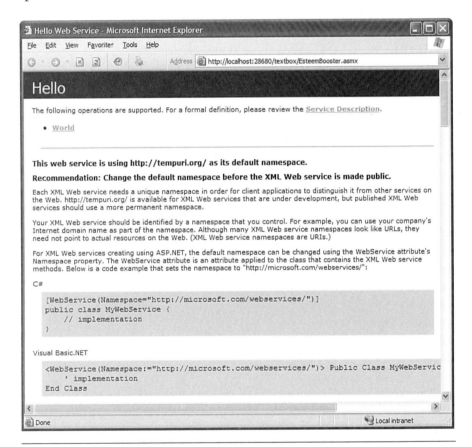

Figure 10.1 The diagnostic Web service page.

If you click on the link for "World," you'll get another page with a button that says "Invoke." Press that button, and you'll get a new page of XML—a response to the Web service. It simply shows the results of the call to the service, as shown in Listing 10.2.

Listing 10.2 The XML generated by the `World` method of the `Hello` Web service

```
<?xml version="1.0" encoding="utf-8" ?>
<string xmlns="http://tempuri.org/">Hello world!</string>
```

Remarkably unimpressive? Perhaps, but it didn't take much code to generate it either. The diagnostic page will give you form fields to send data to the Web service if the methods require them. These are of limited use, though, if you use more complex types, such as classes that contain a number of different properties.

There are a couple useful attributes we can use with the class and methods of our Web service. You've already seen `WebMethod`, and you can add some additional information to it to make it more useful. Listing 10.3 shows all these additional parameters for the `WebMethod` attribute in use, separated by commas. They're all fairly straightforward in their usage:

- `BufferResponse`: A Boolean value that, if true, forces the Web service to generate its entire response before sending it back to the calling client. The default is true.
- `CacheDuration`: Number of seconds to cache the response.
- `Description`: A string indicating what the method does. This is used in the diagnostic page as well as in the generated WSDL (more on that in the next section).
- `EnableSession`: A Boolean value that turns on session state when true. This works by issuing an HTTP cookie to track session state. This is not generally useful because it assumes that the calling system will store and return that cookie.
- `MessageName`: A string that gives a method an alias; necessary when you have two methods with the same name but different method signatures.
- `TransactionOption`: Transactions in Web services are beyond the scope of this discussion.

Listing 10.3 Specifying `WebMethod` attribute with properties

C#
```
[WebMethod(BufferResponse=true, CacheDuration=20, Description="stuff",
EnableSession=false, MessageName="test", TransactionOption =
TransactionOption.Disabled)]
```

(Continues)

Listing 10.3 Specifying `WebMethod` attribute with properties *(Continued)*

VB.NET
```
<WebMethod(BufferResponse:=True, CacheDuration:=20, _
Description:="stuff", EnableSession:=False, MessageName:="test", _
TransactionOption:=TransactionOption.Disabled)>
```

There is also an attribute called `WebService` with three available properties, set just before the class declaration, as shown in Listing 10.4. Its properties are even simpler:

- `Description`: A string explaining the overall purpose of the Web service.
- `Name`: A string naming the service.
- `Namespace`: A string that will appear in the XML of the service indicating its namespace. If you're unfamiliar with XML namespaces, they are simply unique identifiers, usually written as URIs. A namespace doesn't necessarily reflect an actual Web address, but because Web addresses are inherently unique, they are frequently used. Web service authors will frequently use actual URIs that point to documentation for the service, but that's entirely optional. It's acceptable to use something like http://dotnetrules/myservice if that's what you desire.

Listing 10.4 Specifying the `WebService` attribute with properties

C#
```
[WebService(Description="A fun Web
service.",Name="Hello",Namespace="http://happyfun/hello/")]
```

VB.NET
```
<WebService(Description:="A fun Web service.", Name:="Hello", _
Namespace:="http://happyfun/hello/")>
```

To some extent, you need to cast aside the design principles mentioned early in the book when you're building a Web service. As we already discussed, trying to implement a true object-oriented API will cause a great deal of data exchange and result in huge messages being sent back and forth between your Web service and the calling system.

That doesn't mean that you can't build a service with more complex types. The key to keeping the service limited to one trick is in the way you package the exchange of data. This is dictated by the method signatures you'll use.

For example, Amazon.com uses Web services to allow enterprising developers and site publishers to access the Amazon system for product data and even shopping cart manipulation. (The developers do this, of course, because they get a cut of anything bought through their sites via Amazon's affiliate program.) Amazon has a single service called `AmazonSearchService`, with a number of methods that take various types as parameters and return other types. By using this scheme, a chunk of data is sent in one message to the service and a chunk is sent back, all in one round trip.

This is quite different from our earlier design patterns, where we would create various objects and interact with different methods to manipulate them. Doing so in this situation would cause multiple trips to the service to get the desired result, which could cause the system to get bogged down if it got busy. In fact, you could actually put the `WebMethod` attribute on the get and set portions of a property, but you'd pay dearly in terms of performance.

To demonstrate the design of a Web service that serves as an endpoint for a single exchange, we'll create a service that boosts your self-esteem. In the following section, we'll see how to consume the service.

Our new Web service should take an object called `Person`, which contains the person's age and name, and should return an object called `Status`, which contains a self-esteem boosting message and the amount of money the person is entitled to, based on their age (an old person's dream, for sure).

Open a new Visual Studio Web project and add a Web service to the project. Call it `EsteemBooster.asmx`. To create this service, we'll create two container classes, one called `Person` and one called `Status`. The third class, called `EsteemBooster`, will be the one that actually contains our `WebMethod`, which is called `Boost`. The code is shown in Listing 10.5.

Listing 10.5 The `EsteemBooster` class (`EsteemBooster.asmx`)

C#
```
<%@ WebService Language="C#" Class="EsteemBooster" %>
using System;
using System.Web;
using System.Web.Services;
using System.Web.Services.Protocols;
```

(Continues)

Listing 10.5 The `EsteemBooster` class (`EsteemBooster.asmx`) *(Continued)*

```
[WebService(Description="Never feel down again.",
Namespace="http://esteemshack/booster")]
public class EsteemBooster
{
  [WebMethod(Description="Boost the user's self-esteem.")]
  public Status Boost(Person peep)
  {
    Status s = new Status();
    s.Message = peep.Name + " is an outstanding person!";
    s.Dollars = peep.Age * 10000;
    return s;
  }
}

public class Person
{
  public string Name;
  public int Age;
}

public class Status
{
  public string Message;
  public int Dollars;
}
```

VB.NET

```
<%@ WebService Language="VB" Class="EsteemBooster" %>

Imports System
Imports System.Web
Imports System.Web.Services
Imports System.Web.Services.Protocols

<WebService(Description:="Never feel down again.",
Namespace:="http://esteemshack/booster")>  _
Public Class EsteemBooster
    <WebMethod(Description:="Boost the user's self-esteem.")>  _
    Public Function Boost(peep As Person) As Status
        Dim s As New Status()
        s.Message = peep.Name + " is an outstanding person!"
```

```
        s.Dollars = peep.Age * 10000
        Return s
    End Function
End Class

Public Class Person
    Public Name As String
    Public Age As Integer
End Class

Public Class Status
    Public Message As String
    Public Dollars As Integer
End Class
```

The structure of these classes should seem familiar enough to you, with the only significant difference being the attributes added before the class and method declarations. Notice that the actual Web service class has only methods. It does not have any properties. This supports our idea that the service should be an efficient endpoint, where one round trip of data does the job.

Consuming a Web Service

The other end of this process is the consumption of the Web service, and it's just as easy to do. Using Visual Studio, we need only add a Web reference to the service to generate what's called a proxy class. A proxy class does what the name implies—it creates a code interface that acts as a front end to the remote code.

Proxy classes are generated in one of two ways in Visual Studio 2005. If you add a reference to a Web project, several files are generated that describe the service and how to discover it. The proxy class is then generated dynamically at runtime. If you add a Web reference to a class library project, an actual class is generated and added to the project.

For the moment, let's add a reference to a class library project. When you right-click on the project in the solution explorer and choose Add Web Reference, the dialog in Figure 10.2 appears.

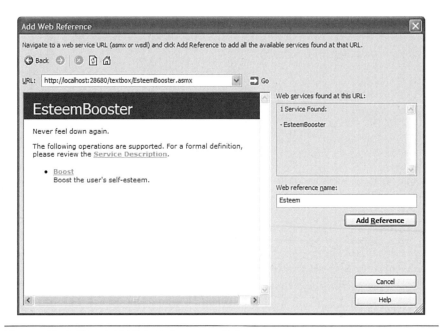

Figure 10.2 The Add Web Reference dialog.

The dialog has a mini-Web browser in it. Type the URL of the Web service, and the browser will attempt to identify it (don't forget the port number if you're using the built-in Web server of Visual Studio 2005). If the Web service is found, the dialog will indicate that on the right side and allow you to name the Web reference. The default is the domain name, but name it something you'll remember because it will be the root namespace used when you call it from code.

After you've added the reference, a number of files are added to the project. If you click the "show all files" button in the solution explorer and drill down under the Web references, you'll see a tree of files similar to those shown in Figure 10.3.

The most important file to look at is `Reference.cs` (or `Reference.vb`). This file contains the actual proxy class. The contents of the proxy class, generated based on the Web service, are shown in Listing 10.6. (We've left out the VB.NET version for the sake of brevity.)

Figure 10.3 The generated files for your Web reference.

Listing 10.6 The proxy class file generated for the `EsteemBooster` Web service

```
//------------------------------------------------------------------
// <autogenerated>
//      This code was generated by a tool.
//      Runtime Version:2.0.40607.16
//
//      Changes to this file may cause incorrect behavior and will be
//      lost if the code is regenerated.
// </autogenerated>
//------------------------------------------------------------------

//
// This source code was auto-generated by Microsoft.VSDesigner, Version
2.0.40607.16.
//
namespace MyProject.Esteem {
  using System.Diagnostics;
  using System.Web.Services;
  using System.ComponentModel;
  using System.Web.Services.Protocols;
  using System;
  using System.Xml.Serialization;


  /// <remarks/>
  [System.Diagnostics.DebuggerStepThroughAttribute()]
  [System.ComponentModel.DesignerCategoryAttribute("code")]
```

(Continues)

Listing 10.6 The proxy class file generated for the `EsteemBooster` Web service
             (Continued)

```
[System.Web.Services.WebServiceBindingAttribute(Name="EsteemBoosterSoap"
, Namespace="http://esteemshack/booster")]
  public class EsteemBooster :
System.Web.Services.Protocols.SoapHttpClientProtocol {

    /// <remarks/>
    public EsteemBooster() {
      string urlSetting =
System.Configuration.ConfigurationSettings.AppSettings["MyProject.Esteem.
EsteemBooster"];
        if ((urlSetting != null)) {
          this.Url = string.Concat(urlSetting, "");
        }
        else {
          this.Url = "http://localhost:28680/textbox/EsteemBooster.asmx";
        }
    }

    /// <remarks/>

[System.Web.Services.Protocols.SoapDocumentMethodAttribute("http://estee
mshack/booster/Boost", RequestNamespace="http://esteemshack/booster",
ResponseNamespace="http://esteemshack/booster",
Use=System.Web.Services.Description.SoapBindingUse.Literal,
ParameterStyle=System.Web.Services.Protocols.SoapParameterStyle.Wrapped)
]
    public Status Boost(Person peep) {
      object[] results = this.Invoke("Boost", new object[] {
                          peep});
      return ((Status)(results[0]));
    }

    /// <remarks/>
    public System.IAsyncResult BeginBoost(Person peep,
System.AsyncCallback callback, object asyncState) {
      return this.BeginInvoke("Boost", new object[] {
                          peep}, callback, asyncState);
    }

    /// <remarks/>
    public Status EndBoost(System.IAsyncResult asyncResult) {
      object[] results = this.EndInvoke(asyncResult);
```

```
    return ((Status)(results[0]));
  }
}

/// <remarks/>
[System.SerializableAttribute()]

[System.Xml.Serialization.XmlTypeAttribute(Namespace="http://esteemshack
/booster")]
  public class Person {

    /// <remarks/>
    public string Name;

    /// <remarks/>
    public int Age;
  }

/// <remarks/>
[System.SerializableAttribute()]

[System.Xml.Serialization.XmlTypeAttribute(Namespace="http://esteemshack
/booster")]
  public class Status {

    /// <remarks/>
    public string Message;

    /// <remarks/>
    public int Dollars;
  }
}
```

For the most part, this generated class looks a lot like your Web service code, only with additional attributes and extra methods to do asynchronous calls to the service. The only thing missing is the actual code—the creation and calculation of a `Status` object, based on a `Person` object.

This code is generated based on the description offered by the Web Service Definition Language (WSDL). This is XML that describes the form of the XML data exchanged via the Web service. When you add a Web reference, Visual Studio checks the address you entered for this WSDL file. For Web services authored in .NET, you can simply append "?WSDL" to the end of an address to view the WSDL.

Although using Visual Studio is in itself a "best practice," you aren't left high and dry by Microsoft if you don't have this tool. The free .NET SDK contains a number of command line tools that can do some of the same work, albeit more manually. To generate a proxy class without Visual Studio, use the `wsdl.exe` program. See the SDK for details.

Let's add a new page to the Web project we created for our `EsteemBooster` service. Add a Web reference to the project. If you right-click the `EsteemBooster.asmx` file in the solution explorer and then click "show in browser," the resulting browser will have the address of the Web service. Use that for your reference. Remember that no proxy class file is generated in a Web project, though you'll still be able to reference the Web service classes and members, starting with the name you gave it (in the previous example we used "Esteem").

Now, in your new page, enter the code in Listing 10.7. Run the page (right-click and select Show in Browser from the solution explorer), and you'll get the resulting page shown in Figure 10.4.

Listing 10.7 A page that calls our Web service

C#
```
<%@ Page Language="C#" %>
<script runat="server">
    void LinkButton1_Click(object sender, EventArgs e)
    {
        Esteem.Person peep = new Esteem.Person();
        peep.Name = NameTextBox.Text;
        peep.Age = Convert.ToInt32(AgeTextBox.Text);
        Esteem.EsteemBooster booster = new Esteem.EsteemBooster();
        Esteem.Status status = booster.Boost(peep);
        ResultLabel.Text = "Message: " + status.Message + " - Dollars:
" + status.Dollars.ToString("c");
    }
</script>
<html>
<body>
    <form id="form1" runat="server">
        Name: <asp:TextBox ID="NameTextBox" Runat="server" /><br />
        Age: <asp:TextBox ID="AgeTextBox" Runat="Server" /><br />
```

```
        <asp:LinkButton ID="LinkButton1" Runat="server"
OnClick="LinkButton1_Click">Get Message</asp:LinkButton><br />
        <asp:Label ID="ResultLabel" Runat="Server" />
    </form>
</body>
</html>
```

VB.NET

```
<%@ Page Language="VB" %>
<script runat="server">
Sub LinkButton1_Click(sender As Object, e As EventArgs)
    Dim peep As New Esteem.Person()
    peep.Name = NameTextBox.Text
    peep.Age = Convert.ToInt32(AgeTextBox.Text)
    Dim booster As New Esteem.EsteemBooster()
    Dim status As Esteem.Status = booster.Boost(peep)
    ResultLabel.Text = "Message: " + status.Message + _
" - Dollars: " + status.Dollars.ToString("c")
End Sub</script>
<html>
... (same as C# version
</html>
```

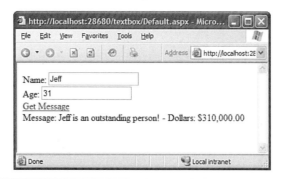

Figure 10.4 The calling page in action.

The code in the page has an event handler for the LinkButton that first creates a new Person object. That object is populated, an EsteemBooster object is created, and its Boost() method is called, passing in the Person object and assigning the returned Status object to a new variable. The results are displayed. This code doesn't look much different than if you were programming with the original classes in the Web services.

Object-Oriented Programming Without "Owning" the Object

Although the introduction for this chapter said we should think of Web services in terms of objects, it doesn't mean that we can consider creating Web services to be full-blown object-oriented programming. As we mentioned earlier, the performance hit you would take by constantly sending messages back and forth could be catastrophic.

In our `EsteemBooster` example, we created simple classes that grouped data together for the purpose of sending and receiving data. These classes didn't actually do anything on their own; they were only containers. By providing these containers, we can send and receive chunks of data all at one time. In fact, you could even exchange arrays of these objects if you wanted to. Think of results from a product search, where you have some product container, and each one in the array has the name, price, and so on.

The individual methods marked with the `WebMethod` attribute do actual work. When consumed, these methods are a lot like calling static methods in your own classes (though to do so, you still need to create an instance of the proxy class). Because of the proxy class, it's like having the class available to you as if it were your own.

Modifying the Proxy Class

You might have noticed that the address of a Web service is hard-coded right into the proxy class. Although this might be handy, it's safe to assume that when you deploy your Web service, it won't be located on a server called "localhost," as shown in Listing 10.6. The constructor in the generated class first looks for a setting in the `web.config` file's `appSettings` section called `MyProject.Esteem.EsteemBooster`. This is a convenient means of setting the location of the Web service without having to modify the code.

This is not present in the older Visual Studio versions prior to 2005. Although you can alter the proxy class, it may be regenerated if you update the Web reference. The easiest way to get around this is to copy and paste the entire proxy class into your own class file and then replace the address with a reference to the `web.config` file's `appSettings` section.

Summary

Web services provide a platform-neutral means of exchanging data between two systems over the Web using XML. Simple Object Access Protocol (SOAP) is a standard used to serialize and transfer object data between these systems. ASP.NET goes a long way to isolate programmers from the actual XML and allows them to concentrate on the implementation in the familiar realm of object-oriented code.

Although it's possible to simulate full object orientation in the design of Web services, consideration should be given to make them act as endpoints for the exchange of data, similarly to the way you'd call a static method from a local class. You can also package data in container classes. It's important to consider the performance implications of a Web service that needs to make many calls back and forth to arrive at an end result, as this kind of solution would not scale well.

Consuming a Web service from Visual Studio 2005 requires little more than adding a reference to the Web service. In a Web project, this reference is created dynamically, while a class library creates a physical proxy class. In both scenarios, you can code against these objects as if they were locally in your own system, releasing you from the details of how the data is exchanged with the remote system.

CHAPTER 11

Membership and Security

If you could pick just one advantage of the Internet over every other popular medium out there, that advantage would be its interactivity. We can communicate with users, customize their content, and most importantly, make sure that they can only see what they're supposed to see.

ASP.NET originally shipped with a fairly slick mechanism for identifying users, and it saved programmers a ton of work. Microsoft has taken this to a new level in ASP.NET v2.0 with the addition of the Membership programming interface. Now we can whip up a mechanism to register and manage users with little to no code in a matter of minutes.

Forms Authentication and Membership

The included forms authentication in v1.x of ASP.NET enables you to easily make a user appear logged in after you've verified his or her credentials. By simply calling the static method `FormsAuthentication.SetAuthCookie(string name, bool saveLogin)`, a cookie is set that enables you to identify the user by name.

This mechanism does not provide a way to check the user's credentials. You still need to create some kind of plumbing and database code to make it work. The ASP.NET team apparently felt that this was more work than you should have to do, and as a result they created the `Membership` class. This class, new to v2.0 of ASP.NET, has a number of static methods that manage user accounts either through a Microsoft SQL Server 2005 database or through some other means as dictated by a provider.

The provider model is a design pattern that puts a specific data access layer between a particular class and a data store. For Membership and other built-in capabilities of ASP.NET v2.0, Microsoft has chosen SQL Server 2005 Express (a free product) as the default data store. Aside from being free, one of the greatest benefits of this product is that it enables you to deploy a database as a file, enabling xcopy deployment. This is significantly easier than using import and export methods to get your data from one place to another.

If you have SQL Server 2005 Express installed, when you use these methods, a database is created and placed in the application's `/App_Data` folder by default, and it's named `ASPNetDB.mdf`. You don't need to do anything else—it's done and ready to go! Table 11.1 provides a brief overview of these methods. Check the .NET documentation for a full list of parameters and return values.

Table 11.1 Static methods of the `Membership` class

Method	Description
`CreateUser()`	Creates a new user in the data store. There are several overloads for this method.
`DeleteUser()`	Deletes a user from the data store. A second overload indicates whether associated user data should be deleted.
`FindUsersByEmail()`	Searches for users by email. A second overload enables the search results to be paged.
`FindUsersByName()`	Same as above, except that the search is conducted against names.
`GeneratePassword()`	A helper function to generate random passwords.
`GetAllUsers()`	The mother of all user data collections. As with the searches, it can be paged.
`GetNumberOfUsersOnline()`	Kind of a vanity function, but you can find out just how many users are on the site.
`GetUser()`	Returns a `MembershipUser` object. Overloads vary from getting the current logged in user to one indicated by name.
`GetUserNameByEmail()`	Does what the name implies.

Method	Description
UpdateUser()	Persists changes made to a MembershipUser object to the data store.
ValidateUser()	Checks user and password to find out if your user is legitimate.

The core of user data manipulation involves the MembershipUser class. This class acts as a bucket to tie your user's basic data together, with properties Comment, CreationDate, Email, IsApproved, LastActivityDate and LastPasswordChangedDate, and read-only properties IsOnline, PasswordQuestion, Provider (gets a reference to the underlying Membership provider), UserId, and UserName. It also has the methods ChangePassword(), ChangePasswordQuestionAndAnswer(), GetPassword(), and ResetPassword().

> The Membership system optionally uses a question-and-answer challenge to verify the identity of the user in the event that the user has lost his or her password. You've probably encountered this mechanism on some Web sites.
>
> One potentially negative aspect of the design of the Membership system is that it identifies users by name instead of email. Some believe that this is less than ideal because although your user name may vary from one site to another, your email address will always be unique. Chances are that two users may want to use the same name, but they'll never have the same email address.

ASP.NET v2.0 also has a role manager that will maintain user roles for you. Prior to this version you had to create your own plumbing, and create some means to assign roles to the user's Principal object on every request. Listing 8.7 did this for you by hitting the database (or the cache) from an HttpModule. So while that was a great example of an HttpModule, and very useful code in v1.x of ASP.NET, you won't need it if you're using v2.0 or later of ASP.NET. The Roles class, like the Membership class, has a number of static methods, shown in Table 11.2. Check the .NET documentation for a full list of parameters and return values.

Table 11.2 Static methods of the `Roles` class

Method	Description

`AddUsersToRole()`
`AddUsersToRoles()`
`AddUserToRole()`
`AddUserToRoles()`
	Adds users to roles in different quantities of each. The plural varieties take string arrays as parameters—i.e., `AddUserToRoles()` takes a user name string and an array of role name strings.

`CreateRole()`	Adds a role to the data store.
`DeleteCookie()`	Deletes the user's cookie used to cache roles.
`DeleteRole()`	Removes a role from the data store. An overload will throw an exception if users are still assigned to the role.
`FindUsersInRole()`	Returns a string array of users in a role.
`GetAllRoles()`	Returns a string array of all roles in the data store.
`GetRolesForUser()`	Returns a string array of roles for a user. Without a parameter, it uses the logged in user. You can also pass in a user name.
`GetUsersInRole()`	Returns a string array of users in a particular role.
`IsUserInRole()`	A lot like `User.IsInRole()`, but this version has an overload to look up a user by name.

`RemoveUserFromRole()`
`RemoveUserFromRoles()`
`RemoveUsersFromRole()`
`RemoveUsersFromRoles()`
	Deletes users from roles in different quantities of each. The plural varieties take string arrays as parameters—i.e., `RemoveUserFromRoles()` takes a user name string and an array of role name strings.

`RoleExists()`	An easy way to see if a role already exists in the data store.

The Built-in Membership Provider

You might be wondering how this "magic" works. As I mentioned earlier, the membership system uses a provider that ties these classes to a data store. In the case of the default provider, a SQL Server 2005 Express database is created, and data is stored there.

To configure the built-in SQL Server provider, called `System.Web.Security.SqlMembershipProvider`, you don't need to add anything to `web.config`, but you may have to specify that you're using Forms authentication. To use the built-in role management that works with the SQL database, you'll need to enable the role manager (the role manager is not "on" by default). At minimum then, your web.config file will need to include the elements shown in Listing 11.1.

Listing 11.1 The minimum web.config elements for Forms authentication and role management

```
<?xml version="1.0"?>
<configuration>
  <system.web>
    <authentication mode="Forms" />
    <roleManager enabled="true" />
  </system.web>
</configuration>
```

Beyond that, the methods found in Membership and Roles are so self-explanatory that I'll leave you to your own devices to explore them. A complete framework is created to manage users and their credentials without a single line of database plumbing on your part.

As a refresher, you'll recall that FormsAuthentication. SetAuthCookie(string name, bool saveLogin) does the actual work of causing a user to physically be logged into your site. Calling the User.Identity.Name property identifies the users, and User.Identity.IsAuthenticated checks if the user is logged in at all.

Role management is particularly useful because you can lock out users from entire folders or pages with simple additions to web.config, and you can redirect the users automatically to a login page. This great feature has been around since the beginning of ASP.NET, and it is demonstrated in Listing 11.2.

Listing 11.2 Specifying permissions on a folder by role from web.config

```
<?xml version="1.0"?>
<configuration>
  <system.web>
    <authentication mode="Forms">
      <forms loginUrl="login.aspx" />
    </authentication>
  </system.web>
  <location path="admin">
    <system.web>
```

(Continues)

Listing 11.2 Specifying permissions on a folder by role from `web.config` *(Continued)*

```
    <authorization>
      <allow roles="Admin" />
      <deny users="*" />
    </authorization>
  </system.web>
 </location>
</configuration>
```

This example shows that a folder in our application called "admin" can only be accessed by users in the role "Admin," while everyone else should be shut out. These rules are enforced one at a time, in sequence, until the user matches the criteria. By putting the `loginUrl` attribute in the `forms` tag of the `authentication` section, we indicate where a user should be directed when they try to go somewhere they shouldn't.

That's all you need to know to get the basics of using `Membership` and role management in your application. It does not replace Forms authentication from the previous versions of ASP.NET, but it does supplement it by taking care of all of this user housekeeping for you.

Because using a SQL Server 2005 Express database in the site's file system might not be ideal for you (because of its 4 gigabyte size limit or your use of a database on another server), Microsoft has provided a way to perform the very same `Membership` functions via an external SQL Server database. An easy-to-use wizard called `aspnet_regsql.exe`, found at `C:\WINDOWS\Microsoft.NET\Framework\v2.0.xxxx`, will take database connection information and create all the necessary database pieces for `Membership`, role management, and personalization. You won't have to mess with running SQL scripts at all.

To make the `SqlMembershipProvider` and role manager work in your application with an external database, you'll need to set `web.config` to include the settings in Listing 11.3 in addition to the previous entries mentioned. The key parts are a connection string that points to the database created with the wizard, the specification of the `SqlRoleProvider` in the `roleManager` element's `provider` section, and the specification of the `SqlMembershipProvider` in the `membership` element's `provider` section. We'll get deeper into this configuration when we build our own providers. Remember that if you use the default Express database, you don't need to make these settings at all because they're taken care of at the machine level.

Listing 11.3 Setting `web.config` to use the `SqlMembershipProvider`

```xml
<?xml version="1.0"?>
<configuration>
  <connectionStrings>
    <add name="SqlServices" connectionString="your string" />
  </connectionStrings>
  <system.web>
    <roleManager enabled="true" defaultProvider="SqlProvider">
      <providers>
        <add name="SqlProvider"
          type="System.Web.Security.SqlRoleProvider"
          connectionStringName="SqlServices" />
      </providers>
    </roleManager>
    <membership defaultProvider="SqlProvider"
      userIsOnlineTimeWindow="20">
      <providers>
        <add
          name="SqlProvider"
          type="System.Web.Security.SqlMembershipProvider"
          connectionStringName="SqlServices"
          applicationName="MyApplication"
          enablePasswordRetrieval="false"
          enablePasswordReset="true"
          requiresQuestionAndAnswer="true"
          requiresUniqueEmail="true"
          passwordFormat="Hashed" />
      </providers>
    </membership>
  </system.web>
</configuration>
```

Building Your Own Provider

The built-in SQL database functionality is adequate for most purposes. You may, however, want to build a provider for some other data store (such as a FoxPro database), or you might have your own existing database that you want to plug into this existing framework. Fortunately, the provider model enables you to pipe all of this `Membership` goodness into your own system by writing you own provider.

To write your own provider, you'll need to create a class that inherits from the abstract `System.Web.Security.MembershipProvider` class. Remember that you can't create an instance of an abstract class, only classes that derive from it. `MembershipProvider` has a number of abstract properties and methods, which means you have to implement these in order for the class to compile.

Your custom provider will sit between your data store and the `Membership` class, as shown in Figure 11.1. It will be configured for use in the same way we used the `SqlMembershipProvider` in Listing 11.3. Let's pretend that our data is stored in our own SQL Server database for the purpose of these code samples.

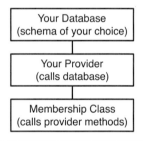

Figure 11.1 Tying Membership to the data store, with your provider in the middle.

We'll also need to create a class that inherits from the `RoleProvider` class, and we'll need to specify that it will manage roles via `web.config`.

Visual Studio makes the implementation of an abstract class fairly easy by helping you fill in the blanks quickly. Figure 11.2 shows how Intellisense pops up a list of methods when you type "`public override.`"

```
public class MyMembershipProvider : MembershipProvider
{
    public override |
    ApplicationName { get; set; }
    ChangePassword (string name, string oldPassword, string newPassword)
    ChangePasswordQuestionAndAnswer (string name, string password, string newPasswordQuestion
    CreateUser (string username, string password, string email, string passwordQuestion, string passw
    DeleteUser (string name, bool deleteAllRelatedData)
    EnablePasswordReset { get; }
    EnablePasswordRetrieval { get; }
    Equals (object obj)
    FindUsersByEmail (string emailToMatch, int pageIndex, int pageSize, out int totalRecords)
    FindUsersByName (string usernameToMatch, int pageIndex, int pageSize, out int totalRecords)
}
```

Figure 11.2 Filling in the blanks with Intellisense.

Note that you don't need to implement every one of these methods, as some are not abstract members. In fact, some are actually from classes further up the inheritance chain (such as the `Equals()` method, which comes from `object`). There are a total of 12 methods and five properties to implement, and we'll go through some of them briefly here, with code samples when necessary.

First let's establish the required properties. There are five of them, and all but `ApplicationName` are read-only. The `Name` property, if null, should return a name that reflects what your provider does. That makes the property section of our provider look something like Listing 11.4.

Listing 11.4 Properties in our derived `MembershipProvider`

C#
```
public class CustomMembershipProvider : MembershipProvider
{
  private string _applicationName;
  public override string ApplicationName
  {
    get { return _applicationName; }
    set { value = _applicationName; }
  }

  private bool _enablePasswordReset;
  public override bool EnablePasswordReset
  {
    get { return _enablePasswordReset; }
  }

  private bool _enablePasswordRetrieval;
  public override bool EnablePasswordRetrieval
  {
    get { return _enablePasswordRetrieval; }
  }

  private string _name;
  public override string Name
  {
    get
    {
      if (_name == null) return "MyMembershipProvider";
      return _name;
```

(Continues)

Listing 11.4 Properties in our derived `MembershipProvider` *(Continued)*

```
      }
   }

   private bool _requiresQuestionAndAnswer;
   public override bool RequiresQuestionAndAnswer
   {
      get { return _requiresQuestionAndAnswer; }
   }
}
```

VB.NET

```
Public Class CustomMembershipProvider
   Inherits MembershipProvider

   Private _applicationName As String
   Public Overrides Property ApplicationName() As String
      Get
         Return _applicationName
      End Get
      Set
         value = _applicationName
      End Set
   End Property

   Private _enablePasswordReset As Boolean
   Public Overrides ReadOnly Property EnablePasswordReset() As Boolean
      Get
         Return _enablePasswordReset
      End Get
   End Property

   Private _enablePasswordRetrieval As Boolean
   Public Overrides ReadOnly Property EnablePasswordRetrieval() As _
Boolean
      Get
         Return _enablePasswordRetrieval
      End Get
   End Property

   Private _name As String
   Public Overrides ReadOnly Property Name() As String
```

```
    Get
      If _name Is Nothing Then
        Return "MyMembershipProvider"
      End If
      Return _name
    End Get
  End Property

  Private _requiresQuestionAndAnswer As Boolean
  Public Overrides ReadOnly Property RequiresQuestionAndAnswer() As _
  Boolean
    Get
      Return _requiresQuestionAndAnswer
    End Get
  End Property
End Class
```

Now that we have a handle on the properties, let's flesh out the
required methods of our provider. The first one we'll need to write is
called `Initialize()`, and it's actually an abstract member in
`System.Configuration.Provider.ProviderBase`, the class that
`MembershipProvider` in turn inherits from. This method is used to populate our read-only properties that we established previously by reading
the matching values from `web.config`. Because the values from
`web.config` are strings, we'll also add a private helper method to interpret
Boolean values. The result is shown in Listing 11.5.

Listing 11.5 The `Initialize()` method of our derived `MembershipProvider`

C#
```csharp
public override void Initialize(string name, NameValueCollection config)
{
  _name = name;
  if (config["applicationName"] == null ||
config["applicationName"].Trim() == "")
  {
    _applicationName = HttpContext.Current.Request.ApplicationPath;
  }
  else
  {
```

(Continues)

Listing 11.5 The `Initialize()` method of our derived `MembershipProvider` *(Continued)*

```
  _applicationName = config["applicationName"];
  }
  _enablePasswordReset = GetBooleanValue(config["enablePasswordReset"],
true);
  _enablePasswordRetrieval =
GetBooleanValue(config["enablePasswordRetrieval"], true);
  _requiresQuestionAndAnswer =
GetBooleanValue(config["requiresQuestionAndAnswer"], false);
}

private bool GetBooleanValue(string configValue, bool defaultValue)
{
  if (configValue != null)
  {
    if (configValue.ToUpper() == "TRUE") { return true; }
    if (configValue.ToUpper() == "FALSE") { return false; }
  }
  return defaultValue;
}
```

VB.NET

```
Public Overrides Sub Initialize(name As String, _
  config As NameValueCollection)
  _name = name
  If config("applicationName") Is Nothing Or _
    config("applicationName").Trim() = "" Then
    _applicationName = HttpContext.Current.Request.ApplicationPath
  Else
    _applicationName = config("applicationName")
  End If
  _enablePasswordReset = _
    GetBooleanValue(config("enablePasswordReset"), True)
  _enablePasswordRetrieval = _
    GetBooleanValue(config("enablePasswordRetrieval"), True)
  _requiresQuestionAndAnswer = _
    GetBooleanValue(config("requiresQuestionAndAnswer"), False)
End Sub

Private Function GetBooleanValue(configValue As String, _
  defaultValue As Boolean) As Boolean
```

```
If Not (configValue Is Nothing) Then
  If configValue.ToUpper() = "TRUE" Then
    Return True
  End If
  If configValue.ToUpper() = "FALSE" Then
    Return False
  End If
End If
Return defaultValue
End Function
```

The `NameValueCollection` is found in the `System.`
`Collections.Specialized` namespace, and as such, you may
need the proper `using/Imports` statements if you don't call it by
its fully qualified name.

If you jump back a moment to the `web.config` in Listing 11.3, you'll notice a number of attributes in the `add` element where we add a provider to the application. The attributes `requiresUniqueEmail` and `passwordFormat` are specific to the `SqlMembershipProvider`, so we don't have to implement those here (unless we want to). We'll still need to get the other five values and assign them to our properties though, and that's what the `Initialize()` method does. The `name` string parameter corresponds to the name we give the provider in `web.config`, while the `NameValueCollection` parameter `config` gets the rest of the values. Because the values are strings and some of our properties are Boolean, we use the private helper method `GetBooleanValue()` to convert the string to an all-uppercase value and interpret it as true or false, or return a default value we supply.

Other methods need to speak the language of the `Membership` class. For example, `GetUser()` must return a `MembershipUser` object, so you'll need to write some plumbing code to convert your data to this expected format. In fact, you'll need to do the same thing for several other methods (such as `GetAllUsers()`), so a helper method that converts the contents of a `SqlDataReader` to a `MembershipUser` object is just what you'll need. That method and `GetUser()` are demonstrated in Listing 11.6.

Listing 11.6 The `GetUser()` method of our derived `MembershipProvider`, with the helper method `PopulateMembershipUser()`

C#

```csharp
public override MembershipUser GetUser(string name, bool userIsOnline)
{
  MembershipUser user;
  SqlConnection connection = new
SqlConnection(ConfigurationSettings.ConnectionStrings["SqlServices"].
ConnectionString);
  SqlCommand command = new SqlCommand("SELECT * FROM MyUsers WHERE Name
= @Name", connection);
  command.Parameters.AddWithValue("@Name", name);
  SqlDataReader reader = command.ExecuteReader();
  if (reader.Read()) user = PopulateMembershipUser(reader);
  else throw new Exception("User not found");
  reader.Close();
  if (userIsOnline)
  {
    command.CommandText = "UPDATE MyUsers SET LastActivity =
@LastActivity WHERE Name = @Name";
    command.Parameters.AddWithValue("@LastActivity", DateTime.Now);
    command.ExecuteNonQuery();
  }
  connection.Close();
  return user;
}

private MembershipUser PopulateMembershipUser(SqlDataReader reader)
{
  return new MembershipUser(this, reader["Name"].ToString(),
    Convert.ToInt32(reader["ID"]), reader["Email"].ToString(),
    reader["PasswordQ"].ToString(), reader["Comment"].ToString(),
    Convert.ToBoolean(reader["Approved"]),
    Convert.ToDateTime(reader["SignedUp"]),
    Convert.ToDateTime(reader["LastLogin"]),
    Convert.ToDateTime(reader["LastActivity"]),
    Convert.ToDateTime(reader["LastPasswordChange"]));
}
```

VB.NET

```vbnet
Public Overrides Function GetUser(name As String, _
  userIsOnline As Boolean) As MembershipUser
```

```
    Dim user As MembershipUser
    Dim connection As New _
SqlConnection(ConfigurationSettings.ConnectionStrings("SqlServices").
ConnectionString)
    Dim command As New SqlCommand(_
       "SELECT * FROM MyUsers WHERE Name = @Name", connection)
    command.Parameters.AddWithValue("@Name", name)
    Dim reader As SqlDataReader = command.ExecuteReader()
    If reader.Read() Then
       user = PopulateMembershipUser(reader)
    Else
       Throw New Exception("User not found")
    End If
    reader.Close()
    If userIsOnline Then
       command.CommandText = _
       "UPDATE MyUsers SET LastActivity = @LastActivity WHERE Name =
@Name"
       command.Parameters.AddWithValue("@LastActivity", DateTime.Now)
       command.ExecuteNonQuery()
    End If
    connection.Close()
    Return user
End Function

Private Function PopulateMembershipUser(reader As SqlDataReader) _
    As MembershipUser
    Return New MembershipUser(Me, reader("Name").ToString(),_
       Convert.ToInt32(reader("ID")), reader("Email").ToString(), _
       reader("PasswordQ").ToString(), _
       reader("Comment").ToString(), _
       Convert.ToBoolean(reader("Approved")), _
       Convert.ToDateTime(reader("SignedUp")), _
       Convert.ToDateTime(reader("LastLogin")), _
       Convert.ToDateTime(reader("LastActivity")), _
       Convert.ToDateTime(reader("LastPasswordChange"))))
End Function
```

The method starts by naming a MembershipUser variable that we'll return at the end of the method. This implementation of the GetUsers() method assumes that we have a table in our database called "MyUsers" and that it has columns named in the helper method called

`PopulateMembershipUser()`. The first step is to create our typical connection and command objects, pass in a parameter to the command object with a name to match (specified in the method's `name` parameter), and finally execute a `SqlDataReader`. If a record is returned, checked by the reader's `Read()` method, we pass the reader to the helper method, which takes the values of the reader and returns them in a new `MembershipUser` object. One of the constructors of the `MembershipUser` class takes all of those values as parameters to populate the object, and that's what our helper method uses.

`GetUser()` has another parameter, the Boolean `userIsOnline`, which according to the documentation is intended to cause the user's "last activity" date stamp to be updated in your data store. Because we track this data in our fictitious database, we'll update that column on the same record if the parameter is true. We're using the same connection and the same command objects because they already exist. The `@Name` parameter we added to the command object when we retrieved the user data is still in the collection, so to update the record, we need only pass in an extra parameter for the new date stamp.

At the end of the method, we return the `MembershipUser` object that our helper method returned. We've successfully implemented one method in our derived `MembershipProvider`! When your custom provider is configured, calling the static method `Membership.GetUser("Jeff")` from your application will in turn call the code from your provider. If you ever change the data store, you'll only need to change the code in your custom provider, not the code that looks up users. This illustrates our tiered application model from Chapter 4, "Application Architecture."

Let's try another one. `UpdateUser()` takes a `MembershipUser` object as a parameter, so in many ways it's the opposite of the `GetUser()` method. We'll take the properties of the `MembershipUser` that aren't read-only and persist those to the database. Listing 11.7 shows this code.

Listing 11.7 The `UpdateUser()` method of our derived `MembershipProvider`

C#
```
public override void UpdateUser(MembershipUser user)
{
  SqlConnection connection = new
SqlConnection(ConfigurationSettings.ConnectionStrings["myConnection"].
ConnectionString);
  string sql = "UPDATE MyUsers SET Comment = @Comment, "
```

```
   + "SignedUp = @SignedUp, Email = @Email, Approved = @Approved, "
   + "LastLogin = @LastLogin, LastActivity = @LastActivity, "
   + "LastPasswordChange = @LastPasswordChange WHERE Name = @Name";
 SqlCommand command = new SqlCommand(sql, connection);
 command.Parameters.AddWithValue("@Comment", user.Comment);
 command.Parameters.AddWithValue("@SignedUp", user.CreationDate);
 command.Parameters.AddWithValue("@Email", user.Email);
 command.Parameters.AddWithValue("@Approved", user.IsApproved);
 command.Parameters.AddWithValue("@LastLogin", user.LastLoginDate);
 command.Parameters.AddWithValue("@LastActivity",
user.LastActivityDate);
 command.Parameters.AddWithValue("@LastPasswordChange",
user.LastPasswordChangedDate);
 command.Parameters.AddWithValue("@Name", name);
 command.ExecuteNonQuery();
 connection.Close();
}
```

VB.NET

```
Public Overrides Sub UpdateUser(user As MembershipUser)
 Dim connection As New
SqlConnection(ConfigurationSettings.ConnectionStrings("myConnection").
ConnectionString)
 Dim sql As String = "UPDATE MyUsers SET Comment = @Comment, "
   + "SignedUp = @SignedUp, Email = @Email, Approved = @Approved, "
   + "LastLogin = @LastLogin, LastActivity = @LastActivity, "
   + "LastPasswordChange = @LastPasswordChange WHERE Name = @Name"
 Dim command As New SqlCommand(sql, connection)
 command.Parameters.AddWithValue("@Comment", user.Comment)
 command.Parameters.AddWithValue("@SignedUp", user.CreationDate)
 command.Parameters.AddWithValue("@Email", user.Email)
 command.Parameters.AddWithValue("@Approved", user.IsApproved)
 command.Parameters.AddWithValue("@LastLogin", user.LastLoginDate)
 command.Parameters.AddWithValue("@LastActivity",
user.LastActivityDate)
 command.Parameters.AddWithValue("@LastPasswordChange",
user.LastPasswordChangedDate)
 command.Parameters.AddWithValue("@Name", name)
 command.ExecuteNonQuery()
 connection.Close()
End Sub
```

You have probably written data access code like this many times before. The only thing that's perhaps unique here is that the parameters you're passing in are properties of the `MembershipUser` parameter of the method. Calling `Membership.UpdateUser(someMembershipUser)` will call the method in your provider. Again, changing the data store means changing the provider, while any code that calls the static `Membership` methods need not be modified.

The end result of all this is that the same code can get and modify user data, regardless of whether you use the Access, SQL Server, or a custom provider. The code in Listing 11.8 works exactly the same for every provider, as long as the code in the provider does what the method description indicates it should do.

One feature we did not use here in our custom `Membership` provider was the `ApplicationName` property as it relates to our own data store. If we were to use the same database for multiple applications, we could use the value from `ApplicationName` as the connection between our data and the specific application. The default database could be used for any number of different applications because user records are marked with the application name.

Listing 11.8 Using provider-neutral code with the `Membership` class

C#
```
MembershipUser user = Membership.GetUser("Jeff");
user.Email = "new@address.com";
Membership.UpdateUser(user);
```

VB.NET
```
Dim user As MembershipUser = Membership.GetUser("Jeff")
user.Email = "new@address.com"
Membership.UpdateUser(user)
```

We won't go through every method in `MembershipProvider`, but between the method names and descriptions in the documentation, it should be fairly obvious what each method should do. Remember that you'll also need to implement a class that inherits from `RoleProvider` to pipe the `Roles` class methods to your data store.

After you have your custom providers for Membership and Roles ready to go, add the correct elements to `web.config`, as in Listing 11.9.

Listing 11.9 Setting `web.config` to use your custom providers

```xml
<?xml version="1.0"?>
<configuration>
  <system.web>
    <roleManager enabled="true" defaultProvider="CustomRoleProvider">
      <providers>
        <add name="CustomRoleProvider"
          type="MyRoleProvider, MyAssembly" />
      </providers>
    </roleManager>
    <membership defaultProvider="CustomMembershipProvider">
      <providers>
        <add
          name="CustomMembershipProvider"
          type="MyMembershipProvider, MyAssembly"
          applicationName="MyApplication"
          enablePasswordRetrieval="false"
          enablePasswordReset="true"
          requiresQuestionAndAnswer="true" />
      </providers>
    </membership>
  </system.web>
</configuration>
```

There are some differences here when using a custom provider. First off, notice that we didn't specify a connection string. Your implementation doesn't need to pass in a connection string via the provider declaration in `web.config`. Your implementation may specify a connection string directly (as we did in Listings 11.6 and 11.7), or it may not need to specify a connection string at all if your provider in turn gets its data from some other data access classes.

We also must specify the assembly where we'll find the custom providers. Notice in the `add` elements for both the `membership` and `roleManager` sections that we specify the class name followed by the assembly name in the `type` attribute. The assembly should of course be compiled and ready in the `/bin` folder of the application. If the class is not compiled and exists as a class file in the `/App_Code` folder, you need not specify the assembly.

Authentication Controls

As impressive as the `Membership` and `Roles` classes are, ASP.NET v2.0 also ships with a number of authentication controls that make life easier by helping you manipulate user data and page elements based on the providers.

The first and arguably most useful of the authentication controls is the `Login` control. This is a composite control that takes user name and password input to authenticate and log in a user. Under the covers, it calls `Membership.ValidateUser()`, and if the user input matches the values in the data store (as determined by the `MembershipProvider`), `FormsAuthentication.SetAuthCookie()` is called, and the user is logged in.

This composite control is rendered by placing just one control in your page with `<asp:Login ID="Login1" Runat="server" />`. A vast array of properties enables you to customize everything from the text to the colors and validation. Everything else is taken care of for you. Figure 11.3 shows the rendered control in the browser.

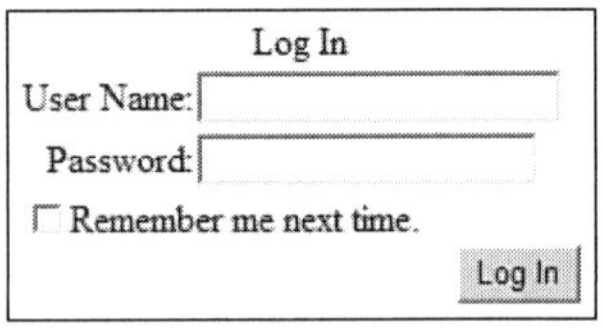

Figure 11.3 The `Login` control as rendered in the browser.

The `LoginName` control simply outputs the name of the currently logged in user. Displaying it in the page requires only `<asp:LoginName ID="LoginName1" Runat="server" />`. It has a `FormatString` property that will let you add in extra text. If no user is logged in, it doesn't display anything.

The `LoginStatus` control is basically the counterpart of the `Login` control. It's added to the page with `<asp:LoginStatus ID="LoginStatus1" Runat="server" />`. When a user is not logged in, it provides a link to the login page specified in the `loginUrl` attribute of the `forms` element (located within the `authentication` section) of `web.config`. When the user is logged in, it provides a `LinkButton` that says "Logout" that will call `FormsAuthentication.SignOut()` and remove the auth cookie of the user. This control also has a number of properties that enable you to alter the text and style of the rendered elements.

The `LoginView` control uses templates to display content based on the user's login status or role. This is useful to show a user only the content that he or she should see. Listing 11.10 shows how straightforward this control is to use.

Listing 11.10 Using the `LoginView` control

```
<asp:LoginView ID="LoginView1" Runat="server">
  <AnonymousTemplate>
    Unknown user
  </AnonymousTemplate>
  <LoggedInTemplate>
    Logged in user
  </LoggedInTemplate>
  <RoleGroups>
    <asp:RoleGroup Roles="Admin">
      <ContentTemplate>A user in the Admin role</ContentTemplate>
    </asp:RoleGroup>
    <asp:RoleGroup Roles="Moderator">
      <ContentTemplate>A user in the Moderator role</ContentTemplate>
    </asp:RoleGroup>
  </RoleGroups>
</asp:LoginView>
```

The `PasswordRecovery` control is probably the most complex of the bunch but also the most powerful. This control provides user interface elements that enable the user to change or receive his or her password by email, depending on the settings of the provider. In the first step, it asks for the user's name. In the second step, it asks for the answer to the user's question, if it's enabled. The third part is a confirmation that the password was sent or reset, again depending on the values set for the `MembershipProvider`.

Summary

The Membership system, new to ASP.NET v2.0, provides an easy way for programmers to manage user data. A well-documented API of static methods and classes enables us to manipulate user data without worrying about the underlying data store. ASP.NET by default provides a Microsoft Access database to store this data.

The provider model creates an abstraction layer between the `Membership` and `Roles` classes and a data store. This means that programmers can always use these familiar classes, but they can still alter the underlying data access to suit their needs. With classes derived from the abstract `MembershipProvider` and `RoleProvider` classes, these custom providers can be specified for use in place of the default provider that uses an Access database. Configuration is a simple matter of altering the `web.config` file.

Several ready-to-use server controls are available to largely automate the process of identifying registered users. These controls can be declaratively used within a page with little to no programming necessary.

CHAPTER 12

Profiles, Themes, and Skins

Membership solves the common problem of storing basic information about our users and authenticating them. What it does not do is store other details about users, such as their favorite color or their birthday. Fortunately, the profile system in ASP.NET v2.0 makes it easy to store data in the same database or in your own data store with your own provider.

Profiles in Relation to Membership Records

As you learned in Chapter 11, "Membership and Security," the Membership system only stores basic user data for the purpose of authenticating a user. The realm of storing other data is a huge area to cover, as different applications have different needs. Fortunately, the Profile system will store whatever data you need, as configured by your `web.config` file. Using the default `System.Web.Profile.SqlProfileProvider` class, ASP.NET will store this data in the very same database used to store Membership data by default.

> The same auto-generated SQL Server 2005 Express database used by `SqlMembershipProvider` is used by this provider and created in the `/App_Data` folder. As before, you can use the `aspnet_regsql.exe` utility to generate this database at another location.

Let's first look at the use of the `Profile` property without consideration for the underlying data store. This property is of the type `HttpProfileBase` and is a property of the `HttpContext` class (just like `Request`, `Response`, `Session`, and `Cache`, among others). The properties that are in turn available from Profile are generated at runtime (and design time, in Visual Studio) by reading them from web.config. Listing 12.1 shows a sample <profile> section from web.config.

Listing 12.1 The <profile> section of web.config

```
<?xml version="1.0" ?>
<configuration>
  <system.web>
    <profile defaultProvider="CustomProvider">
      <providers>
        <add name="CustomProvider" type="CustomProvider, MyAssembly" />
      </providers>
      <properties>
        <add name="Happy" type="System.Boolean" />
        <add name="HairColor" type="System.String" />
      </properties>
    </profile>
  </system.web>
</configuration>
```

This very basic configuration creates two properties that we'll be able to set from code. The first one is called "Happy" and is of type Boolean, while the second one is called "HairColor" and is a string. Properties are listed between the properties elements. The providers that take care of the data plumbing are listed between the providers elements (more on providers in a minute). Figure 12.1 shows what happens in Visual Studio when we type a period after Profile.

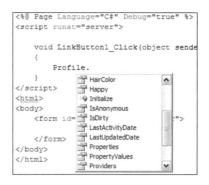

Figure 12.1 Intellisense showing our Profile properties.

You can see that the two properties we declared in web.config appear for us, and because they're strongly typed, we know by mousing over the property that it's a Boolean or string (or whatever we declared it to be). When we try to read one of these properties, the provider tries to fetch the profile values from the database. After we change them, they are saved when we call Profile.Save().

In the profile element, we name a default provider, which must appear in the following providers section. The default SqlProfileProvider is assumed if you don't specify one.

If you'd like to further group your properties together, you can do so by enclosing them in a group. If you wanted to set up Profile.Pets.CatName, for example, you would set web.config as shown in Listing 12.2.

Listing 12.2 Grouping Profile properties

```xml
<?xml version="1.0" ?>
<configuration>
  <system.web>
    <profile>
      <properties>
        <add name="Happy" type="System.Boolean" />
        <add name="HairColor" type="System.String" />
        <group name="Pets">
          <add name="CatName" type="System.String" />
        </group>
      </properties>
    </profile>
  </system.web>
</configuration>
```

Profile data is tied to the logged in user, as identified by User.Identity.Name. If you try to get profile data when no user is logged in and you aren't allowing for anonymous identification (more on that in a minute), you'll get an exception.

The profile system can also persist anonymous user data that's associated with the user's browser. By adding <anonymousIdentification enabled="true" /> between the <system.web> elements, a cookie is sent to the user for identification. Any properties that have their allowAnonymous attribute set to true will then be saved, and you won't get the error we described. In these cases, the user data is associated

with the string set in the cookie (a `Guid`, actually) instead of
`User.Identity.Name`. Listing 12.3 shows the `Profile.Pets.CatName`
configured for anonymous use.

Listing 12.3 Enabling anonymous identification and profile properties

```
<?xml version="1.0" ?>
<configuration>
  <system.web>
    <anonymousIdentification enabled="true" />
    <profile>
      <properties>
        <group name="Pets">
          <add name="CatName" type="System.String"
          allowAnonymous="true" />
        </group>
      </properties>
    </profile>
  </system.web>
</configuration>
```

> There are several other attributes that you can place in the
> `anonymousIdentification` tag that determine how the cookie
> is handled. Please consult the ASP.NET documentation for more
> information.

If you want a specific provider to handle a particular property, simply
add a `provider` attribute to the `add` element and set it to the name of the
provider in the `providers` section. This is a really useful feature because
you can mix and match providers to handle data in different ways, poten-
tially from totally separate data sources. For example, if `CatName` is handled by one provider but `CarType` would be handled by a different
provider, you would add lines like this between the `properties` (or
`group`) elements:

```
<add name="CatName" type="System.String"
provider="MyAnimalProvider" />
<add name="CarType" type="System.String"
provider="MyVehicleProvider" />
```

Profile's provider mechanism works just like Membership's does. An underlying class handles the plumbing between the class you use and the data store. In the case of the default `SqlProfileProvider`, profile data is stored in the default database or the database you specify as a combination of strings and binary objects, serializing the data as needed. The `add` elements in the `<profile>` section have an optional `serializeAs` attribute, which can be set to `Binary`, `String`, `Xml`, or `ProviderSpecific`. The first three will format the data as their names suggest, while the last will rely on the underlying provider to make the decision. Your own custom providers may choose to ignore this setting entirely, but that's up to you.

Building Your Own Profile Provider

The Membership and Profile systems are undoubtedly something you'll want to use on new projects as is. They'll save you a ton of work because they handle the grunt work of managing user data. There will be times, however, when you have specific needs or existing data that you'd like to use in the context of these systems. That's why ASP.NET enables you to write your own providers. Let's walk through an example of a custom Profile provider to match our Membership provider.

Just as our custom Membership provider had to inherit from and implement members of an abstract class, our custom Profile provider will do the same, this time using `System.Web.Profile.ProfileProvider` as the base. This provider, however, only has two properties, `Name` and `ApplicationName`. It also has an `Initialize()` method like the Membership provider. Listing 12.4 shows the two properties and the `Initialize()` method.

> If you're curious about the lineage of these providers, they do share some common ground. `ProfileProvider` inherits from `System.Configuration.SettingsProvider`, which in turn inherits from `System.Configuration.Provider.ProviderBase`. `MembershipProvider` inherits directly from `ProviderBase`. You can see by looking at the "roots" of the class where they get their members.

Listing 12.4 The two required properties and `Initialize()` method of our Profile provider

C#

```csharp
public class CustomProfileProvider : ProfileProvider
{
  public override void Initialize(string name, NameValueCollection
config)
  {
    _name = name;
    if (config["applicationName"] == null ||
config["applicationName"].Trim() == "")
    {
      _applicationName = HttpContext.Current.Request.ApplicationPath;
    }
    else
    {
      _applicationName = config["applicationName"];
    }
  }

  private string _name;
  public override string Name
  {
    get { return _name; }
  }

  private string _applicationName;
  public override string ApplicationName
  {
    get { return _applicationName; }
    set { _applicationName = value; }
  }
}
```

VB.NET

```vbnet
Public Class CustomProfileProvider
  Inherits ProfileProvider

  Public Overrides Sub Initialize(name As String, _
config As NameValueCollection)
    _name = name
    If config("applicationName") Is Nothing Or _
config("applicationName").Trim() = "" Then
      _applicationName = HttpContext.Current.Request.ApplicationPath
```

```
      Else
        _applicationName = config("applicationName")
      End If
   End Sub

   Private _name As String
   Public Overrides ReadOnly Property Name() As String
      Get
         Return _name
      End Get
   End Property

   Private _applicationName As String
   Public Overrides Property ApplicationName() As String
      Get
         Return _applicationName
      End Get
      Set
         _applicationName = value
      End Set
   End Property
End Class
```

If this code looks familiar to you, that's probably because it isn't that different from the humble start of our custom Membership class in Listing 11.5. The difference here is that we don't have the extra properties to deal with. We set the properties in the Initialize() method, where Name is still read-only and comes from web.config, while ApplicationName is still determined by the path of the application or the application name.

> As with the custom Membership provider we created in Chapter 11, we aren't going to make use of the ApplicationName here. As with Membership, this property can be used to associate profile data with a specific application in a shared database.

> We could provide a connection string property here as well, similar again to those used in Membership providers. The same principles apply when passing in values via attributes in the web.config provider add elements, setting them up in the provider itself via the Initialize() method.

We need to be concerned about two primary methods to get data in and out of our data store. `GetPropertyValues()` pulls data out of the store, while `SetPropertyValues()` persists them when `Profile.Save()` is called.

`GetPropertyValues()` takes a `System.Configuration.SettingsContext` object and a `System.Configuration.SettingsPropertyCollection` object as parameters and returns a `System.Configuration.SettingsPropertyValueCollection`. This returned collection is used by the `Profile` property to return property values. Let's sort these out, one at a time.

The `SettingsContext` object is derived from `Hashtable` and contains two key-value pairs. The first value is "UserName," which not surprisingly is a string of the name of the user whose profile we want to retrieve. The second value, "IsAuthenticated," is a Boolean and indicates what the name implies. The temptation here is to not look up profile data if the user isn't authenticated, but keep in mind that you can load any user's profile data into an `HttpProfile` object using `Profile.GetProfile()`. If anonymous identification is enabled (as in Listing 12.3), you may want to store and retrieve anonymous user data. If the user is not authenticated and a call is made to the anonymous user's profile, the "UserName" value returned is a Guid (in string form) used to identify the anonymous user.

The `SettingsPropertyCollection` is, believe it or not, a collection of `SettingsProperty` objects. The method will get one of these objects for every property you declared in `web.config`. If your provider is configured as the default provider, then any property not specifically set to use another provider (with the `provider` attribute) will be in this collection. If it's not the default provider, then only those properties specified to use your provider will be in the collection. Grouped properties will have a name like the one you'd use in the calling code. In our previous grouping example, calling for `Profile.Pets.CatName` would correspond to a `SettingsProperty` object with the name "Pets.CatName" here.

The `SettingsPropertyValueCollection` object should return a collection of `SettingsPropertyValue` objects, one for each of the `SettingsProperty` objects passed in to the method.

Now that you're familiar with the parameters and return value for `GetPropertyValues()`, you need to make some design decisions. You'll need to decide if your provider will be capable of storing any property you specify in `web.config`, or if it will handle only properties you specify. The default SQL provider does a good job of accommodating any property, so duplicating that functionality is a lot like reinventing the wheel. Chances are that if you're writing a custom provider, you've got very specific needs in mind, and therefore you only need to handle specific properties.

In case you're wondering, the default SQL provider stores the data in a single row for a particular user. In the `aspnet_Profile` table, the UserId column references an entry in the `aspnet_Users` table (where the name of the user, or Guid as a string for anonymous users, is stored). Two columns hold the actual property values, `PropertyValuesString` and `PropertyValuesBinary`, which store strings and binary values, respectively. The `PropertyNames` column stores the property name, a flag indicating whether the value is stored as a string or binary object, the starting position of the property value in either the `PropertyValuesString` or `PropertyValuesBinary` columns, and the length of the value. So if we had a binary property called "Test" and a string value called "Age," the `PropertyNames` column would say:

`Test:B:0:40:Age:S:0:2`

`PropertyValuesString` would say something like "21" for the age (causing the length of "2" in `PropertyNames`), and `PropertyValuesBinary` would have some binary value for test that was 40 bytes long.

Let's assume we're only going to return values for specific properties, namely those we set up in Listing 12.1. "Happy" and "HairColor" are two data items associated with a particular user's profile data. Our profile database table in SQL Server has three columns: Name (nvarchar), Happy (bit), and HairColor (nvarchar). We'll match up these database values with our properties, as shown in Listing 12.5, our complete `GetPropertyValues()` method. Depending on your needs, you may want to store additional data such as a DateTime that indicates when the profile data was updated or accessed. These are handy when implementing other members in the provider, as we'll see later.

Listing 12.5 Our `GetPropertyValues()` method

C#

```
public override SettingsPropertyValueCollection
GetPropertyValues(SettingsContext context, SettingsPropertyCollection
ppc)
{
  if ((bool)context["IsAuthenticated"] == false) throw new
Exception("Anonymous profile data is not supported by this Profile
Provider.");
  SettingsPropertyValueCollection settings = new
SettingsPropertyValueCollection();
  SqlConnection connection = new SqlConnection("my connection string");
  Connection.Open();
  SqlCommand command = new SqlCommand("SELECT Happy, HairColor FROM
ProfileData WHERE Name = @Name", connection);
  command.Parameters.AddWithValue("@Name",
context["UserName"].ToString());
  SqlDataReader reader = command.ExecuteReader();
  bool dataAvailable = false;
  if (reader.Read()) dataAvailable = true
  foreach (SettingsProperty property in ppc)
  {
    SettingsPropertyValue value = new
SettingsPropertyValue(ppc[property.Name]);
    switch (property.Name)
    {
      case "Happy":
        if (dataAvailable) value.PropertyValue = reader.GetBoolean(0);
        else value.PropertyValue = false;
        break;
      case "HairColor":
        if (dataAvailable) value.PropertyValue = reader.GetString(1);
        else value.PropertyValue = "";
        break;
      default:
        throw new Exception("This profile provider doesn't process the
\"" + property.Name
        + "\" profile property.");
    }
    settings.Add(value);
  }
  reader.Close();
```

```
    connection.Close();
    return settings;
}
```

VB.NET

```
Public Overrides Function GetPropertyValues(context As SettingsContext,_
ppc As SettingsPropertyCollection) As SettingsPropertyValueCollection
    If CBool(context("IsAuthenticated")) = False Then
        Throw New Exception("Anonymous profile data is not supported by this
Profile Provider.")
    End If
    Dim settings As New SettingsPropertyValueCollection()
    Dim connection As New SqlConnection("my connection string")
    Connection.Open()
    Dim command As New _
SqlCommand("SELECT Happy, HairColor FROM ProfileData WHERE Name=@Name",_
connection)
    command.Parameters.AddWithValue("@Name", _
context("UserName").ToString())
    Dim reader As SqlDataReader = command.ExecuteReader()
    Dim dataAvailable As Boolean = False
    If reader.Read() Then
        dataAvailable = True
    End If
    Dim property As SettingsProperty
    For Each property In  ppc
        Dim value As New SettingsPropertyValue(ppc([property].Name))
        Select Case [property].Name
            Case "Happy"
                If dataAvailable Then
                    value.PropertyValue = reader.GetBoolean(0)
                Else
                    value.PropertyValue = False
                End If
            Case "HairColor"
                If dataAvailable Then
                    value.PropertyValue = reader.GetString(1)
                Else
                    value.PropertyValue = ""
                End If
            Case Else
                Throw New _
Exception("This profile provider doesn't process the """ + _
[property].Name + """ profile property.")
```

(Continues)

Listing 12.5 Our `GetPropertyValues()` method   *(Continued)*

```
    End Select
    settings.Add(value)
  Next property
  reader.Close()
  connection.Close()
  Return settings
End Function
```

At first glance, it looks like there's a lot going on here, but there's not. The method starts by checking the value of the "IsAuthenticated" item in the context hash, and if it's false, it throws an exception. Remember that we decided not to persist anonymous data with our provider.

Next we declare a `SettingsPropertyValueCollection` object, which is where we'll put all the values we want to return.

The next bit is typical SQL code that looks for the profile data from our database, based on the "UserName" string passed in via the settings context. It's possible that the user may not have any profile data stored yet, so we create a test with the `SqlDataReader`'s `Read()` method.

Finally we loop through the `SettingsProperty` objects passed in via the `SettingsPropertyCollection` parameter. First we create the `SettingsPropertyValue` object, based on the `SettingsProperty` that we're going to add to the returning `SettingsPropertyValueCollection`. For each object, we'll run a `switch` (`Select` in **VB.NET**) block to determine which property we're dealing with. For each match, we'll assign the value from the database if our `Read()` test was successful; otherwise we'll assign a default value. If the property name doesn't match any of our cases, we'll throw an exception indicating that our provider doesn't handle the particular profile property. As long as one of the items in the switch block is called, we'll add the new `SettingsPropertyValue` object to our `SettingsPropertyValueCollection`. When we're done, we close our data connection and return the new collection. This method now acts as the plumbing between our `Profile` property and our data store.

`SetPropertyValues()` should do nearly the same thing, only in reverse. It acts as the plumbing when the `Save()` method of the `HttpProfile` object is called. Perhaps the biggest difference is that we'll delete the user's old profile data before saving the new data. This method has no return value, but it again has the `SettingsContext` object and this time a `SettingsPropertyValueCollection` as parameters. The code is shown in Listing 12.6.

Listing 12.6 Our `SetPropertyValues()` method

C#

```csharp
public override void SetPropertyValues(SettingsContext context,
SettingsPropertyValueCollection ppvc)
{
  SqlConnection connection = new SqlConnection("my connection string");
  connection.Open();
  SqlCommand command = new
SqlCommand("DELETE FROM ProfileData WHERE Name = @Name", connection);
  command.Parameters.AddWithValue("@Name",
context["UserName"].ToString());
  command.ExecuteNonQuery();
  command.CommandText = "INSERT INTO ProfileData "
+ "(Name, Happy, HairColor) VALUES (@Name, @Happy, @HairColor)";
  foreach (SettingsPropertyValue propertyvalue in ppvc)
  {
    switch (propertyvalue.Name)
    {
      case "Happy":
        command.Parameters.AddWithValue("@Happy",
(bool)propertyvalue.PropertyValue);
        break;
      case "HairColor":
        command.Parameters.AddWithValue("@HairColor",
(string)propertyvalue.PropertyValue);
        break;
      default:
        throw new Exception("This profile provider doesn't process the
\"" + propertyvalue.Name
        + "\" profile property.");
    }
  }
  command.ExecuteNonQuery();
  connection.Close();
}
```

VB.NET

```vbnet
Public Overrides Sub SetPropertyValues(context As SettingsContext, ppvc
As SettingsPropertyValueCollection)
  Dim connection As New SqlConnection("my connection string")
  connection.Open()
  Dim command As New _
SqlCommand("DELETE FROM ProfileData WHERE Name = @Name", connection)
```

(Continues)

Listing 12.6 Our `SetPropertyValues()` method   *(Continued)*

```
  command.Parameters.AddWithValue("@Name",
context("UserName").ToString())
  command.ExecuteNonQuery()
  command.CommandText = "INSERT INTO ProfileData (Name, Happy, HairColor)
VALUES (@Name, @Happy, @HairColor)"
  Dim propertyvalue As SettingsPropertyValue
  For Each propertyvalue In  ppvc
    Select Case propertyvalue.Name
      Case "Happy"
        command.Parameters.AddWithValue("@Happy",
CBool(propertyvalue.PropertyValue))
      Case "HairColor"
        command.Parameters.AddWithValue("@HairColor",
CStr(propertyvalue.PropertyValue))
      Case Else
        Throw New Exception("This profile provider doesn't process the
""" + propertyvalue.Name + """ profile property.")
    End Select
  Next propertyvalue
  command.ExecuteNonQuery()
  connection.Close()
End Sub
```

This method is a bit more straightforward. As before, our user is identified by the "UserName" value in the `SettingsContext` hash. First we delete any profile data for the user. We could also look for existing data, and if it exists, perform an UPDATE instead of an INSERT, but this requires an extra step if the data does not already exist. Next we create the command that will insert the data and add parameters to our command object by looping through the `SettingsPropertyValueCollection`. We get the new value from the `SettingsPropertyValue` objects' `PropertyValue` properties. (Is that enough use of the word "property?") When we're done, we execute the command and clean up our connection.

The remaining methods to implement in the provider get or delete profile data. These methods act as the plumbing under the static methods of the `ProfileManager` class. Most of these methods use `ProfileInfo` objects grouped in `ProfileInfoCollection` objects.

The `ProfileInfo` class does not contain any of the actual profile data, but it does contain several properties that describe it: `IsAnonymous` (Boolean), `LastActivityDate` (DateTime), `LastUpdatedDate`

(DateTime), Size (Int32), and UserName (String). The class is little more than a container class, so you're free to populate whichever properties you want. Instances of the class can be added to a ProfileInfoCollection object in the same way as most other collections, using its Add() method. Listing 12.7 shows a simple example of manipulating these two objects.

Listing 12.7 Using `ProfileInfo` with `ProfileInfoCollection`

C#
```
ProfileInfoCollection pic = new ProfileInfoCollection();
ProfileInfo info = new ProfileInfo();
info.UserName = "Jeff";
info.LastUpdatedDate = DateTime.Now;
pic.Add(info);
```

VB.NET
```
Dim pic As New ProfileInfoCollection()
Dim info As New ProfileInfo()
info.UserName = "Jeff"
info.LastUpdatedDate = DateTime.Now
pic.Add(info)
```

Let's look at the other eight methods required for a profile provider. If your requirements don't call for these methods, as used via ProfileManager, you can add just one line of code to these methods:

```
throw new NotImplementedException();
```

Visual Studio 2005 actually generates this line for you in each of the methods when you declare your intention to inherit from the base class.

DeleteProfiles() has two overloads, one that takes a string array of user names as a parameter, and one that takes a ProfileInfoCollection. These methods are intended to delete the profiles of those users indicated. Both return an integer indicating the number of deleted profiles.

DeleteInactiveProfiles() takes two parameters, a ProfileAuthenticationOption enumeration (whose values are All, Anonymous, or Authenticated) and a DateTime indicating the cut-off date for inactive profiles. The method returns an integer indicating the number of deleted profiles. Implementing this method requires that your profile data use some kind of date stamp that is updated any time the profile is accessed. It also requires that you differentiate between the profiles of anonymous and authenticated users. `GetNumberOfInactiveProfiles()` works just like your `DeleteInactiveProfiles()`, except that it doesn't delete the profile data.

`GetAllProfiles()` returns a `ProfileInfoCollection` and limits the number of `ProfileInfo` objects returned by providing a paging mechanism. Its first parameter is a `ProfileAuthenticationOption` value, followed by integers for the page index and page size, and an integer output parameter that indicates the total number of records. In the case of most data stores, it's probably a good idea to implement some kind of server-side logic (such as a stored procedure in SQL Server) to page the results and send them back to the ASP.NET application.

Output parameters rest in a method signature like other parameters, but the difference is that they actually must have a value assigned to them before the method is finished executing. They're marked in C# with the `out` keyword, and `ByRef` in VB.NET. You need a variable declared when calling a method with an output value to hold the output value. Imagine you have the following method:

C#
```
public void OutputTest(out int totalRecords)
{
    totalRecords = 32;
}
```

VB.NET
```
Public Sub OutputTest(ByRef totalRecords As Integer)
    totalRecords = 32
End Sub
```

Before calling this method, you'll have an integer declared to pass in a parameter, and when the method is finished, the value of that integer will have changed.

```
int x = 0;
OutputTest(out x);
Trace.Write(x.ToString()); ' x now has a value of 32
```

`GetAllInactiveProfiles()` works almost the same as `GetAllProfiles()`, except that its second parameter is a `DateTime` indicating the cut-off for inactive profiles. As with `DeleteInactiveProfiles()`, this requires that you've put some kind of activity date stamp in your profile data.

`FindProfilesByUserName()` and `FindInactiveProfilesByUserName()` also work similarly, except that they take a string parameter to search for profiles by name.

More specifics about this and the other ASP.NET providers are available in the .NET SDK documentation, including full-blown sample implementations. Simply search for the provider's base class, where you'll find links to the sample implementations. The documentation has details on the method signatures, return values, and the intended function of each member.

Themes

The theme mechanism introduced in ASP.NET v2.0 is an incredibly easy way to change the entire look of your site programmatically and in a hurry. This system applies style information to your pages via style sheets or control "skin" declarations.

To use themes, you'll need a `/App_Themes` folder in the root of your application. Below that, create another folder with the name of the theme you want to create. At that point, you can set the theme for a page in a number of ways.

The first way is to set the `Theme` attribute in the `@Page` directive by indicating the theme's folder name. If you have a folder called `/App_Themes/bluetheme`, you'd use `Theme="bluetheme"` in the directive. This is demonstrated in the first line of the "MyPage.aspx" section of Listing 12.9.

Another way is to set the theme at runtime, which enables you to alter the appearance based on user preference, for example. The key to doing this is that the setting of the theme must occur in the `Page_PreInit()` event handler for the page (this event was added for ASP.NET v2.0).

Listing 12.8 shows the event handler code in the page (either from code-behind or in a code block).

Listing 12.8 Setting a theme programmatically

C#

```
void Page_PreInit(object sender, EventArgs e)
{
  Theme = "bluetheme";
}
```

VB.NET

```
Sub Page_PreInit(sender As Object, e As EventArgs)
  Theme = "bluetheme"
End Sub
```

You can also theme an entire site by placing an element in `web.config` between the `system.web` elements like this: `<pages theme="bluetheme" />`

What happens when a theme is set? The page framework looks in `/App_Themes` for the folder that you specify and scans that folder for style sheet files (`.css`) and skin files (`.skin`). We'll talk about skins in a moment. For each style sheet found, an HTML `link` element is injected in between the page's `head` tags. The style sheets can be named anything you want, as long as they end in `.css`. In the previous example, the rendered HTML would include the `link` element shown in the rendered HTML of Listing 12.9.

> In order for these style sheet links to be added to the page, the head tag must have the `runat="stylesheet"` attribute, so it's processed by the server. You'll need this anyway if you want to programmatically manipulate the page title.

ASP.NET also scans the skin files and applies the control style declarations to every control on the page. Note that these declarations only apply to ASP.NET controls and not to static HTML.

Skinning Controls

Skin files are simple text files where you declare controls just as you would in a page, only without an `ID` attribute. The idea is to specify all of the various properties of a control to get it to look a certain way. That "template" of sorts is then applied to all of the controls of the same type on the page. If we add a file called `MyControlStyles.skin` and put it in the `/App_Themes/bluetheme` folder we've been working with, all of the style properties in each control declaration will be applied to the controls of the same type in the page. For example, we could declare a drop-down list to have a black background and white text in the skin file, and all of the drop-down controls on the page would have the same properties applied in the page when we assign the "bluetheme" theme. Listing 12.9 illustrates this.

Listing 12.9 Skin controls, controls in the page, and their rendered output

MyControlStyles.skin

```
<asp:DropDownList runat="server" BackColor="Black" ForeColor="White" />
```

MyPage.aspx

```
<%@ Page Language="C#" Theme="bluetheme" %>
<html>
<head runat="server">
  <title>Themed Page</title>
</head>
<body>
  <form id="form1" runat="server">
    <asp:DropDownList ID="Ddl1" Runat="Server">
      <asp:ListItem>test</asp:ListItem>
    </asp:DropDownList>
  </form>
</body>
</html>
```

Rendered HTML

```
<html>
<head id="Head1">
  <title>Themed Page</title>
  <link rel="stylesheet" href="Themes/BlueTheme/BlueStyle.css"
type="text/css" />
```

(Continues)

Listing 12.9 Skin controls, controls in the page, and their rendered output
            (Continued)

```
</head>
<body>
  <form method="post" action="Default.aspx" id="form1">
    <select name="Ddl1" id="Ddl1" style="color:White;background-
color:Black;">
      <option value="test">test</option>
    </select>
  </form>
</body>
</html>
```

The two most important things to notice in the rendered HTML are the inclusion of the style sheet link that we talked about earlier and the style information included in the `select` element's `style` attribute. We declared the theme for the page in the `@Page` directive.

The style information is applied just as if we had set the `ForeColor` and `BackColor` properties in the page itself. You can see how this would be useful if you wanted to change the look of controls throughout the site, especially if they're complex, like the `Calendar` control. Instead of having to change the information on every page, you would only need to do it once.

You can specify alternate skins for the same control by adding a `SkinID` attribute to both the declaration in the skin file and the control itself. Listing 12.10 shows the declarations to set a drop-down list that has black text on a white background, and one that is the reverse.

Listing 12.10 Multiple skins for the same control type

MyControlStyles.skin

```
<asp:DropDownList runat="server" BackColor="White" ForeColor="Black" />
<asp:DropDownList runat="server" BackColor="Black" ForeColor="White"
SkinID="Reverse" />
```

MyPage.aspx

```
<asp:DropDownList ID="Ddl1" Runat="Server">
  <asp:ListItem>test</asp:ListItem>
</asp:DropDownList>
<asp:DropDownList ID="Ddl2" Runat="Server" SkinID="Reverse">
  <asp:ListItem>test</asp:ListItem>
</asp:DropDownList>
```

All Web controls in ASP.NET v2.0 have a `SkinID` property that can be used to programmatically set the control's skin.

Skin files, like the style sheets, can be named whatever you want, and you can have more than one. The skin files are treated together as one in the theme's folder, so you can organize the control declarations by `SkinID` (or any way you see fit).

As cool as the use of skins may be, it does have some drawbacks. First of all, if you work in a team with graphic designers, chances are they understand CSS but not the proprietary syntax of ASP.NET controls. Therefore, it's much easier for programmers to set the `CssClass` property of a control and know that the designers have a CSS class that will apply styles to that control. This way you can still use themes, but you can also have the style information stored in a format that is easily understood by programmers and designers. As a side effect, the style sheet will likely be cached in the user's browser instead of having all of that inline style information transmitted with every page.

Another downside, as we already discussed, is that this style information applies only to server controls and not to static HTML. If you wanted to apply the same styles to both a static HTML table and a `DataGrid`, you would need to create the `DataGrid` skin declaration and the style sheet. It's a lot less work to do it once and apply it to both.

Tying the Look to User Profiles

To make a theme "stick" with a user, you'll need a profile property to store his or her favorite theme name. Going back to our first `web.config` example in Listing 12.1, you simply need to add a profile property called `Theme` and set its type to `System.String`. Regardless of the profile provider you use (unless of course your own custom provider doesn't deal with the `Theme` property), Listing 12.11 shows how your page can set the theme for the user.

Listing 12.11 Setting the theme for a user with Profile

C#
```csharp
void Page_PreInit(object sender, EventArgs e)
{
  Theme = Profile.Theme;
}
```

(Continues)

Listing 12.11 Setting the theme for a user with Profile   *(Continued)*

VB.NET
```
Sub Page_PreInit(sender As Object, e As EventArgs)
  Theme = Profile.Theme
End Sub
```

Summary

The profile system introduced in ASP.NET v2.0 provides a powerful means to store user data. The built-in SQL Server provider that works with SQL Server 2005 Express Edition enables you to quickly create a robust system to store user data by simply adding configuration information to the profile section of web.config.

If your needs aren't met by the built-in provider, or if you want to interface the profile system to your own data, you may create your own profile provider by inheriting from the abstract ProfileProvider base class and overriding the required members.

The theme engine introduced in ASP.NET v2.0 enables you to alter the look and feel of pages or even the entire site by specifying a theme consisting of style sheets and skin files. The style sheets are dynamically linked into the page, while skin files apply style properties to controls in the pages.

CHAPTER 13

Declarative Programming

Declarative programming, as the name would imply, enables you to declare high-level objects that address a problem. Declarative programming has been a component of ASP.NET since the beginning. Controls that you declare in the page that do something without additional code, such as a `RequiredFieldValidator`, are declarative.

It's not unreasonable to guess that the ASP.NET team may feel very strongly about declarative components in Web applications because they added a lot of them in v2.0. We'll take a closer look at these controls in this chapter.

Overview

It appears that there is a new emphasis on declarative programming in ASP.NET with the release of v2.0. This approach has two serious benefits. The first is that it saves a great deal of time because you don't need to write as much code yourself to perform routine tasks. The second is that declarative programming, when implemented right, can be used by less experienced coders to perform complex tasks.

> It's also worth noting that the forthcoming version of Windows, code-named "Longhorn," will make use of XAML, Extensible Application Markup Language. XAML is to Windows applications much as HTML is to Web applications. It's a declarative language that will enable Windows developers to declare controls on a form, such as a button, in much the same way that we declare controls on a Web form. A simple Windows form using XAML might contain the following:
>
> ```
> <?xml version="1.0" standalone="yes"?>
> <Window>
> ```

```
<Button>Hello World</Button>
</Window>
```

For more information about XAML, check out http://www.xaml.net.

For example, the `RequiredFieldValidator` control saves time because you don't need to write a block of code to do the work that it can do by itself. That code, while not complex by most people's standards, isn't something a beginner would need to understand in terms of checking the length of the input of a control and displaying an error message (not to mention wiring into the `Page` object's `IsValid` property).

Declarative controls aren't just something you'll find in the .NET Framework; you can build your own as well. The `DataSourceControl` abstract class acts as the base for other classes like `SqlDataSource`, which acts as a UI element on your page but does the work of binding data to a data control for you without having to create the typical connection and command objects. You can derive your own controls from `DataSourceControl` that grab specific data for binding to other controls.

Validation Controls

The ASP.NET validation controls are one of the first "gee whiz" features that are introduced to a lot of developers, and rightfully so. These controls take some of the grunt work out of making sure that user input meets certain criteria. If any of these controls finds the input to be invalid, it can display an error message, and the `Page` object's `IsValid` property returns false.

Six validation controls are included in ASP.NET. Their names indicate their functions: `CompareValidator`, `CustomValidator`, `RangeValidator`, `RegularExpressionValidator`, `RequiredFieldValidator`, and `ValidationSummary`. All of these can be used without any additional code, except for the `CustomValidator`. The `ValidationSummary` control is particularly interesting because it can take the error messages from other validation controls, group them together, and display them in one place.

What makes the controls declarative? Their use is dictated entirely by the way they are declared in the page. For example, consider this `RequiredFieldValidator`:

```
<asp:RequiredFieldValidator id="checkName" runat="server"
controlToValidate="NameTextBox" text="Please enter a name." />
```

All of the details required to make this control work are declared right there on the page. You've seen the `id` and `runat` attributes in every control, but `controlToValidate` instructs the control to check on a `TextBox` control, while the `text` attribute indicates what the error message to the user should be.

These are among the simplest declarative controls in ASP.NET, but they still save us a bit of work. Using them in Visual Studio is even easier, as we can drag and drop them from the toolbox and set the attributes in the property window.

Data Controls

We've been able to declaratively code data controls in ASP.NET since the start. Using simple templates, we've been able to format `DataGrids` and `Repeaters` with ease. The slightly more tricky part has been binding data to these controls. That got easier in v2.0 of ASP.NET with the addition of data source controls.

Consider a typical scenario where we need the name and city of our customers from a database, and we need to bind the resulting data to a `DataGrid`. Listing 13.1 demonstrates this scenario through the use of traditional means, in code, and declaratively using a `SqlDataSource` control.

> The code listing shows the reference to a connection string using an ASP.NET expression. We'll get to expressions at the end of the chapter. For now, just understand that it references a connection string in `web.config`.
>
> This is also a good time to point out that, despite having "Sql" in the name, the `SqlDataSource` control can actually get data from most OleDb data sources, including Microsoft Access, by using the attribute `provider="System.Data.OleDb"` in the control's declaration.

Listing 13.1 Traditional code vs. declarative code

Traditional code

```
SqlConnection connection =
  new
SqlConnection(ConfigurationSettings.ConnectionStrings["MyDatabase"].
ConnectionString);
string sql = "SELECT Name, City FROM Customers";
SqlCommand command = new SqlCommand(sql, connection);
SqlDataReader reader = command.ExecuteReader();
CustomerGrid.DataSource = reader;
CustomerGrid.DataBind();
reader.Close();
connection.Close();
```

Declarative code

```
<asp:SqlDataSource id="SqlDataSource1" runat="server"
dataSourceMode="DataReader"
connectionString="<%$ ConnectionStrings:MyDatabase %>"
selectCommand="SELECT ID, Name, City FROM Customers" />

<asp:DataGrid id="CustomerGrid" runat="server"
dataSourceID="SqlDataSource1" />
```

Although one could certainly argue that this declarative approach to data binding doesn't represent a "best practice" of separating your application into discrete layers, it's hard to deny that this programming method saves time and is perfectly suited for a small application. It might also seem odd to put a control on the page like this when it doesn't actually render anything to the browser, but this is what declarative programming is all about! Instead of writing an extensive block of code in a traditional class, we simply declare it right in the HTML.

Perhaps a more realistic use of `SqlDataSource` is to pass in some kind of parameter. Imagine you have a form that enables you to search for customers by name. You can feed in a parameter to the SQL statement by providing the ID of the other control on the page, and that control's property to use as a parameter. This is shown in Listing 13.2, between the `SelectParameters` elements.

Listing 13.2 Passing in parameters to the `SqlDataSource` control

```
<asp:TextBox id="NameTextBox" runat="server" />

<asp:SqlDataSource id="SqlDataSource1" runat="server"
```

```
dataSourceMode="DataReader"
connectionString="<%$ ConnectionStrings:MyDatabase %>"
selectCommand="SELECT ID, Name, City FROM Customers WHERE Name = @Name">
  <SelectParameters>
    <asp:ControlParameter Name="Name" ControlID="NameTextBox"
PropertyName="Text" />
  </SelectParameters>
</asp:SqlDataSource>

<asp:DataGrid id="CustomerGrid" runat="server"
dataSourceID="SqlDataSource1" />
```

This code isn't that different from the code in Listing 13.1, except that the SQL statement has a parameter in its `WHERE` clause, and we've added the `SelectParameters` section to the control. There still isn't any "normal" code to go along with this; it all works with these simple declarations. The `ControlParameter` is one of several that we can use to feed data into the select command, including `CookieParameter`, `FormParameter`, `Parameter`, `ProfileParameter`, `QueryStringParameter`, and `SessionParameter`. That's a lot of flexibility because it lets you feed parameters in from virtually anywhere.

One of the examples frequently given to demonstrate data binding and updating data involves the combination of an editable `DataGrid` and a `DataSet`. The `DataSet` is populated in code, and event handlers are tied to the `DataGrid` to make it all work. Although this task is much easier than it might be on other platforms, it still requires a lot of work. The good news is that you can do it declaratively in ASP.NET v2.0.

Listing 13.3 shows an example using `GridView` and `SqlDataSource` controls together to make data editable. Figure 13.1 shows how the grid is rendered in the browser after one of the row's "edit" buttons has been clicked.

Listing 13.3 Using `GridView` and `SqlDataSource` together to declaratively create an editable table

```
<asp:SqlDataSource ID="SqlDataSource1" Runat="server"
  DataSourceMode="DataReader"
  ConnectionString="<%$ ConnectionStrings:MyDatabase %>"
  SelectCommand="SELECT CustomerID, Name, City FROM Customers"
  UpdateCommand="UPDATE Customers SET Name = @Name, City = @City WHERE
CustomerID = @original_CustomerID"
  DeleteCommand="DELETE FROM Customers WHERE CustomerID =
```

(Continues)

Listing 13.3 Using `GridView` and `SqlDataSource` together to declaratively create an editable table   (*Continues*)

```
@original_CustomerID">
</asp:SqlDataSource>

<asp:GridView ID="MyGrid" Runat="Server" DataSourceID="SqlDataSource1"
   AutoGenerateEditButton="true"
   AutoGenerateDeleteButton="true" DataKeyNames="CustomerID" />
```

	CustomerID	Name	City
Edit Delete	1	Jeffrey	Cleveland
Update Cancel	2	Stephanie	Columbus
Edit Delete	3	Mike	Cincinnati

Figure 13.1 The `GridView` rendered in the browser.

By adding the `UpdateCommand` and `DeleteCommand` attributes to the `SqlDataSource` control and adding the list of attributes to the `GridView`, including `DataKeyNames` to indicate our primary key, we can edit our data with ease. Gone are the many lines of plumbing code we would ordinarily have to write to achieve this functionality.

This discussion only scratches the surface of what you can do with declarative data controls, and I'm sure that countless books will be dedicated to the subject. ASP.NET v2.0 adds these new controls (including `GridView` and `DetailsView`) to make data manipulation even easier in general and significantly easier for a less experienced programmer.

Web Parts

Microsoft has unified a portal structure that crosses several products, including ASP.NET v2.0, Microsoft Content Management Server, SharePoint, and Office. This portal structure is commonly referred to as Web Parts.

Web Parts are a fairly simple means of creating a rich, customizable portal structure on a Web page. A `WebPartManager` control is placed on the page, but like the data source controls, it does not have any user interface. Other controls work with this control to create a customizable portal structure that ties into ASP.NET's personalization features to save individual users' preferences and layouts.

The topic of using this portal framework is huge, worthy of its own book, and as such we won't dive into it here.

Navigation Controls

The `TreeView` and `SiteMapPath` controls, introduced in ASP.NET v2.0, are fantastic additions to the built-in controls. As with the other controls mentioned in this chapter, they can be programmatically manipulated, but they can also be programmed declaratively.

`TreeView` has been around for a long time; it was originally offered in a somewhat less robust form as part of a control package downloadable from Microsoft. Listing 13.4 demonstrates the simple declaration of a `TreeView` to create the navigation shown in Figure 13.2.

Listing 13.4 `TreeView` declaration

```
<asp:TreeView ID="MyTree" Runat="Server" ShowLines="true" Font-
Names="Verdana, Arial">
   <Nodes>
     <asp:TreeNode Text="Home" NavigateUrl="~/Default.aspx"
Expanded="true">
       <asp:TreeNode Text="Page 1" NavigateUrl="~/Page1.aspx" />
       <asp:TreeNode Text="Page 2" NavigateUrl="~/Page2.aspx" />
     </asp:TreeNode>
   </Nodes>
</asp:TreeView>
```

Figure 13.2 The `TreeView` rendered in the browser.

What's the deal with the tilde (~) in the navigation path? Using the tilde references the root of an application. If you have a subfolder in the site acting as an application, the tilde points to that root, not the site root. In Listing 13.4, an application residing in http://www.mysite.com/myapp would resolve the above path to http://www.mysite.com/myapp/Page1.aspx.

If you prefer to separate the data from the control, you can bind an external XML file to the `TreeView` and an `XmlDataSource` control. Just as you used a `SqlDataSource` control to bind to various data controls, a `SiteMapDataSource` control can be used to bind hierarchical data to a `TreeView`. Listing 13.5 shows the `web.sitemap` file, where `SiteMapDataSource` gets its data. This functionally produces the same output shown in Figure 13.2

Listing 13.5 Using `SiteMapDataSource` with `TreeView` and `web.sitemap`

Code from an .aspx page
```
<asp:TreeView ID="MyTree" Runat="Server" ShowLines="true" Font-
Names="Verdana, Arial" DataSourceID="MapSource" />

<asp:SiteMapDataSource id="MapSource" runat="server" />
```

web.sitemap
```
<?xml version="1.0" encoding="utf-8" ?>
<siteMap>
  <siteMapNode title="Home" url="~/Default.aspx">
    <siteMapNode title="Page 1" url="~/Page1.aspx" />
    <siteMapNode title="Page 2" url="~/Page2.aspx" />
  </siteMapNode>
</siteMap>
```

The `SiteMapPath` control creates a breadcrumb trail of links through the site, based on the `web.sitemap` file. All it requires is declaration in the page like this: `<asp:SiteMapPath ID="SiteMapPath1" Runat= "server" />`. If you were on `Page1.aspx` described in the `web.sitemap` file from Listing 13.5, and it contained this control, you'd get the output shown in Figure 13.3. This is another great example of how little work is required on your part with some declarative controls.

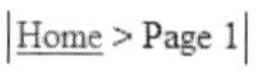

|Home > Page 1|

Figure 13.3 The `SiteMapPath` control rendered in the browser.

Expressions

Expressions are little shortcuts that enable you to declaratively link data to objects in the page. We saw an example of an expression in Listing 13.1 when we passed in the connection string to a `SqlDataSource` object. The syntax is simple: `<%$ prefix: value %>`.

ASP.NET expressions are dictated by a section of `machine.config` (and `web.config`, if you add it) called `<expressionBuilders>`. Each entry in this section adds a prefix name and the class that implements the abstract `ExpressionBuilder` class to handle the expression.

The default expressions include the `ConnectionStrings` prefix shown in Listing 13.1, the `AppSettings` prefix, and the `Resources` prefix. `AppSettings` works just like `ConnectionStrings`, in that it reads a value right out of `web.config` and passes it into the page. The only difference is that it looks in `web.config`'s `<appSettings>` element instead of the `<connectionStrings>` element.

The `Resources` prefix gets values out of resource (.resx) files. Resource files are generally used to break out the UI elements of an application to allow for easy localization. Under the hood, they're XML files, but they can be edited in Visual Studio as a simple table. Accessing the data of a particular field in the resource file is accomplished with the syntax `<%$ Resources: MyResourceFile, MyKeyValue %>`, where "MyResourceFile" is the name of the resource file without the .resx extension and "MyKeyValue" is the name of the field from which you want to extract a value.

Summary

Declarative programming is a means of using declared elements, namely controls, to create functionality without having to write procedural code. Declarative controls enable the programmer to perform tasks quickly, and they provide enhanced functionality to less experienced programmers.

In this chapter, we looked at several groups of declarative controls, including validation controls, data controls, Web parts, and navigation controls. We also reviewed ASP.NET expressions as a means of getting configuration and resource information.

PART III

Development Issues

CHAPTER 14

Developing with Visual Studio

Visual Studio is easily the most prized piece of software on a .NET developer's computer. This integrated development environment (IDE) is incredibly powerful, complex, and vast in terms of its features. On one hand, Visual Studio could be credited with the .NET platform's success, as many critics will argue that it's the best IDE ever created. On the other hand, it might be somewhat hard for a beginner to sink his or her teeth into this huge beast and all it has to offer.

Regardless of the software's reputation, Visual Studio is an essential tool for quickly building ASP.NET applications. That said, it's not without its issues, and we hope to explore some of those in this chapter.

Versions

Back in the "old days" (and by old, we mean before 2002), several development products were packaged under the name Visual Studio, and each was its own standalone product. Visual Studio v6.0 included Visual C++, Visual Basic, and Visual InterDev. InterDev was the Web development tool used for the old Active Server Pages. I doubt you'll find many developers these days who have anything nice to say about InterDev.

During .NET's first beta period in 2001, Visual Studio .NET (version 2002 or v7.0) was widely available in what became a massive preview program. The new IDE was a single, unified product that could be used for any of the .NET languages and for both Windows development and Web development using ASP.NET. This version was released in early 2002 with v1.0 of the .NET Framework.

Visual Studio .NET 2003, or v7.1, was a mostly minor upgrade that accompanied the release of v1.1 of the .NET Framework. Despite the upgrade, the Web form designer could be absolutely miserable to work with because of the way it mangled HTML and used the old code-behind methods we covered in Chapter 6, "The Nuts and Bolts of IIS and Web Applications."

Meanwhile, a free tool called WebMatrix was released on Microsoft's www.asp.net Web site. Remember that the .NET Framework and the software development kit (SDK) have always been available as free downloads, so in theory you could code a Windows application with Notepad and the compiler included in the SDK. WebMatrix gave users a somewhat nicer "mini-IDE" to get their feet wet with ASP.NET. Although it lacked the hardcore features found in Visual Studio, it did provide kind of a preview and testing ground for features that would make their way into the next version of Visual Studio.

Visual Studio 2005 (note that they dropped ".NET" from the name) is the latest version of the product, and it accompanies the release of v2.0 of the .NET Framework. This version is loaded with enhancements, especially for Web developers. In addition to the newer code-behind model, it facilitates deployment and offers Intellisense everywhere (including in pages), a visual designer that doesn't mangle your HTML, XHTML compliance (which comes in combination with improved server controls), visual designing of master template pages, no-compile coding, a built-in Web server that allows for project-less development without IIS, and more.

Along with Visual Studio 2005, Microsoft has also produced inexpensive, slightly less functional, individual "express" products. There is one for each primary language, plus a lighter version of SQL Server 2005 and Visual Web Developer 2005 Express (VWD). VWD is a steal because it offers a new class of developer access to the power of Visual Studio. It does have a few limitations, though. It doesn't allow multiple projects because there are no "solutions," so you can't build a class library in one project and then reference it from a Web project. It lacks the built-in pre-compilation feature, though this can still be accomplished with a command line tool in the SDK. It also lacks the server explorer feature. It doesn't do Windows forms development at all. Conversely, the language-specific products do not allow you to develop ASP.NET applications.

Because corporate spending can be a serious roller coaster, we understand that not everyone will have the latest version of Visual Studio, so we'll cover some of the issues involved with all versions.

Default Behavior of the IDE

The 2002 and 2003 versions of Visual Studio, by default, use the old code-behind model. There are no partial classes at all because these versions are based on v1.x of the .NET Framework. If you want to use the `Page` directive's `src` attribute, you'll have to manually add it and enter the name of the class file you want to use as code-behind. Keep in mind that building the Web project will cause a compiled version of the code-behind class to appear in the generated assembly in the `/bin` folder. Be sure that it doesn't appear in both places or you'll get an error.

The old versions also set `autoeventwireup` to false in the `Page` directive by default. When set this way, indicating a method to fire by a button's `onClick` attribute, for example, will not work. To get around this, you can either delete the attribute or double-click the button in the designer to generate code similar to that in Listing 7.6. It's a bit less straightforward, but you'll spend less time fighting the IDE.

Visual Studio 2005 works differently, as we described in Chapter 6, but the biggest "issue" is just getting used to it if you've been developing with one of the previous versions for a couple years. The biggest change is that all of the class files are not compiled to a single assembly. Instead, the class files are all compiled when the application is used for the first time. That means you can make changes on-the-fly and not have to rebuild the project with every change.

Pitfalls of the Designer

The Web form designer in versions 2002 and 2003 isn't entirely broken, but it can be a serious pain to work with. The aforementioned event wire up is an issue, though it is by design most of the time. There were other issues where the designer would lose wire ups.

More serious is the synchronization between the page and the code-behind file. When you drag and drop a control on the page in design view, a reference is added in the code-behind file. However, if you manually type in a control in the HTML view, that reference is not created until you switch back to design view. This in turn will likely destroy whatever formatting you had in the HTML.

If you want to generate that reference in code-behind, you can switch to design and then back to HTML. To undo the format mangling, click the undo button two or three times, and this will get your formatting back.

Visual Studio 2005 doesn't suffer from these issues. Because partial classes work without references, you don't need to worry about this synchronization. Your HTML formatting is also preserved.

Multiple Projects and References

In Chapter 4, "Application Architecture," we explored the idea of dividing up our applications into layers. Visual Studio makes this easier than ever by grouping projects together as solutions. A project can be a Web site or a class library, among other things, and you can work on them together as a solution.

Figure 14.1 shows the Solution Explorer with a Web project at the top and a class library right below it. You'll notice that the assembly from the class library appears in the Web project's /bin folder.

Figure 14.1 The Solution Explorer.

By creating a reference from one project to another, you can access all of the compiled code from the referenced project. Figure 14.2 shows how to add a reference from the Web project shown in the Solution Explorer to another project. Right-clicking the project name and choosing Add Reference brings up the dialog.

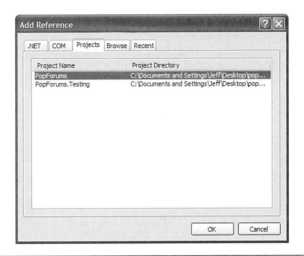

Figure 14.2 Add Reference dialog.

Using multiple projects can help you divide up your project into layers where appropriate. For example, you can create a class library that does the "heavy lifting" and logic for your application and not worry about the implementation of the user interface. Good class design also lets you unit test the classes in your class library (something we'll go into more in Chapter 16, "Testing, Deployment, and Code Management"). By getting your logic absolutely right and thoroughly tested, implementing the user interface becomes less error-prone.

Working Locally

Visual Studio 2005 allows for the development of sites in folders, outside of your local IIS installation. The IDE turns on its own Web server to host your application. Working locally, therefore, is as easy as picking a folder anywhere on your computer.

> Well, it's mostly that easy. Chances are that you have administrative rights on your own machine and can do anything you like. When you migrate your application to a production environment, you may have to set folder or file permissions if you upload or change files to the site. This is also true for local data files, such as Access databases.

Visual Studio 2002 and 2003 require Web apps to live in a folder in IIS. This process works by associating a URL such as `http://localhost/folder` with a path to the administrator file share, `/wwwroot$`. Generally this share maps to `c:\inetpub\wwwroot`, unless you've altered it. If Visual Studio can't match these two locations as the same place, it won't allow you to create a project there.

Working from Another Server on Your LAN

In Visual Studio 2005, trying to execute code from a remote server in its Web server won't work for security reasons. A better solution is to use some kind of source control (such as Visual Source Safe) to check out the code and work with it on a local folder.

Working remotely with Visual Studio 2002 and 2003 operates a lot like the local scheme, using a URL and an administrator share to access the code. To make it work, the machine you're working from must have administrator privileges on the remote server to access the file share. The fastest and easiest way to accomplish this on a Windows network is to put your user account in the remote server's administrator group. That's something you may have to "negotiate" with your IT department.

Working on a server in this manner also requires that remote debugging be installed on the server if you plan to use the debugger.

Working from a Web Server

All versions of Visual Studio can work remotely on a Web server by using Microsoft FrontPage extensions. These extensions retrieve files via HTTP, cache them locally, and send them back to the server when you save them. There are two drawbacks—the retrieving and saving of files can be slow, and you can't use the debugger in this fashion.

In order to compile assemblies and edit files, Visual Studio saves the files locally on your computer. The default location for this is `c:\Documents and Settings\YourUserName\VSWebCache`. A sub-folder is created for every site you work on, including your local IIS folders. When you issue a build command in 2002 or 2003, all of the `.cs` (or `.vb`) files are used as the source code for the compiled assembly. The assembly is saved in the `/bin` folder of this temporary cache of your project, and then uploaded to the Web server.

Other files that are not compiled (`.aspx` files, for example) are also stored in the same location. However, if you happen to be editing someone else's work, that file will not exist in your cache structure until you open it.

> In the event of some catastrophic failure (and your reluctance to back things up), you may be able to salvage much of your application from these cached folders. Keep in mind though that if the file on the Web server was not originally created by you, and you haven't attempted to edit it, or it's not a file you used to compile an assembly, it will not yet be in your cache folder.

Working with a Source Control Provider

Source control is a means of versioning and sharing code among a team of developers. Generally speaking, a central database keeps copies of the code files, and new copies are created every time the file is changed. Developers check out files to alter them. A checked out file can't be (or rather shouldn't be) checked out by other developers. In some cases, the source control can track the changes between two developers and then merge the changes.

Visual Source Safe has shipped with Visual Studio for years, and it went relatively unchanged through several versions until Visual Studio 2005. The latest version works on a local network as well as the Web. Visual Studio has the built-in capability to access source control from the solution explorer. In Figure 14.1, you can see the little padlock icons next to files, which indicate that a file is checked in.

A number of other products such as Source Gear's Vault are compatible with Visual Studio.

The Debugger

The debugger in Visual Studio is one of the most under-appreciated features of the product among Web developers. The debugger enables you to "spy" on your code in the middle of its execution cycle and see the decisions it makes and the values of every object in the code. Windows developers have enjoyed this debugging capability for a long time, and now it's just as straightforward for Web jockeys.

Using the debugger is fairly simple—just push F5 or click Debug -> Run from the menu, and you're on your way. The default page will run, and the debugger will "attach" to ASP.NET. At this point, you can do anything you might normally do with your running application. The excitement occurs when the debugger encounters a *break point* in your code, a notification to the debugger that it should stop the execution so you can see what's going on. You set a break point by clicking in the left margin next to your code.

Figure 14.3 shows the debugger in action. The small red sphere is a break point.

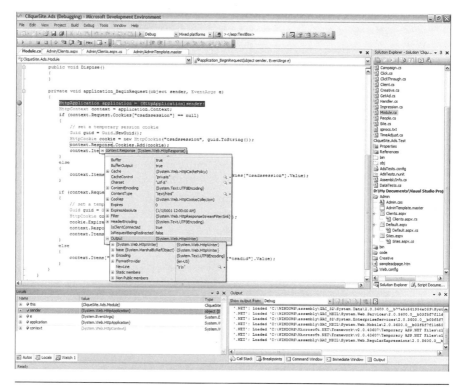

Figure 14.3 The debugger in action.

When the debugger hits a break point, you can either continue by pressing the continue button (shaped like a play button) or press F5. Even more useful, you can step through the code one line at a time by pressing F11. The line with the arrow in Figure 14.3 shows where the debugger currently is in the code. Every press of F11 will move to the next line, opening other class files if it has to show you where the execution is going.

While you're stepping through the code, you can explore the value of every object that currently exists in the context of this execution. In our example screen, you can see that simply mousing over the `Response` object has enabled us to drill down through properties and sub-properties. You can do virtually the same thing in the Locals window at the bottom of the screen. In fact, if any of those objects changes when you step into the next line of code, that object's name changes color to let you know.

This means of debugging is a lot easier than placing `Trace.Write()` statements in your code, and it gives you the big picture of everything happening during code execution.

Summary

Visual Studio is the most powerful and comprehensive tool for developing applications for ASP.NET. Several versions have come along since the release of the .NET Framework, with 2002 and 2003 supporting versions 1.0 and 1.1, respectively, and 2005 supporting v2.0.

Developing with the earlier versions introduces some issues and "gotchas" when developing ASP.NET applications. Version 2005 has solved many of the problems for Web developers and has made great strides in making Web development more flexible.

Source control solutions such as Visual Source Safe enable developers to share and version code. A system of checkouts and code comparison keeps everyone up-to-date.

The debugger in Visual Studio can be the developer's best friend when trying to stomp out bugs. The debugger enables you to step through your code one line at a time and peek in to see what values objects contain.

CHAPTER 15

Performance, Scalability, and Metrics

ASP.NET makes it possible to develop Web applications quickly and easily, but the relative ease of use doesn't mean that the resulting product will perform or scale well. What is perfectly adequate for a small intranet site may very well buckle under the pressure of a huge audience on the Internet.

In this chapter, we'll look at performance, the capability of your application to scale, and a number of ways to measure performance and scalability.

Terms Defined

When we speak of *performance*, we generally speak of the capability of an application to perform fast enough for our needs. That means different things to different people, but it's safe to say that if your application doesn't do what your user needs in a reasonable amount of time, it doesn't perform well. In the case of a commercial application or site, this could be a disaster because your audience might find somewhere else to go, and that could cost you money.

Scalability is the capability of your application and systems to perform well as their user count grows. Chances are that a couple of sloppy database queries every few seconds will not bring your system to its knees, but if suddenly your user base climbs into the tens of thousands, and the application can't handle it, it doesn't scale.

Fragment Caching

The OutputCache directive, placed in pages and user controls, causes the rendered contents to be cached in memory, without any of the page or user control code executing on the new request. This is certainly an outstanding way to save resource use because it reads the content from memory instead of going through the process of executing code and all the object instantiation that this involves.

However, in a world of dynamic sites with personalized and frequently changing data, it's not practical to cache an entire page. Fragment caching is the process of caching only a user control. User controls are essentially "fragments" of pages, with their own execution, so we can cluster content into these smaller units and cache them. The rest of the page hosting a user control can execute normally.

Caching user controls works just like caching a page, by placing the OutputCache directive right after the Control directive:

```
<%@ OutputCache Duration="120" VaryByParam="None" %>
```

Data Caching

Because of the dynamic nature of our sites, caching data is often more practical than an entire page. We already gave you a fairly extensive data caching example in Chapter 5, "Object-Oriented Programming Applied: A Custom Data Class," with our custom data class. As we said then, the key to using the Cache object is to make sure that changing data in the data store invalidates the cached data. Encapsulating your data access in something like our example class makes the validity of the cached data easy.

There are trade-offs to consider when you're caching data. Reading data from memory instead of the database is certainly faster, but while your disk space is relatively "endless," your server only has a finite amount of memory. Your server situation has a lot to do with the amount of caching you can do. If the server has a gigabyte of memory with no other applications running on it, and the data you cache totals 100 megabytes, you obviously have no problem. If your application is running on a server farm, then you can't cache in memory because different servers would have different values for the data.

Inserting data into the cache takes several parameters:

```
Cache.Insert(nameString, objectToCache, cacheDependency,
    absoluteExpirationTime, slidingExpirationTimeSpan);
```

The first parameter is a name used to look up the cached item. Our example in Chapter 5 used a prefix and the primary key relative to the database record we were caching in object form. The second parameter is the object to actually place into the cache. The third parameter is a `CacheDependency` object, which is used to monitor file changes or other cache entries. It's not very useful for most data stores, and a `null` (Nothing) value is often passed in. The fourth parameter indicates an absolute `DateTime`, after which the item expires and is removed from the cache. When this value is used, the last parameter must be `TimeSpan.Zero`. The last value is a sliding expiration, where the item continues to be cached as long as the specified `TimeSpan` hasn't passed without the item being accessed. If this parameter is specified, the absolute expiration must be set to `DataTime.MaxValue`.

A more useful cache dependency object is one based on the `SqlCacheDependency` class (starting in ASP.NET v2.0). It monitors changes to a SQL Server table to invalidate cached items. It's a lot more work to set up. It works differently for SQL Server 7.0 or 2000 and SQL Server 2005 (formerly known as "Yukon").

For 7.0 and 2000, the class depends on a polling mechanism and a special series of tables and triggers added to your database. The cache is invalidated any time the table is changed. To make this work, you must run the `aspnet_regsql.exe` tool from the command line.

> `aspnet_regsql.exe` does a lot of things, as this is the same tool you used to set up the membership features in a SQL database. This particular function, however, requires the use of the command line, not the program's GUI.

To enable this caching functionality on your SQL database, first run the following from the command line:

```
aspnet_regsql -ed -d aspnetdb -E
```

This says "Enable cache dependency on the database named aspnetdb and use a trusted connection." Other options can be found by simply using `aspnet_regsql -?`. This creates a new table and some stored procedures. To make the rest work, triggers have to be placed on the tables you want to monitor for dependencies. This is done with the following on the command line:

```
aspnet_regsql -et -t tableName -d aspnetdb -E
```

This particular command means "Enable cache dependency on a table, the table called tableName in database aspnetdb using a trusted connection." Finally, you'll need the `web.config` settings shown in Listing 15.1.

Listing 15.1 Setting `SqlCacheDependency` in `web.config`

```
<configuration>
  <connectionStrings>
    <add name="MyDatabase" connectionString="Data
Source=localhost;Integrated Security=SSPI;Initial Catalog=MyDataBase;"
/>
  </connectionStrings>
  <system.web>
    <cache>
      <sqlCacheDependency enabled="true" pollTime="60">
        <add name="MyDep" connectionName="MyDatabase" pollTime="60" />
      </sqlCacheDependency>
    </cache>
  </system.web>
</configuration>
```

You're already familiar with the connection string and the general format of <add> elements in the file. The `pollTime` attribute determines how often ASP.NET should check to see if the tables have had an insert, update, or delete. This introduces a bit of overhead itself, but finding a good polling time will help you with the trade-off. The downside in this case is that with SQL Server 7.0 and 2000, you can only monitor entire tables, not individual records.

In the `Cache.Insert()` syntax we showed you earlier, you can pass in an instance of `SqlCacheDependency` as your final step to invalidate a cache entry. This is as easy as replacing "cacheDependency" with:

```
new SqlCacheDependency("MyDep", "tableName")
```

"MyDep" comes from the dependency we named in Listing 15.1, in the `web.config` file, and the table name is whatever table you want to monitor for changes, making sure of course that you set it up as described earlier using the `aspnet_regsql.exe` tool.

This caching affair is even easier to use with SQL Server 2005, as it has a built-in notification system that will create a callback to ASP.NET, letting it know that a record has been changed. To use this feature, forget the previous discussion with regards to setup and simply use this overload of the `SqlCacheDependency` constructor:

```
new SqlCacheDependency(command)
```

...where `command` is the `SqlCommand` object that originally fetched the data. Recall Listing 5.9 from Chapter 5, where we revised our constructor with our cache lookup and insert. We could change the cache insertion to look like this:

```
context.Cache.Insert("UberCustomer" +
    _CustomerID.ToString(), this, new
SqlCacheDependency(command),
    DateTime.Now.AddSeconds(60), new TimeSpan.Zero);
```

Instead of passing null into the third parameter, we've added a `SqlCacheDependency` object that will automatically listen for SQL Server 2005's notification that our record has changed. This means that the `Update()` and `Delete()` methods of our sample class in Chapter 5 don't need to fire the `DeleteCache()` method we wrote either because SQL Server 2005 and the .NET Framework will take care of this cache invalidation for us.

Managing Viewstate

Viewstate can be a blessing and a curse in ASP.NET. You've already learned that viewstate helps ASP.NET simulate statefulness on a page. The problem is that too much viewstate can slow down your page for three reasons. First, a control's state must be saved into viewstate before the page is sent to the user. Then the actual sending of that viewstate uses precious bandwidth to get to the user. Finally, the viewstate has to be decoded when it is returned back to the server from the user. This process can take up precious CPU time, and it can fill your pipe with redundant data. If you don't need it, don't use it!

Fortunately, disabling viewstate is easy to do, by page or individual control. The `Page` directive (and `Control` directive, if you're using a user control) has an `enableViewState` attribute that you can set to false. This means that no controls on the page will use viewstate, and the hidden field in the HTML will result in just a handful of bytes. It's important to know that this high-level declaration affects everything below it, so you can't turn on viewstate for any controls on the page.

Every control has an `EnableViewState` property because all controls inherit from `System.Web.UI.Control` (including the `Page` object). You can set this property declaratively or programmatically. The general rule I use is that if the control can't be altered by the user (like a `Label` control), and I can set the control's value on the server side, it's safe to turn off viewstate.

Variations in Data Access Methods

By now you've realized that there are essentially two ways to get data out of the database using .NET: readers and `DataSets`. Data readers (using `SqlDataReader` with SQL Server) are often called the "fire hose" of data access because they provide for a fast and efficient one-way data stream. You can't step through the data in reverse or persist changes back to the database; it's just a one-way affair.

`DataSets`, on the other hand, provide a more robust way of manipulating an in-memory version of data that enables you to persist changes to the database, scroll about in your data, and even store more than one `DataTable` together in memory.

You've heard it said before that everything in .NET is an object, so guess which method of data access involves more objects? If you guessed the `DataSet`, you are correct! With every `DataSet`, you are creating at least one `DataTable` object, `DataRow` objects, `DataColumn` objects, and objects that likely need to be cast to their proper types (`int`, `string`, etc.) if the columns are not typed. That's a lot of different objects to create just to bind a couple news items to a `Repeater`!

Needless to say, using a reader to get data and specific command objects to insert, update, and delete data is far more efficient. One solution to use is the data class we created in Chapter 5. It has many advantages in that we use specific SQL commands, the properties are strongly typed, we can build in caching schemes, CRUD (create, retrieve, update, and delete) methods are available, and so on. It seems like extra work, but careful construction of this kind of class will yield fewer objects and a more intuitive interface to your data.

String Concatenation vs. *StringBuilder*

Getting developers to use the `StringBuilder` class can be a hard sell because when viewed one instance at a time, string concatenation doesn't seem like a big deal. When you multiply it by hundreds or thousands of operations, though, it's suddenly very obvious that string concatenation is slow.

Strings are immutable, which means they can't be changed. So to arrive at a concatenated string, we need to create a new string based on the combination of two other strings. Imagine creating a long string in your own custom server control, having to create a new object with every additional line you added to the string. Each time you concatenate, a new object is created, and the contents of two other string objects must be copied over to the new object.

`StringBuilder` works differently by creating an expandable buffer in memory. By using its `Append()` method, and its `ToString()` method when you're done, you avoid all of that memory copying and object creation. The easiest way to demonstrate its efficiency compared to plain string concatenation is with a little code. Listing 15.2 shows the sample. The `Trace` output on the page yields the results shown in Table 15.1.

Listing 15.2 String concatenation vs. `StringBuilder`

C#

```
using System;
using System.Text;
using System.Web;

public partial class StringBuild_aspx
{
  void Page_Load(object sender, EventArgs e)
  {
    string sentence = "I really like riding roller coasters because
they're super fun and have ups and downs, just like life!";
    string[] words = sentence.Split(new char[] { ' ' });
```

(Continues)

Listing 15.2 String concatenation vs. `StringBuilder`   (*Continued*)

```
  string result = "";
  Trace.Warn("Start concatenation");
  for (int i = 0; i < 1000; i++)
  {
    foreach (string word in words)
    {
      result = result + word + " ";
    }
  }
  Trace.Warn("End concatenation");
  Trace.Warn("Start StringBuilder");
  StringBuilder builder = new StringBuilder();
  for (int i = 0; i < 1000; i++)
  {
    foreach (string word in words)
    {
      builder.Append(word);
      builder.Append(" ");
    }
  }
  result = builder.ToString();
  Trace.Warn("End StringBuilder");
  }
}
```

VB.NET

```
Imports System
Imports System.Text
Imports System.Web

Public Partial Class StringBuild_aspx
  Sub Page_Load(sender As Object, e As EventArgs)
    Dim sentence As String = "I really like riding roller coasters
because they're super fun and have ups and downs, just like life!"
    Dim words As String() = sentence.Split(New Char() {" "c})
    Dim result As String = ""
    Trace.Warn("Start concatenation")
    Dim i As Integer
    For i = 0 To 999
      Dim word As String
      For Each word In words
        result = result + word + " "
      Next word
    Next i
```

```
    Trace.Warn("End concatenation")
    Trace.Warn("Start StringBuilder")
    Dim builder As New StringBuilder()
    Dim i As Integer
    For i = 0 To 999
      Dim word As String
        For Each word In words
           builder.Append(word)
           builder.Append(" ")
        Next word
    Next i
    result = builder.ToString()
    Trace.Warn("End StringBuilder")
  End Sub
End Class
```

Table 15.1 Trace results from `StringBuilder` vs. concatenation

Message	From Last
Start concatenation	0.000157
End concatenation	22.377516
Start StringBuilder	0.000212
End StringBuilder	0.013082

The code first splits up a sentence into a string array of words, using the `Split()` method to divide the sentence by its spaces. Next, it concatenates a string by recombining the words with spaces in between them, repeating this action a thousand times. The same task is then repeated using a `StringBuilder` object. Messages are sent to the page's trace output, marking the start and end times of each action.

Although it's pretty ridiculous to think that you would ever concatenate a couple words a thousand times over, this exercise does demonstrate how string concatenation doesn't scale well. It took more than 22 seconds to do the straight concatenation, compared to a little over a hundredth of a second to accomplish the same thing with `StringBuilder`. On a smaller scale, the difference might not be as huge, but when thousands of users are hitting your site and this kind of concatenation must occur, which method would you rather use?

Using *Trace* to Measure Time

Our string concatenation exercise introduces a quick and dirty way to measure the time it takes to complete an operation in the execution of your page. When `Trace` is on for the page or your application, every item in the `Trace` output is marked with two times, once from the start of execution, and once from the previous item.

Because we've talked a lot about application layering and breaking out your "heavy lifting" into its own application layer, you might be writing code outside of the context of a page, and therefore outside of the normal ASP.NET runtime. To get around this, remember that you can access most of the same objects by accessing `HttpContext.Current`. This provides a reference, cleverly enough, to the current instance of the `HttpContext` in which your code is running. You can access `Cache`, `Trace`, and the usual suspects this way.

If you find your page is not responsive when you're testing, try surrounding an action in `Trace.Warn()` (or `Trace.Write()`) methods to output messages to the page trace, as we did in Listing 15.2. Typical slow points might include database access, calls to Web services, or generation of dynamic images.

ACT and WAS

Application Center Test (ACT) and the Web Application Stress Tool (WAS) are two tools used to simulate "real world" use of your application. ACT was released with the enterprise versions of Visual Studio .NET 2002 and 2003, while WAS is a free download from Microsoft.

WAS has many admirable qualities, the most prominent of which is that it's free. It's a great tool to create blunt-force traffic simulations against your application. It works by recording your actions in Internet Explorer to create a script that simulates the requests of your browser. This script can be deployed to several machines and coordinated to fire off multiple sessions from each box.

ACT does very much the same thing, but it includes an object model that you can write VBScript and Jscript scripts against. This enables you to tailor the next step in the script depending on the kind of response that you get from the server.

Both applications create reports that tell you how fast the server is responding, how many requests it can handle per second, and so on. These reports give you a good 10,000-foot view of how well your application can respond to heavy traffic. They can isolate problems to single pages or requests, but they don't get to the heart of any underlying problems. You'll need to use other methods in this chapter to get these details.

Both applications have walkthroughs and extensive documentation on http://msdn.microsoft.com.

Microsoft is planning to include load testing and unit testing tools in Visual Studio 2005. At the time of this writing, Microsoft has announced Team System, though it has not yet reached beta stage. It is expected to be included only in the enterprise-level versions.

Performance Monitor

The Performance monitor built into Windows 2000, XP, and Windows Server 2003 can give you a peek into all kinds of activity on your server. It can be found under the Administrator Tools in your Start menu. Figure 15.1 shows the Performance monitor in action.

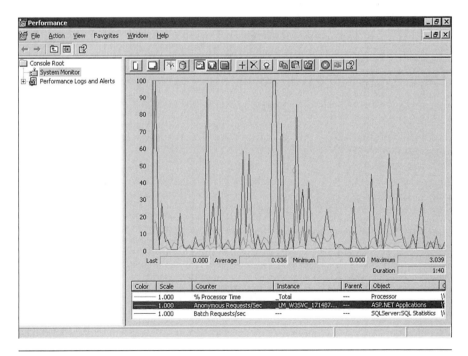

Figure 15.1 The Performance monitor.

In the screenshot, we can see that we're monitoring the total CPU time used, the number of requests being made in a specific IIS application, and the number of batch requests per second being made to SQL Server. Clicking the + button in the toolbar will show you literally hundreds of other things you can measure in real time.

Of course, the first thing you can check when your server appears to be choking is whether its CPU is getting maxed out. This is easy enough to see in the Task Manager, shown in Figure 15.2. You can get to this screen by pressing Ctrl-Alt-Del and choosing it or by right-clicking the task bar and choosing it.

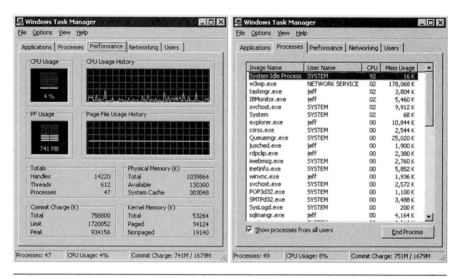

Figure 15.2 The Task Manager Performance and Processes tabs.

The left side shows the Performance tab, which includes a CPU meter and graph. The right side shows the Processes tab, which lists all of the running processes. You can click the column headings to sort these processes. Here we have the processes sorted by CPU time. You can see that `w3wp.exe`, the IIS Web serving process, is using a little more CPU than everything else right now. If you watched it in real time, you'd likely see the SQL Server process jump up there from time to time.

Hardware

Given the many metrics you can explore in the Performance Monitor, it's almost too obvious that your server hardware comes into play with regards to performance.

Server hardware is, relatively speaking, inexpensive. As Intel and AMD keep pushing CPUs faster and faster, processing power becomes less of an issue, while the other physical aspects create bottlenecks. Fast and redundant disks, redundant power supplies, lots of high-performance network equipment, and load balancing can keep your application humming.

I recently read a case study for an online dating site where a load balancer sent requests to one of several dozen relatively inexpensive servers. Those servers then shared several industrial-strength database servers to share state information and data. Splitting up these responsibilities kept everything running smoothly regardless of the load on the site. This goes back to the careful separation of different application duties into various layers, as we discussed in Chapter 4, "Application Architecture."

At the opposite end of the spectrum, many developers need only one or two servers to operate a site. Dedicated servers, even Windows-based servers, can now be rented for under $100 USD per month, with hundreds or even thousands of gigabytes of monthly data transfer allowed. With prices so low, it almost doesn't make sense anymore to risk putting your application on a shared server.

SQL Profiler and Query Analyzer

SQL Server comes with a couple tools that are as underappreciated by Web developers as the Visual Studio debugger. The Profiler and Query Analyzer let you find those pesky SQL queries and stored procedures that bring your server to its knees and take forever to complete.

The Query Analyzer can be run directly from the Start menu or from the Tools menu of the Enterprise Manager. At its most simple, it's a place to experiment with queries to make them do exactly what you want. The status bar will show you how long the query took. A simple SELECT from the analyzer is shown in Figure 15.3. To make your query go, just click the Play button in the toolbar.

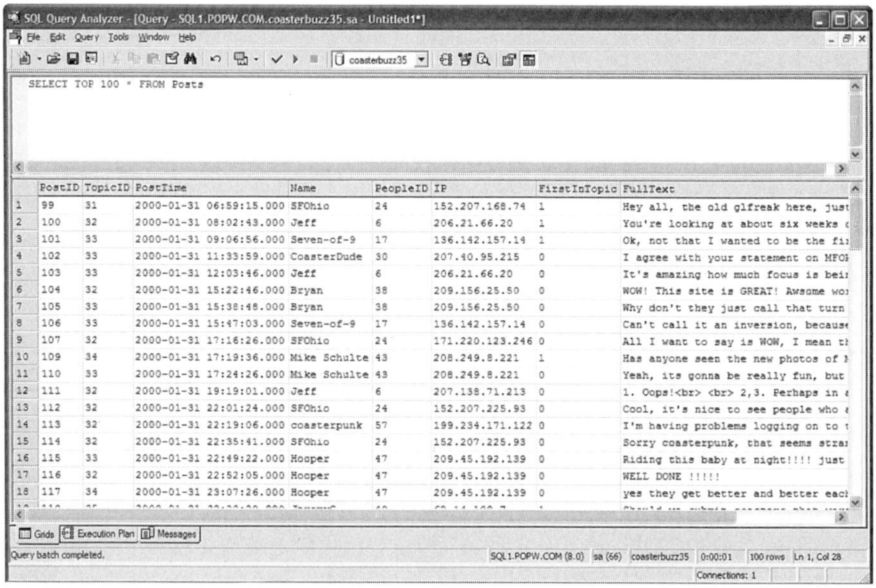

Figure 15.3 Performing a simple query in the Query Analyzer.

One of the more useful operations of the analyzer is to explore the details of a query's execution plan. An execution plan describes how SQL Server will go about performing the operations you've specified. Execution plans are well beyond the scope of this book, but understanding what SQL Server is doing under the hood makes for a fascinating discipline. Figure 15.4 shows the graphical representation of an execution plan.

Although the analyzer can help you gauge performance before you start to test your application, the Profiler can help you find problems while your application is running. This program peeks into SQL Server's operation and monitors every single query executed against its databases. Among other things, it can show you what values are actually being passed into a query, rather than the values you *think* are being passed in. It is also available from your Start menu and from the Tools menu in the Enterprise Manager.

The first clue that indicates that you need to use the Profiler is that SQL Server is using a lot of CPU time on the Processes tab of the Task Manager. When your database is well tuned, SQL Server generally doesn't use much CPU time in most Web applications.

The easiest way to start a new trace is to specify an ending time for the trace. Generally a couple minutes worth of data will provide plenty of opportunities to find problem spots. Figure 15.5 shows a complete trace with one item selected, whose details are shown in the lower pane.

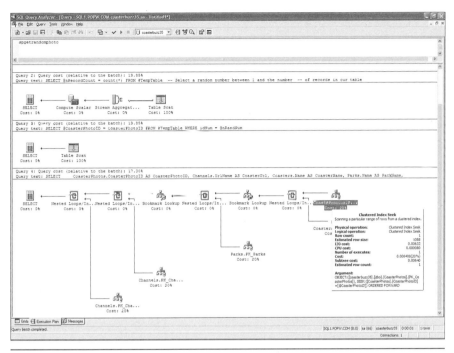

Figure 15.4 An execution plan.

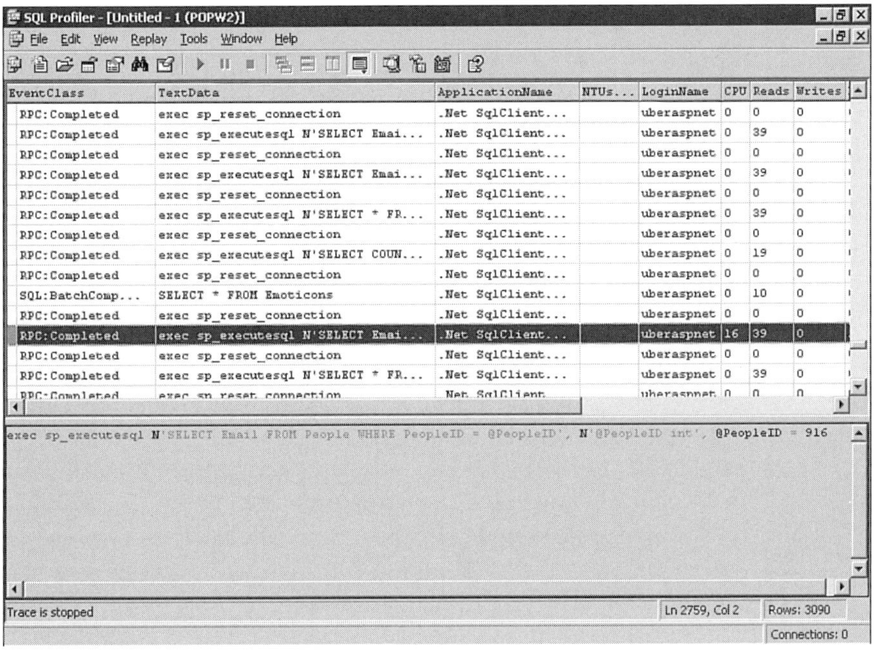

Figure 15.5 The SQL Profiler in action.

In this case, I noticed that one query stood out in terms of CPU usage (scrolling right will show additional attributes associated with the query). Selecting the item shows what the underlying query was, and it gives me a clue as to where I should look for problems. The query shown is a simple SELECT statement with a single parameter, so the problem probably isn't the query itself, but the way the table is indexed. You'll find that indexing issues account for many SQL Server performance issues.

Getting the most out of SQL Server would be a book unto itself, so if you don't happen to have a database administrator on your staff (what staff?), I strongly suggest reading up on designing and maintaining SQL Server databases.

> It might be out of scope for this book, but as we mentioned, indexing has a lot to do with how fast your database can find data. As a very general rule, it's a good idea to index any column that is frequently searched. Primary key columns are indexed by default. There is a performance trade-off in indexing columns because the index must be modified every time a new row is inserted into the column, so index carefully!
>
> What about stored procedures? Stored procedures (or "sprocs," as they're often called) are intended to group complex queries into single units or to limit the amount of data that a user account may access. The long-standing myth is that it's faster for a sproc to get data than "ad hoc" SQL statements in your code because the sproc's execution plan is compiled and ready to go. However, simple parameterized queries like the one shown in Figure 15.5 do have their execution plans cached, so there is little to no performance benefit to using sprocs for this kind of simple access.

Summary

Application performance is critical to serving your users because a system that doesn't perform isn't meeting the users' needs. Scalability is the capability of an application to handle an ever-increasing workload. A number of techniques enable you to increase performance and measure the results.

Caching a page or portions of it certainly makes your application run faster because the underlying code isn't executed. The contents of the page, or user control in the case of fragment caching, are stored in memory and sent to the user.

Data caching saves time and keeps your application responsive by keeping data ready to go in memory, instead of having to read it from a data store. You can use a combination of caching techniques that range from your own data classes to dependency schemes built into the .NET Framework.

String concatenation can be a huge resource drain, as data is repeatedly copied from one location in memory to the next to build the larger string. Using a `StringBuilder` object in lieu of traditional concatenation can be thousands of times faster.

Using the `Trace` object in your code can enable you to gauge how fast (or slow) blocks of code execute, and it enables you to isolate specific problems with your code.

The Application Center Test and the Web Application Stress tools enable you to create scripts that simulate access to your application and report on the number of requests it can handle.

The Performance monitor built into Windows acts as a tool to measure hundreds of different operations on your server. It provides a real-time peek into specific tasks to give you a good overview of how your application (and server in general) is handling the load.

SQL Server's Query Analyzer and Profiler can help diagnose problem queries by measuring execution time, CPU usage, and read/write activity to your database.

CHAPTER 16

Testing, Deployment, and Code Management

It's easy to get so wrapped up in creating the greatest Web application ever that we allow testing to become somewhat of an afterthought. Even the novice developer knows the kind of disaster that this can cause, so it's important to have a plan for testing and deployment.

Testing can be like a religion to some developers, and in this chapter we'll give you an overview of the methodologies that have taken hold in corporate culture and private shops alike.

Test, Test, and Retest with All Stakeholders

Let's start by explaining what testing is not. Testing is not a written script for the intern to click on buttons and arrive at some expected result. Unfortunately, this is the way many development shops operate, and it's a ridiculously narrow view that misses most of the big picture.

In my frequently less-than-humble opinion, testing actually begins with the development of specifications and requirements. Before any developer types "public class" in Visual Studio, an extensive discovery process must take place to flesh out exactly what your application is supposed to do. This requires involvement from every stakeholder in the process. End-users, subject matter experts (generally the "business people"), DBAs, hardware people...everyone. What's more, these people should stay involved throughout the entire process. It's easier to view development as an evolutionary process than getting a sign-off at the start of the project and delivering what you think they wanted.

Using test-driven development (TDD) principles (more on that in a moment), you'll write tests before the actual code. These tests are frequently simple enough that requirements analysts (yeah, that might be the same person as you) can read the code to understand what's going on and determine whether they match the stated goals or use cases of the application's function.

As development progresses, your suite of tests must still pass. If one or more of the tests fails, you'll have to revisit the code and fix it so that it passes the tests. This absolutely must not be a process that comes when you're "done" writing code.

When the code is closer to "done," then you can start to get into some of the traditional testing and use human beings to find out if your user interface does what it should (along with automated tools such as ACT). The theory is that your underlying business logic already works because you've been testing it all along.

Right up to the end of this process, to the release of the greatest software ever, all your stakeholders should be involved to make sure that the application performs as it should.

Test-Driven Development

"Agile" and "extreme programming" have been around for quite awhile, and it's quickly dominating corporate development culture as the fastest and least expensive means of getting large projects finished in a high-quality manner. One of the core tenents of this philosophy is test-driven development. As we mentioned, test-driven development requires that you write testing code first and write your code to satisfy those tests.

An open-source tool called NUnit (http://nunit.org) is a free application that allows you to unit test your code using "test fixtures," special classes that contain suites of tests. After you install NUnit, its classes will be installed in the global assembly cache, so they'll appear in the .NET tab of the Add References dialog of Visual Studio.

> NUnit is inspired by JUnit, a similar tool created by the Java community to unit test Java code. Many of the open-source testing and building tools in the .NET world are directly inspired by Java counterparts.

The first piece of the puzzle is to determine how we set up our projects. In Visual Studio, we can create a solution that includes two class library projects. The first will be the actual class library we intend to use in production, while the second will be our testing class library. The testing class library needs a project reference to the production class library. Figure 14.2 showed the Add Reference dialog. You'll also need a reference to the `NUnit.Framework.dll` and `System.Web.dll` assemblies in your test project (these are not added to class library projects by default). Figure 16.1 shows the Solution Explorer with a test project referencing both the production class library (in this case named "CliqueSite.Ads") and the NUnit framework. Note that we'll also need to add `using` (`Imports` in VB.NET) statements in our class file, as you'll see in Listing 16.1.

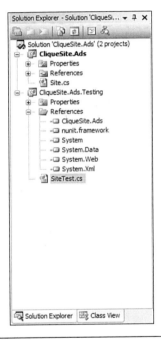

Figure 16.1 Solution Explorer showing project and NUnit references.

Consistent naming conventions are important in any development environment. For most projects, I append the namespace and project folder for test code with ".Testing" to signify that it's test code for a particular class library. In this case, I called my testing code project "CliqueSite.Ads.Testing" and put it in a folder of the same name. You can use whatever you want, but be consistent. Also, be sure to put this code in its own project because you don't want to deploy test code to production.

A class that contains tests must be marked with the `TestFixture` attribute, and it must be declared public. Similarly, individual tests in the class should be public methods that don't return anything (`void` in C#, `Sub` in VB.NET), and each method needs the `Test` attribute. You can optionally create methods that are marked with the `TestFixtureSetUp` and `TestFixtureTearDown` attributes to do some initialization before the tests are run and to clean up afterward.

Because we're going to execute code completely out of the context of the ASP.NET environment, we need to simulate it. To do this, we need a spot of setup code to create an `HttpContext` that we can work with. That code goes in our setup method, which is shown together with the rest of our initial test code in Listing 16.1. Replace the application path with the actual location of your test assembly.

Listing 16.1 A bare-bones test fixture

C#

```csharp
using System;
using System.IO;
using System.Web;
using System.Web.Hosting;
using NUnit.Framework;
using CliqueSite.Ads;

namespace CliqueSite.Ads.Testing
{
  [TestFixture]
  public class SiteTest
  {
    [TestFixtureSetUp]
    public void Setup()
    {
      TextWriter tw = new StringWriter();
      HttpWorkerRequest wr = new SimpleWorkerRequest(
        "/",
        "C:\\applicationpath",
        "default.aspx", "", tw);
      HttpContext.Current = new HttpContext(wr);
    }
```

```
    [Test]
    public void FirstTest()
    {
    }
  }
}
```

VB.NET

```
Imports System
Imports System.IO
Imports System.Web
Imports System.Web.Hosting
Imports NUnit.Framework
Imports CliqueSite.Ads

Namespace CliqueSite.Ads.Testing
  <TestFixture()> Public Class SiteTest
    <TestFixtureSetUp()> Public Sub Setup()
      Dim tw = New StringWriter()
      Dim wr = New SimpleWorkerRequest("/", "C:\applicationpath", _
"default.aspx", "", tw)
      HttpContext.Current = New HttpContext(wr)
    End Sub

    <Test()> Public Sub FirstTest()
    End Sub
  End Class
End Namespace
```

With all our skeleton test code in place, we're ready to write tests! Keep in mind that, at this point, we haven't written any production code. Let's say that our goal is to write a custom data class, similar to the one in Chapter 5, "Object-Oriented Programming Applied: A Custom Data Class," where we mimic columns in a table called "Site" with properties in our class, and we use create, update, and delete methods to manipulate data in the database. Our first design choice is probably to have a constructor that populates the object with default values. To test this, we'll create the code in Listing 16.2 (we'll leave out the VB.NET version because it's so straightforward).

Listing 16.2 Our first test

```
[Test]
public void FirstTest()
{
  Site s = new Site();
  Assert.AreEqual(0, s.SiteID);
  Assert.AreEqual(String.Empty, s.Contact);
  Assert.AreEqual(String.Empty, s.Email);
  Assert.AreEqual(String.Empty, s.Phone);
  Assert.AreEqual(String.Empty, s.SiteName);
  Assert.AreEqual(String.Empty, s.SiteUrl);
}
```

If we try to compile our test class library project, it won't work because it has absolutely no idea what the Site class is. This means our test has failed, and that's a good thing! Our code tries to create an instance of the Site class, which doesn't exist. Then it uses the Assert class and its static AreEqual method from the NUnit framework to compare two values. We'll see what these assertions do in a moment, but note that Assert has several other useful methods such as IsNull() and IsFalse(), among others.

At this point, we're ready to write some real production code in our production class library. Our goal in writing this code is simply to pass the test we've written—no more and no less. To make test-driven development work, we must stay mercilessly focused on passing the tests and nothing else. These tests determine the requirements, so there's no need to interpret them to be something else, a habit that you might have during the conventional coding process. To pass the test, our test code needs to be able to compile first of all, and then when it's executed in NUnit (we're getting to that soon, I promise), the new Site object will have the default values we've indicated in our test. Listing 16.3 shows what that code will look like.

Listing 16.3 The start of our class, designed to pass the test in Listing 16.2

```
using System;
using System.Configuration;
using System.Data;
using System.Data.SqlClient;
```

```
namespace CliqueSite.Ads
{
  public class Site
  {
    public Site()
    {
      _siteID = 0;
      _siteUrl = "";
      _siteName = "";
      _contact = "";
      _email = "";
      _phone = "";
    }

    private int _siteID;
    public int SiteID
    {
      get {return _siteID;}
      set {_siteID = value;}
    }

    //
    // more properties and private members here
    //

    private string _phone;
    public string Phone
    {
      get {return _phone;}
      set {_phone = value;}
    }

  }
}
```

This simple code creates a number of properties and private members, and a constructor that assigns default values. That's what we want to perform, according to our test. Now when we attempt to build our solution, Visual Studio will build the production class library first because it's referenced by the test class library. The assembly is copied into test library's project, and with its reference, the test library compiles! Finally, we get to use NUnit.

When we start NUnit, we're asked to save a new project. Choose the same folder as the compiled test assembly, which from the root project folder will be \bin\Debug. Next, choose Project and then Add assembly from the menu, and select the assembly that contains our test (ours was called CliqueSite.Ads.Testing.dll). Items appear in the following order (with gray spots next to them): A tree that starts with the NUnit project file, then the assembly, then the elements of the namespace, then the test fixture class, and finally our tests.

This is where the magic happens. Click the Run button. NUnit loads the assembly and looks for the classes marked with the TestFixture attribute, and then in those classes, it searches for methods marked with the attributes we mentioned earlier. In our example, it finds the SiteTest class and runs the Setup method because it's marked with the TestFixtureSetup attribute. Next it finds methods with the Test attribute. We have only one, and that's FirstTest. When NUnit gets to a line with one of the Assert methods, it tests to see if the condition is true. If it is true, it moves on. If not, it stops and moves on to the next test. If all the tests pass, the "lights" in the tree turn green and a big green bar is shown under the Run button, showing that we've passed our tests! Figure 16.2 shows the happy NUnit.

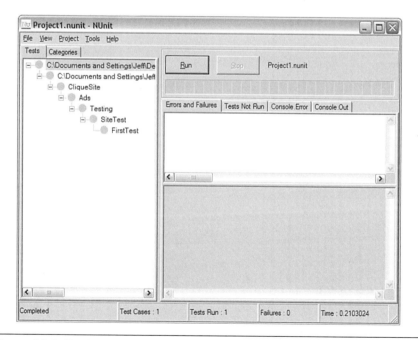

Figure 16.2 Nunit, with all our tests passed.

The next step is to write more tests. Ordinarily we would create a number of tests that test and confirm the selection, insertion, updating, and deletion of data, calling on methods similar to those in Chapter 5. The difference this time is that we're writing these tests first, before we write the actual code. Finally, to be sure we're really going to get it right with our final code (again, before the actual code is written), we can write a more comprehensive test like the one in Listing 16.4.

> Your application will likely contain configuration information that includes connection strings and other information. Because you're running outside of a normal ASP.NET process, your web.config file should be placed in the same folder as your .nunit project file. It should have the same name, replacing .nunit with .config. For example, if your project name is Project1.nunit, name your config file Project1.config.

Listing 16.4 A more comprehensive test to supplement our smaller tests

```
[Test]
public void CrudTest()
{
   Site s = new Site();
   s.Contact = "jeff";
   s.Email = "jeff@popw.com";
   s.Phone = "555.1212";
   s.SiteName = "MySite";
   s.SiteUrl = "http://www.popw.com";
   int siteID = s.Create();

   s = new Site(siteID);
   Assert.AreEqual("jeff", s.Contact);
   Assert.AreEqual("jeff@popw.com", s.Email);
   Assert.AreEqual("555.1212", s.Phone);
   Assert.AreEqual("MySite", s.SiteName);
   Assert.AreEqual("http://www.popw.com", s.SiteUrl);

   s.Contact = "jeffz";
   s.Email = "jeff@popw.comz";
   s.Phone = "555.1212z";
```

(Continues)

Listing 16.4 A more comprehensive test to supplement our smaller tests   (*Continued*)

```
        s.SiteName = "MySitez";
        s.SiteUrl = "http://www.popw.comz";
        s.Update();

        s = new Site(siteID);
        Assert.AreEqual("jeffz", s.Contact);
        Assert.AreEqual("jeff@popw.comz", s.Email);
        Assert.AreEqual("555.1212z", s.Phone);
        Assert.AreEqual("MySitez", s.SiteName);
        Assert.AreEqual("http://www.popw.comz", s.SiteUrl);

        s.Delete();
        Assert.AreEqual(0, s.SiteID);
        s = new Site(siteID);
        Assert.AreEqual(0, s.SiteID);
}
```

This test runs the whole range of manipulating a `Site` object. Keeping in mind that our `Site` class will be similar to the example class in Chapter 5 (which is why we aren't going to actually write it here), we first create a `Site` object, assign its properties, call the `Create()` method to persist the values to a database, and then read them back to see if they match. We update the values and then read them back to see if they match. Finally, we delete the record and ensure that the `SiteID` property returns 0, just as we specified. Our testing project won't compile, of course, because so far we haven't written the `Create()`, `Update()`, and `Delete()` methods. After we do, we can compile and run the tests.

It might seem like a lot of work to develop in this manner, but consider these benefits. First, you are creating code that is only meant to pass a test, which is a single requirement. You are sure of what you need to do, so you don't become a victim of scope creep. The test defines a specific requirement, and you stick to it.

Your finished code is also more likely to be bug-free. Although no developer can entirely separate himself or herself from the code he or she writes, this methodology allows for a certain amount of bias removal. Writing tests that tested code you already wrote would be unfair and biased because you would be testing what you *think* your code is supposed to do. Writing the tests firsts helps reduce that bias.

Best of all, you can have high confidence in your code because it has been so thoroughly tested. If code somewhere else in your project is incompatible, it will cause tests to fail. You don't have to worry about breaking something else because the failed tests will tell you right away where the problem is.

The one remaining issue is that you may have to debug your code when something isn't working right. To do this, you must attach the debugger to a running process, in this case, to NUnit. Figure 16.3 shows the Attach to Process dialog found under Visual Studio's Debug menu.

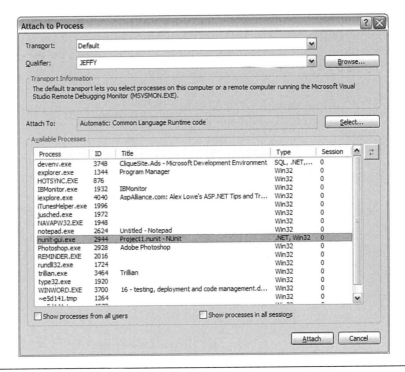

Figure 16.3 Attach to Process dialog.

By selecting the `nunit-gui.exe` process and clicking the Attach button, the debugger "listens" to NUnit. When you click the Run button in NUnit, it begins running the code in your tests. Just as you could set break points in your application code (see Chapter 14, "Developing with Visual Studio"), you can do the very same here. All the same information is available, as well as the ability to step through your code.

Additionally, you can use the static method `Console.WriteLine()` to write out strings to NUnit's Console Out tab. This is similar to using `Trace.Write()` in a page.

Hopefully you can see the benefit of test-driven development. It appears to be more work at first, but the more you do it, the more you will see that the quality of your code increases.

Getting the Bits Out to Production

Deploying your site out to production can work in a number of ways. In Visual Studio 2002 and 2003, the easiest way with the fewest files is to copy the project (from the Project menu). You can use FrontPage or a file share and select to copy Only Files Needed to Run This Application. This means that all your code behind will not be copied, only the compiled assembly.

The other choice is to simply copy up the files using your favorite FTP program. One of the benefits of .NET is what's known as "xcopy deployment," meaning you need only copy the files and go, without having to "install" anything ("install" implies making registry entries and such).

> If you were born after 1980, you probably didn't have much exposure to MS-DOS, the old disk operating system. Back in the day, computers didn't have hard drives, and when they did, they were small. One of the commands you could run was xcopy, which copied not just files but folders as well. This kind of copying is what we're talking about when we deploy code this way, so the name has stuck around.

Choosing Copy Website from the Website menu in Visual Studio 2005 brings up something different, namely a nice file transfer client. You can connect to your local file system, to your local IIS installation, to Web servers using FrontPage extensions, or to the good old reliable FTP sites. Figure 16.4 shows the copy utility.

Perhaps the most impressive feature in 2005 is the Publish option under the Website menu. This function pre-compiles the entire site, including .aspx and .ascx files, and copies the compiled lot to the folder of your choice. This is a nice feature in particular for publishers who want to hide even the HTML of the Web application. A series of placeholder files and a number of assemblies are created, and that's all there is to upload to make your site work.

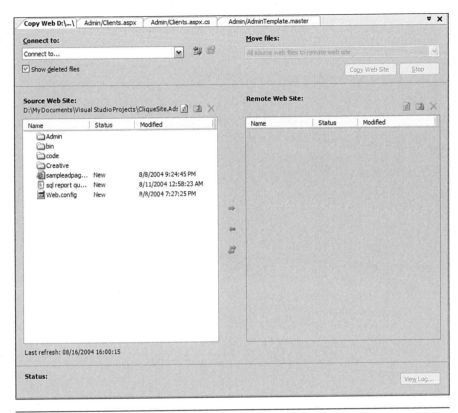

Figure 16.4 The Copy Website window in Visual Studio 2005.

Versioning and Splitting Up the Work

As we discussed in Chapter 14, Visual Source Safe is a tool used to version code and act as a code repository for team members.

One of the most useful features of Visual Source Safe is the capability to go back and check on earlier versions of a particular source code file. A new version is created every time you check in a file. You can get a line-by-line summary of changes, insertions, and deletions between any two versions, and you can restore a previous version if you want. Figure 16.5 shows a change report for a source file.

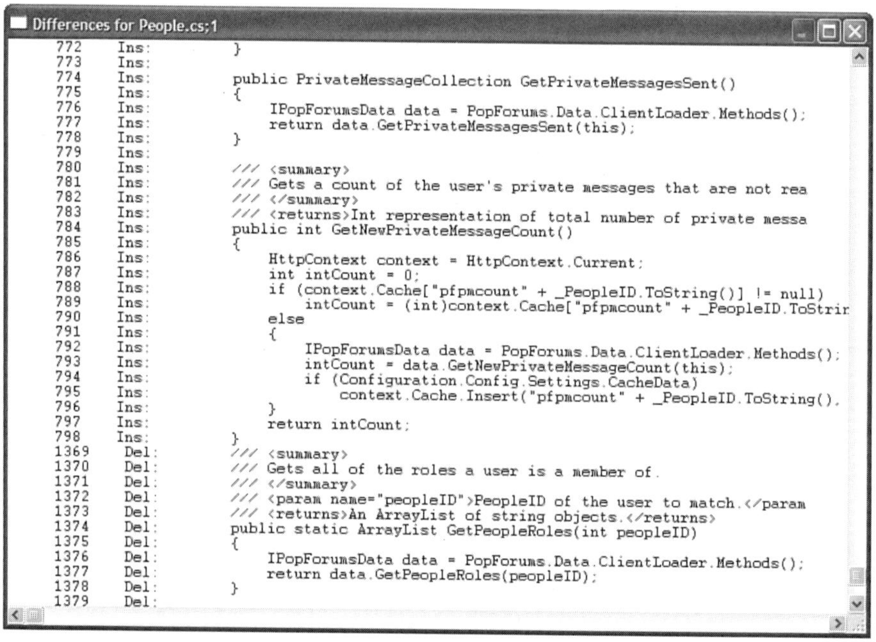

Figure 16.5 A change report in Visual Source Safe.

Summary

Keeping testing on your mind from the beginning of a project can lead to higher-quality code throughout the development process. Test-driven development requires that you write test code before the actual production code and that you write production code to pass the tests. By taking this seemingly backward approach, you can be considerably more confident that your code functions as intended because the tests are less colored by your knowledge of the code.

NUnit is an open-source application used to run unit tests against your code. The application loads an assembly and looks for test fixtures, each of which contains one or more tests to run. If each test passes, evaluating a number of different conditions offered by the NUnit framework, the test appears green in the app. You can further debug your applications by attaching the Visual Studio debugger to NUnit.

Test-driven development borders on religion for some developers, and it really is a fascinating and efficient way to write code. To learn more about TDD with .NET, I recommend *Test-Driven Development in Microsoft .NET* (Microsoft Professional, 2004) by James W. Newkirk and Alexei A. Vorontsov. Their book covers this approach to development extensively with plenty of information on NUnit.

The various versions of Visual Studio offer a number of methods to deploy your finished application to a production site. The pre-compilation option in Visual Studio 2005 in particular offers easy "xcopy" deployment of the files to production.

Visual Source Safe allows teams of developers to version code and compare changes from one check-in to the next.

CHAPTER 17

More Advanced Topics

There are a few more topics that you should have a general knowledge about to round out your .NET experience. Instead of taking entire chapters to cover them, we'll briefly introduce you to them in this chapter.

Streams

Streams don't get much love in the .NET world. You don't read much about them in blogs, on Web sites, or in books. Despite the lack of respect, streams are used in a number of different I/O operations, including working with files, networking, data compression, and cryptography. This is your peek into the secret lives of streams.

> I have some entrepreneurial friends who, upon searching .NET documentation, couldn't find the specific classes used to manipulate files. That's because they were looking more for something that sounds file-centric instead of streams. Make no mistake though—streams are where it's at!

A stream is just a sequence of bytes. The various stream classes all derive from `System.IO.Stream`. It's an abstract class, so by itself it helps no one. The class does however have a number of members that provide the base functionality to the classes that inherit it. Read and write methods complement properties that tell you something about the class's abilities and your place in the stream. Table 17.1 shows the `Stream` properties, while Table 17.2 shows the `Stream` methods. Again, these behave differently in different derived classes.

Table 17.1 `Stream` properties

Property	Description
CanRead	Boolean value that says whether you can read from the stream. A closed stream, for example, can't be read.
CanSeek	Boolean value that returns false if the stream is closed but also indicates whether a stream enables you to seek a particular position. You can't seek a position in a `NetworkStream`, for example.
CanTimeout	Indicates if the stream can timeout. Used by `NetworkStream`.
CanWrite	Boolean value that indicates if you can write to the stream. Again, a closed stream can't be written to.
Length	A long value indicating the length of the stream. Not supported where `CanSeek` is false.
Position	A long value indicating your position in the stream. This is also not supported if `CanSeek` is false.
ReadTimeout	Used to set a read timeout for `NetworkStream`.
WriteTimeout	Used to set a write timeout for `NetworkStream`.

Table 17.2 `Stream` methods

Property	Description
BeginRead()	Asynchronously begins reading the stream. Calls an event handler when the reading is complete. We won't get into this or the other asynchronous methods here for simplicity's sake.
BeginWrite()	Asynchronously begins writing to the stream.
Close()	Closes the stream.
EndRead()	Waits for an asynchronous read to complete.
EndWrite()	Ends asynchronous writing to the stream.
Flush()	Clears the stream buffers and causes buffered data to be written to the stream.
Read()	Reads bytes from the stream.
ReadByte()	Reads a single byte from the stream.
Seek()	Goes to a position in the stream.
SetLength()	Sets the length of the stream, in bytes. Can only be used if `CanSeek` and `CanWrite` are true. Calling this method will truncate part of the stream if it's made smaller.
Write()	Writes bytes to the stream.
WriteByte()	Writes a single byte to the stream.

The `FileStream` class is probably the most commonly used of the stream classes because it operates on (believe it or not) files. A `FileStream` object can be created with any of ten constructors (plus several that are obsolete starting in .NET v2.0), enabling you to specify the file name you want and how you'll work with it. In its most basic use, let's look at creating a file, writing to it, reading from it, and appending it.

Keep in mind that when manipulating files, your application must have the right permissions on a folder to create and alter its contents.

The most basic constructor takes a file name and a `FileMode` parameter, the latter of which is an enumeration indicating how you'll open it, as shown in Table 17.3.

Table 17.3 `FileMode` enumeration

Member name	Action
`Append`	Opens the file to add data to the end of it.
`Create`	Starts a new file or overwrites an existing one.
`CreateNew`	Also starts a new file, but throws an exception if it already exists.
`Open`	Opens an existing file.
`OpenOrCreate`	Opens a file or creates a new one if it doesn't exist.
`Truncate`	Opens a file and truncates all of its data.

Another constructor takes a third parameter indicating the read and write mode of the file. This parameter is of the `FileAccess` enumeration, and not surprisingly, it only has three self-explanatory values: `Read`, `ReadWrite`, and `Write`.

After we have a `FileStream`, we can use the methods mentioned previously to move around it and manipulate it. Listing 17.1 shows the `FileStream` in action. The comments in the code describe what happens in every step.

Listing 17.1 Manipulating a file from our page in the code-behind file

C#
```
using System;
using System.IO;
using System.Text;
using System.Web;
```

(Continues)

.

Listing 17.1 Manipulating a file from our page in the code-behind file   (*Continued*)

```
public partial class FileFun_aspx
{
  public void Page_Load(object sender, EventArgs e)
  {
    // open a new FileStream
    FileStream fs = new FileStream(@"C:\Documents and
Settings\Jeff\Desktop\test.txt", FileMode.Create);
    // create a byte array to write to the stream
    byte[] bytes = Encoding.ASCII.GetBytes("This is my string!");
    fs.Write(bytes, 0, bytes.Length);
    // move to the 11 index position
    fs.Seek(11, SeekOrigin.Begin);
    // write new text there
    bytes = Encoding.ASCII.GetBytes("special code!");
    fs.Write(bytes, 0, bytes.Length);
    // go to the same position, but only write enough bytes to
overwrite "special"
    fs.Seek(11, SeekOrigin.Begin);
    // perform the overwrite
    bytes = Encoding.ASCII.GetBytes("waycool");
    fs.Write(bytes, 0, bytes.Length);
    // now read back the stream into our byte array
    fs.Seek(0, SeekOrigin.Begin);
    byte[] readBytes = new byte[fs.Length];
    fs.Read(readBytes, 0, Convert.ToInt32(fs.Length));
    // convert the byte array into a string and output to Trace
    // Output: "This is my waycool code!"
    Trace.Warn(Encoding.ASCII.GetString(readBytes));
    fs.Close();

    // open a new FileStream in Append mode
    fs = new FileStream(@"C:\Documents and
Settings\Jeff\Desktop\test.txt", FileMode.Append);
    bytes = Encoding.ASCII.GetBytes(" This was appended.");
    fs.Write(bytes, 0, bytes.Length);
    fs.Close();

    // open a new FileStream, read-only
    fs = new FileStream(@"C:\Documents and
Settings\Jeff\Desktop\test.txt", FileMode.Open, FileAccess.Read);
    readBytes = new byte[fs.Length];
    fs.Read(readBytes, 0, Convert.ToInt32(fs.Length));
    // convert the byte array into a string and output to Trace
```

```
    // Output: "This is my waycool code! This was appended."
    Trace.Warn(Encoding.ASCII.GetString(readBytes));
    fs.Close();
  }
}
```

VB.NET

```
Imports System
Imports System.IO
Imports System.Text
Imports System.Web

Public Partial Class FileFun_aspx

  Public Sub Page_Load(sender As Object, e As EventArgs)
    ' open a new FileStream
    Dim fs As New FileStream("C:\Documents and
Settings\Jeff\Desktop\test.txt", FileMode.Create)
    ' create a byte array to write to the stream
    Dim bytes As Byte() = Encoding.ASCII.GetBytes("This is my string!")
    fs.Write(bytes, 0, bytes.Length)
    ' move to the 11 index position
    fs.Seek(11, SeekOrigin.Begin)
    ' write new text there
    bytes = Encoding.ASCII.GetBytes("special code!")
    fs.Write(bytes, 0, bytes.Length)
    ' go to the same position, but only write enough bytes to
    ' overwrite "special"
    fs.Seek(11, SeekOrigin.Begin)
    ' perform the overwrite
    bytes = Encoding.ASCII.GetBytes("waycool")
    fs.Write(bytes, 0, bytes.Length)
    ' now read back the stream into our byte array
    fs.Seek(0, SeekOrigin.Begin)
    Dim readBytes(fs.Length) As Byte
    fs.Read(readBytes, 0, Convert.ToInt32(fs.Length))
    ' convert the byte array into a string and output to Trace
    ' Output: "This is my waycool code!"
    Trace.Warn(Encoding.ASCII.GetString(readBytes))
    fs.Close()

    ' open a new FileStream in Append mode
    fs = New FileStream("C:\Documents and
```

(Continues)

Listing 17.1 Manipulating a file from our page in the code-behind file   *(Continued)*

```
Settings\Jeff\Desktop\test.txt", FileMode.Append)
    bytes = Encoding.ASCII.GetBytes(" This was appended.")
    fs.Write(bytes, 0, bytes.Length)
    fs.Close()

    ' open a new FileStream, read-only
    fs = New FileStream("C:\Documents and
Settings\Jeff\Desktop\test.txt", FileMode.Open, FileAccess.Read)
    readBytes = New Byte(fs.Length) {}
    fs.Read(readBytes, 0, Convert.ToInt32(fs.Length))
    ' convert the byte array into a string and output to Trace
    ' Output: "This is my waycool code! This was appended."
    Trace.Warn(Encoding.ASCII.GetString(readBytes))
    fs.Close()
  End Sub
End Class
```

As the code demonstrates, manipulating a stream can involve a bit of conversion when it comes to writing and reading text. You can just as easily read and write bytes that mean virtually anything. We use static properties of `System.Text.Encoding` to do these conversions. These properties (we use `ASCII`, but there are others) are actually of the `Encoding` type themselves.

Another important thing to note here is that we call the `Close()` method of our `FileStream` objects. This releases the file from our use so that other processes can use it. If you don't explicitly release a resource like this, it will eventually be released, but in the meantime it might be locked up by our process, causing errors in other processes or even our own application.

Reading and writing text to files is probably one of the best-documented concepts in the .NET documentation. The definition for the `FileStream` class alone has nearly two dozen links to various file operations.

This raw manipulation of the `FileStream` is straightforward, but there are two helper classes that can get the job done just as easily. These classes are the `StreamWriter` and `StreamReader` classes. What makes them particularly useful is that you can use them with any of the `Stream` derived classes to write and read characters to a stream. Listing 17.2 shows how to read and write using these classes.

Listing 17.2 Using the `StreamWriter` and `StreamReader` classes

C#

```
// open a new FileStream
FileStream fs = new FileStream(@"C:\Documents and
Settings\Jeff\Desktop\test.txt", FileMode.Create);
// create a StreamWriter, based on our FileStream
StreamWriter sw = new StreamWriter(fs);
// write to the stream
sw.Write("This is my string!");
sw.Close();
fs.Close();

fs = new FileStream(@"C:\Documents and Settings\Jeff\Desktop\test.txt",
FileMode.Open, FileAccess.Read);
// create a StreamReader, based on our FileStream
StreamReader sr = new StreamReader(fs);
// Output: "This is my string!"
Trace.Warn(sr.ReadLine());
sr.Close();
fs.Close();
```

VB.NET

```
' open a new FileStream
Dim fs As New FileStream("C:\Documents and
Settings\Jeff\Desktop\test.txt", FileMode.Create)
' create a StreamWriter, based on our FileStream
Dim sw As New StreamWriter(fs)
' write to the stream
sw.Write("This is my string!")
sw.Close()
fs.Close()

fs = New FileStream("C:\Documents and Settings\Jeff\Desktop\test.txt",
FileMode.Open, FileAccess.Read)
' create a StreamReader, based on our FileStream
Dim sr As New StreamReader(fs)
```

(Continues)

Listing 17.2 Using the `StreamWriter` and `StreamReader` classes   *(Continued)*

```
' Output: "This is my string!"
Trace.Warn(sr.ReadLine())
sr.Close()
fs.Close()
```

Networking

Before we get into the networking classes in .NET, it might be a good idea to define the network. The International Organization for Standardization (ISO) describes the network as having seven layers to it, but as programmers, we're most concerned with the transport layer, where two machines "chat" using the TCP (Transmission Control Protocol) and UDP (User Datagram Protocol) protocols.

The primary difference between TCP and UDP is that TCP requires a connection between the two machines. Responses are sent to make sure that every packet of data is received successfully. UDP does not make any promises about whether data lands at its destination, and as such, it is useful for streaming media where a couple of missing packets won't hurt. This grossly simplifies what goes on between two networked machines, but like so many other things in .NET (remember Web services?), a thorough understanding of the underlying activity is not necessary to use the framework's many classes.

We can send whatever data we want using these protocols, as long as the other end knows what to expect and how to respond. A number of well-established higher-level protocols have been written to make life easier. You already know about HTTP (HyperText Transfer Protocol), and you've used SMTP (Simple Mail Transfer Protocol) to send mail, FTP (File Transfer Protocol) to transfer files, and DNS (Domain Name Service) to resolve domain names.

The .NET Framework has a rich set of classes to manipulate network IO. At the most basic level of TCP, the `TcpClient` and `TcpListener` classes, found in `System.Net.Sockets`, enable us to create a session with a remote machine or listen and wait for an incoming connection. UDP uses the `UdpClient` class (there is no listener equivalent because UDP doesn't require a connection).

The end points of this communication are called sockets. A socket on a computer is defined by the computer's IP address and the port it is using.

Think of a port as any of the driveways on your street that lead up to houses. The end of your street is like the network connection, and the driveways are all ports. These ports aren't physical objects in your computer, but they are there as discrete listening "channels." Certain high-level protocols have ports assigned to them where they listen. HTTP uses port 80, and SMTP listens on 25, for example. Often the computer that initiates the connection will listen on any port that isn't already reserved for a particular protocol.

At a higher level, the framework provides us with `HttpWebResponse` and `HttpWebRequest` to represent HTTP responses and requests and `WebClient` to send and receive data via HTTP. A number of other classes help us deal with URIs, DNS, authentication, and permissions across a network.

The most possibilities lie in the realm of sending and receiving bytes in whatever form we want. For a practical example using `NetworkStream` and `TcpClient`, let's look at the exchange of data between a client and an SMTP server when we attempt to send mail.

> This is a particularly useful example because the existing mail classes in .NET are actually just wrappers around the old CDO (Collaboration Data Objects). Microsoft has been criticized for these classes that call outside of the managed code of the .NET Framework to an "old" COM object, especially considering that sending mail is a relatively easy thing to accomplish, as you'll see in a moment.

To understand what goes on in an SMTP exchange, we'll look at a typical client-server interaction in terms of the text sent back and forth across the network. The full specification can be found at the site of the Internet Engineering Task Force (IETF) as RFC 821. The specification is 68 pages long, so I think a simple visual example is a lot easier to understand for now. See Listing 17.3.

Listing 17.3 An SMTP exchange

```
Server: 220 someservername.com (IMail 8.12 32453-3) NT-ESMTP Server X1
Client: HELO MyServerName
Server: 250 ok
Client: MAIL FROM: <sender@somedomainname.com>
```

(Continues)

Listing 17.3 An SMTP exchange   (*Continued*)

```
Server: ok sender
Client: RCPT TO: <someuser@somedomainname.com>
Server: 250 ok its for <someuser@somedomainname.com>
Client: DATA
Server: 354 ok, send it; end with <CRLF>.<CRLF>
Client: SUBJECT: Test subject
Client: Body of message
Client: .
Server: 250 Message queued
Client: QUIT
Server: 221 Goodbye.
```

The chatting between the two computers is easy to understand. Every time data is sent to the server, it replies with some message, beginning with a numeric code. As long as the code doesn't start with a 4 or 5, it means that the server was OK with the data we sent to it. The only real mystery might be the period on a line by itself, but that's what we use to signal the end of the mail message, preceded and followed by a carriage return and line feed. (In case you're wondering, you can send a period on a line by itself by making it a double period.)

To duplicate this behavior on our page, we'll need to create a `TcpClient` instance and get a reference to its `NetworkStream`. Because we'll be writing and reading to the stream over and over, we'll create two methods that do the work for us by taking and returning a string. These methods will be called `GetResponse()` and `SendRequest()`. In our page load event handler, we'll create the exchange and write the server responses to the `Trace` output (the page will need to have `Trace` enabled). The final code is shown in Listing 17.4.

Listing 17.4 Creating the SMTP exchange in code

C#
```
using System;
using System.Net.Sockets;
using System.Text;
using System.Web;

public partial class Mailer_aspx
{
   public void Page_Load(object sender, EventArgs e)
   {
     TcpClient client = new TcpClient("someservername.com", 25);
```

```
    stream = client.GetStream();

    SendRequest("HELO MyServerName" + "\r\n");
    Trace.Warn(GetResponse());

    SendRequest("MAIL FROM: <sender@somedomainname.com>\r\n");
    Trace.Warn(GetResponse());

    SendRequest("RCPT TO: <someuser@somedomainname.com>\r\n");
    Trace.Warn(GetResponse());

    SendRequest("DATA\r\n");
    Trace.Warn(GetResponse());

    SendRequest("Subject: Test subject\r\n");
    SendRequest("\r\nBody of the message.");
    SendRequest("\r\n.\r\n");
    Trace.Warn(GetResponse());

    SendRequest("QUIT\r\n");
    Trace.Warn(GetResponse());
}

private NetworkStream stream;

private string GetResponse()
{
    byte[] readBuffer = new byte[4096];
    int length = stream.Read(readBuffer, 0, readBuffer.Length);
    string response = Encoding.ASCII.GetString(readBuffer, 0, length);
    if (response.StartsWith("4") || response.StartsWith("5"))
    {
        SendRequest("QUIT\r\n");
        throw new Exception("Mailer error: " + response);
    }
    return response;
}

private void SendRequest(string text)
{
    byte[] send = Encoding.ASCII.GetBytes(text);
    stream.Write(send, 0, send.Length);
}
}
```

(Continues)

Listing 17.4 Creating the SMTP exchange in code   (*Continued*)

VB.NET

```vbnet
Imports System
Imports System.Net.Sockets
Imports System.Text
Imports System.Web

Public Partial Class Mailer_aspx

  Public Sub Page_Load(sender As Object, e As EventArgs)
    Dim client As New TcpClient("someservername.com", 25)
    stream = client.GetStream()

    SendRequest("HELO MyServerName" + CrLf)
    Trace.Warn(GetResponse())

    SendRequest("MAIL FROM: <sender@somedomainname.com>" + CrLf)
    Trace.Warn(GetResponse())

    SendRequest("RCPT TO: <someuser@somedomainname.com>" + CrLf)
    Trace.Warn(GetResponse())

    SendRequest("DATA" + CrLf)
    Trace.Warn(GetResponse())

    SendRequest("Subject: Test subject" + CrLf)
    SendRequest(CrLf + "Body of the message.")
    SendRequest(CrLf + "." + CrLf)
    Trace.Warn(GetResponse())

    SendRequest("QUIT" + CrLf)
    Trace.Warn(GetResponse())
  End Sub

  Private stream As NetworkStream
  Private CrLf As String = ControlChars.Cr + ControlChars.Lf

  Private Function GetResponse() As String
    Dim readBuffer(4096) As Byte
    Dim length As Integer = stream.Read(readBuffer,0,readBuffer.Length)
    Dim response As String = _
Encoding.ASCII.GetString(readBuffer,0,length)
    If response.StartsWith("4") Or response.StartsWith("5") Then
```

```
      SendRequest("QUIT" + CrLf)
      Throw New Exception("Mailer error: " + response)
    End If
    Return response
  End Function

  Private Sub SendRequest([text] As String)
    Dim send As Byte() = Encoding.ASCII.GetBytes([text])
    stream.Write(send, 0, send.Length)
  End Sub
End Class
```

To kick things off, we need to create an instance of `TcpClient` and pass in the name of the server we want to talk to, as well as the port number that we expect the server will be listening on. Because port 25 is reserved for SMTP, that's the one we'll use. To get a reference to the `TcpClient`'s `NetworkStream`, we'll use its `GetStream()` method and assign the stream to our `stream` class member so that it's available to our helper methods.

Our `SendRequest()` method takes a string parameter and encodes it as a byte array. That byte array is passed into the `NetworkStream`'s `Write()` method, using exactly the same method we used to write to a `FileStream` earlier in the chapter. It's that easy to write to a network stream.

Our `GetResponse()` method processes the data coming back from the server. Reading the data back is a little different from how it was for our `FileStream` object. We create a byte array that holds 4K (more than enough, in this case) and then use the stream's `Read()` method to populate that array. The `Read()` method returns an integer to let us know how many bytes were read. We need that in the next step to turn the byte array into a string we can understand. After we have the string, we can do a little error checking. If the first number of the response is a 4 or 5, it means something went wrong, so we throw an exception.

Our `Page_Load` calls `SendRequest()` and `GetResponse()` in sequence after opening the connection. The output to trace will be something like that of the server responses in Listing 17.3.

Because this is an ASP.NET book, and a listening server application generally lives outside the context of a Web app, we'll forego a tutorial on using the `TcpListener` class. An instance of the class waits after its

`Start()` method is called, listening to a specified port for an incoming connection. After it gets a connection, it can begin communicating by accepting a `TcpClient` via its `AcceptTcpClient()` method. Generally you'll spawn the interaction with the calling client in a new thread because a server application will interact with several clients simultaneously.

Threading

Most computers can do more than one thing at once. This is accomplished by running certain programs or components in their own threads. The CPU divides its time between the various threads running, doing some work on one thread during its allotted slice of time and then moving to the next. At any given time, your computer is probably running several hundred different threads, especially if you have several applications open at once.

In the world of Web applications, threading isn't generally a concern for us because most of what we do happens in the context of an incoming request and the response we send back to the browser. A page is stateless; after it has been rendered and sent off to the browser, the server forgets about it forever. This is very different from a Windows application, where several things might be going on at once. For example, if an FTP program worked entirely in one thread, you wouldn't be able to press a Cancel button because the program would be busy sending or receiving a file. By executing that transfer in its own thread, the rest of the application remains responsive.

Web developers may encounter some special needs from time to time that do require threading. Say your application needs to send email to ten different people when a record is updated in your database. Sending all ten messages in the page will cause a delay in sending the response (the page) to the user. That's probably not acceptable.

Another frequent need is to perform some kind of action on a regular interval. A good example of this is to delete incomplete shopping cart data from a database after it has aged a certain amount of time.

Let's start with an example where we perform some kind of action outside of a page. Listing 17.5 shows how we can launch a simple method in its own thread, letting the rest of the page continue its execution at the same time.

Listing 17.5 Launching a new thread

C#
```csharp
using System;
using System.Threading;
using System.Web;

public partial class ThreadFun_aspx
{
  public void Page_Load(object sender, EventArgs e)
  {
    ThreadStart ts = new ThrcadStart(RebelThread);
    Thread t = new Thread(ts);
    t.Start();
  }

  private void RebelThread()
  {
    // do something here
  }
}
```

VB.NET
```vbnet
Imports System
Imports System.Threading
Imports System.Web

Public Class ThreadFun_aspx

  Public Sub Page_Load(sender As Object, e As EventArgs)
    Dim ts As New ThreadStart(RebelThread)
    Dim t As New Thread(ts)
    t.Start()
  End Sub

  Private Sub RebelThread()
    ' do something here
  End Sub
End Class
```

Launching the method `RebelThread()` in its own thread is a three-step process. First, we create a `ThreadStart` delegate, passing in the name of the method as its only parameter. Next we create the `Thread` object, passing in the `ThreadStart` object. Finally, we call the thread's `Start()` method, and the method code fires on its own. The page finishes its execution, and (if it's still working) the method continues on its own.

> .NET v2.0 adds a new `ParameterizedThreadStart` delegate that lets you pass in a parameter to the `Start()` method, which is in turn passed to the method you want to execute in a new thread. The method you want to run should have a single `object` parameter. This could be a handy way to pass in the `HttpContext.Current` object to the new thread, where you'll find information about the original request and have access to `Cache`. Be sure to cast the object from the parameter to whatever type you'll need.

Getting some code to execute on a regular interval can be accomplished using a `Timer` object. A `Timer` object can be instantiated in an HttpModule. Recall from Chapter 8, "HttpHandlers and HttpModules," that a module must implement an `Init()` method, which is called when the application is first run. In this method, we'll assign a new `Timer` to a static member in the module, based on the method that we want to run at a given time interval. For good housekeeping, we'll dispose of the `Timer` in the module's required `Dispose()` method. The basic syntax for all this is shown in Listing 17.6, keeping in mind that we have to add the module to our `web.config` file (refer to Listing 8.7 in Chapter 8).

Listing 17.6 Creating a `Timer` in an HttpModule

C#
```
using System;
using System.Web;
using System.Threading;

public class MyHttpModule : IHttpModule
{
  public void Init(HttpApplication application)
  {
```

```
      myTimer = new Timer(new TimerCallback(this.TimerMethod),
application.Context, 60000, 60000);
   }

   public void Dispose()
   {
      myTimer.Dispose();
   }

   static Timer myTimer;

   private void TimerMethod(object sender)
   {
      HttpContext context = (HttpContext)sender;
      // do something here
   }
}
```

VB.NET

```
Imports System
Imports System.Web
Imports System.Threading

Public Class MyHttpModule
   Implements IHttpModule

   Public Sub Init(application As HttpApplication)
      myTimer = New Timer(New TimerCallback(Me.TimerMethod), _
application.Context, 60000, 60000)
   End Sub

   Public Sub Dispose()
      myTimer.Dispose()
   End Sub

   Private Shared myTimer As Timer

   Private Sub TimerMethod(sender As Object)
      Dim context As HttpContext = CType(sender, HttpContext)
      ' do something here
   End Sub
End Class
```

According to the `IHttpModule` interface, the `Init()` method must take a parameter of the `HttpApplication` type, which provides us with a reference to the application. We have a static `Timer` object declared, which is what we'll use to hold the `Timer` we declare in `Init()`. The method that we want to run in the timer must take an object parameter. This is required by any method that will be declared as a `TimerCallback` delegate.

The actual declaration of our timer takes four parameters. The first is a new `TimerCallback` delegate, which is created with our `TimerMethod()` method as a parameter. Note that we don't include the parameters or parentheses when naming the method. The second parameter for our `Timer` constructor is an object that is used to pass along application state. Because we have a reference to the application as a parameter for the `Init()` method, we'll pass in the application's `Context` property. The last two parameters are integers representing the number of milliseconds that should pass before we start the timer, and then the time that should pass between invocations of our method. We chose 60 seconds (60,000 milliseconds) for both on our example.

Because it's often useful to get various properties from the application, especially its `Cache` property, we can cast the object parameter of our recurring method to `HttpContext`, which is what we passed in when we created the timer.

Index

301

Register
Your Book

at www.awprofessional.com/register

You may be eligible to receive:

- Advance notice of forthcoming editions of the book
- Related book recommendations
- Chapter excerpts and supplements of forthcoming titles
- Information about special contests and promotions throughout the year
- Notices and reminders about author appearances, tradeshows, and online chats with special guests

Contact us

If you are interested in writing a book or reviewing manuscripts prior to publication, please write to us at:

Editorial Department
Addison-Wesley Professional
75 Arlington Street, Suite 300
Boston, MA 02116 USA
Email: AWPro@aw.com

Addison-Wesley

Visit us on the Web: http://www.awprofessional.com

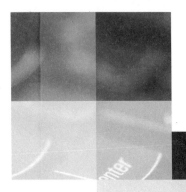

informIT

YOUR GUIDE TO IT REFERENCE

Articles

Keep your edge with thousands of free articles, in-depth features, interviews, and IT reference recommendations – all written by experts you know and trust.

Online Books

Answers in an instant from **InformIT Online Book's** 600+ fully searchable on line books. For a limited time, you can get your first 14 days **free**.

Catalog

Review online sample chapters, author biographies and customer rankings and choose exactly the right book from a selection of over 5,000 titles.